THE HISTORICAL DIMENSIONS OF A RATIONAL FAITH:

The Role of History in Kant's Religious Thought

G. E. Michaelson, Jr.
Oberlin College

University Press
of America™

To my mother and father

FOREWORD

Someone once said of the philosopher Leibniz that he wrote "many puzzling things about many puzzling things." The same, of course, could be said of Immanuel Kant (1724-1804), the subject of this book. The difficulty of Kant's work guarantees disagreement about what he meant, and this--combined with the sheer scope and originality of his thinking--makes it worth returning to him again and again. Such a task may prove frustrating, but the effort always seems to be repaid handsomely.

The aim of what follows is to offer a general introduction to Kant's religious thought that gradually focuses on the relation between religion and history in his thinking. This traditionally neglected area is generating increasing interest within the world of Kant scholarship, and the present work is a modest effort toward describing and clarifying some of the issues involved in this topic.

The relationship between religion and history seems to assume two forms in Kant's philosophy. On the one hand, there is the cluster of issues tied up with the traditional topic of revealed or historical religion. Kant is generally thought to have little or no use for the historical dimensions of religion, such as revelation, scripture, church, and tradition. But while there is undoubtedly a reductionistic side to Kant's thinking on such issues, I suggest that there is a genuinely constructive side as well. Simply expressed, the "historical dimensions" of Kant's "rational faith" give tangible, concrete form to moral ideas, and history thereby assumes a kind of pedagogical role in Kant's thinking. Thus, rational beings learn from the historical side of religion what they implicitly knew all along; through the symbolic forms of revealed religion, history becomes the mediator to a sensuous humanity of supersensuous moral ideas.

Here as elsewhere, Kant shows the unique position he occupies among the thinkers of the eighteenth century Enlightenment. The stringency of Kant's theory of knowledge is fairly applied: it offers him no more latitude in what he can reject than in what he can accept. Consequently, unlike certain exponents of a purely "natural" religion, Kant does not simply dismiss the possibility of a divine revelation. He will instead invoke what he calls the "principle of reasonable modesty" in all discussions of revelation, thereby giving himself an excuse to treat the subject of revealed religion in a philosophically respectable way. The result is what I am calling the constructive side of his theory of historical religion, something which leads Kant to some surprisingly positive remarks about the role of the institutional church in the religious life of mankind.

To be sure, the pedagogically beneficial role played by historical religion is, for Kant, simply a stage on the road to a pure moral faith. Kant looks forward to the day when mankind will no longer require teaching aids in religious matters. Yet this fact in itself suggests a second point of contact between religion and history for Kant, insofar as he clearly endorses a theory of "progress" by which mankind moves from one religious stage to another. After all, history, as a sheer temporal medium, is necessary if such progress is to occur. Much like Lessing, Kant seems implicated in a theory of the divine education of the human race.

Unlike Lessing, however, Kant works against the background of a philosophy which makes such a thing as moral or religious "progress" unintelligible. The only way Kant manages to embrace both the Newtonian world of determinism and a theory of human freedom is by creating two separate realms in which space and time, on the one hand, and freedom, morality, and religion, on the other, go their separate ways. Kant achieves this with his distinction between phenomena and noumena. But the effect of this dichotomy is to make impossible any effort to mix time (including the temporality of history) and religion; there is simply no way for the one to gain any purchase on the other, without threatening the idea of human freedom. As a result, even though Kant's religious thought may demand a theory of moral and religious progress, there is no way that his philosophy can possibly satisfy that demand: the "historical dimensions of a rational faith" end in an impasse.

vi

By design, what follows is a combination of elementary material, intended for introducing Kant to a college-level audience, and more specialized and technical material, intended as a contribution to the contemporary discussion of Kant's religious thought. The reader coming upon Kant for the first time may want to skip the Introduction and begin with Chapter I; such a reader may also wish to skip pp. 91-113 and 157-180. Otherwise, the reader hopefully will find the text to be as clear and intelligible as is possible, given the basic difficulty of the thinker under consideration.

It is well known that any work on Kant relies heavily on the work of others. This is particularly true in my case, since the issue of religion and history has recently been explored in illuminating detail by a number of highly competent scholars, with the works of Michel Despland and Yirmiahu Yovel being especially helpful to me. The fact that I ultimately argue against certain interpretations offered by both Despland and Yovel should not obscure the fact of my indebtedness to them. On the whole, their achievements set a standard of excellence on this topic which I can only hope to approximate and not duplicate.

I am happy to acknowledge a number of more personal debts accrued in the writing of this work. My good friends and former teachers, Malcolm L. Diamond of Princeton University and Hans W. Frei of Yale University, were the main source of constructive criticism and helpful advice while this project was originally taking form as a doctoral dissertation in Princeton's Department of Religion. I am grateful to them both for their warm encouragement and their uncommon patience.

Much of what I know about philosophy of religion generally, and about Kant in particular, I have learned from Victor Preller and Richard Rorty, both of Princeton. And Douglas Langston of the University of California at Irvine, Henry Levinson of Stanford University, and Jeffrey Stout of Princeton, have not only read and criticized portions of the original manuscript, but have contributed to my intellectual growth in ways that defy appropriate expressions of gratitude.

I am thankful to Davidson College for providing me with a fellowship for study in Germany during the summer of 1976. I would also like to thank Daniel D. Rhodes, the chairman of Davidson's Religion Department, for. creating the kind of departmental atmosphere in which it was a joy to work.

Finally, my debt to Linda Michalson is so great that, in many ways, this work is a joint project. Someday I hope to return the favor.

CONTENTS

INTRODUCTION: THE AIMS OF THE INQUIRY

The Problem

There is much in Kant's philosophy that remains problematic in our own time. This is not simply because, as Kant himself once remarked, "the truth of a theory...is that it survives being laughed at";[1] it is also because Kant understood the true character of genuinely lasting philosophical issues. This means it is difficult to criticize Kant on the basis of an aspect of a problem he failed to see, because--more often than not--he did not fail to see it. His treatment of a particular issue may prove to be highly unsatisfactory, and his philosophical system as a whole may fail on a number of counts. But Kant's breadth of vision insured that the important issues would not escape his notice, and his critical methodology guaranteed that whatever he had to say would be interesting and worthwhile. It is in many different senses that Kant can rightly be called "our contemporary."[2]

Kant's views on religion are no exception to this general characterization. Various themes in his philosophy--such as the theoretical-practical dichotomy--still undergird certain religious and theological outlooks of our own time.[3] Furthermore, his systematic advocacy of the interconnection between religion and morality, though more fashionable in some periods than in others, always retains a certain number of sophisticated adherents. Indeed, the influence of Kant on modern religious thought has been so great as to make it extremely difficult to achieve an interpretation of his own religious philosophy which is not filtered through a set of distorting presuppositions. Within theology, for example, Kant's name immediately connotes Ritschlian patterns of thought and their subsequent devaluation by the neo-orthodox movement. And, from the standpoint of philosophy of religion, Kant's views automatically suggest an untenable dualism as well as

1

a philosophical standpoint antedating the rise of historicistic philosophy, with all its corrosive implications for a rationalistic, morally-based religion. The
conceptual accretions of the last two hundred years
have made a genuine pilgrimage "back to Kant" an enor-
mously difficult project.

Largely as a result of this situation, certain key
areas of Kant's religious philosophy have been neglected, distorted, or ignored altogether. Kant is correctly and habitually characterized as the "great water-
shed," but often with little regard for the fine distinction between the reasons for his influence and the
full contours of his own religious vision. As a result, a kind of caricature of Kant's religious philosophy is promoted, as exemplified by T.M. Greene's assessment in his introduction to the English translation of Religion within the Limits of Reason Alone:

> Kant's absolute insistence upon
> the reduction of true religion to
> morality, arising from his distrust
> of mysticism and a stiff-necked re-
> fusal to bow down even before God
> Himself, rendered him incapable of
> appreciating true religious devotion...
> His whole religious theory...is an-
> thropocentric, not theocentric, and...
> his God is certainly, by all reli-
> gious standards, related to the world
> and man in no vital way...We must con-
> clude, then, that Kant's explicit ac-
> count of religion is in many ways a
> typified product of a scientific age
> and a rationalistic mood.[4]

The whole tone of this characterization suggests an
extremely one-sided and narrow view of Kant. To
characterize Kant's religion as "the reduction of true
religicn to morality" and the "typified product of a
scientific age" is to imply, as many have done, that
Kant's religious thought results from a process of
running traditional religious topics through the
wringer of a stringent epistemology. In this kind of
characterization, Kant's "critical" methodology has
become "skeptical"; contrary to Kant's stated intentions, religion has been placed at the service of
epistemology, rather than the other way around.

2

Kant himself, of course, is partly to blame for this stereotype. After all, he _is_ a rationalist in religious matters, and the universal consciousness of moral obligation _is_ the foundation of his religious philosophy. But _it_ is not enough, as so often happens, to speak of Kant's demolition of natural theology (Critique of Pure Reason), his reformulation of religious concepts in terms of ethical rather than metaphysical categories (Critique of Practical Reason), and his subsequent espousal of a pure rational religion over against a positive historical faith (Religion within the Limits of Reason Alone), to get a full measure of Kant's overall religious vision. Such a procedure correctly accounts for Kant's enormous influence, but it fails to balance adequately a concern for the seemingly reductionistic aspects of his thinking with an equal concern for the positive and constructive aspects. If, in fact, Kant is something more than the skeptical product of a rationalistic, scientific age, then more must be said about his religious philosophy.

Perhaps most importantly, more must be said about Kant's understanding of the relationship between religion and history. Because his religious teaching is based upon what he takes to be a necessarily and universally valid doctrine of moral obligation, Kant's view of the connection between the rational world of moral religion and the empirical world of history is, understandably enough, a virtually unknown aspect of his philosophical outlook. At first glance, the relevance of history to Kantian religious themes appears especially dubious, given the fact that, within the Kantian scheme itself, history must be consigned to the world of mere appearance. Furthermore, there is the difficulty of the obvious conflict between historical categories and Kant's transcendental theory of reason. Superficially, at least, it seems entirely appropriate, when viewing Kant's philosophy of religion, to paraphrase Tertullian's celebrated, "What has Athens to do with Jerusalem?" by asking, "What has rational faith to do with history?"

In what follows, I wish to defend the claim that-- for Kant himself--religion and history have a great deal to do with each other. Furthermore, I hope to demonstrate that the connection between religion and history, far from being a Kantian afterthought or the product of a commentator's imagination, arises system-

atically out of Kant's own critical methodology. That
this is so is being increasingly recognized within
Kantian scholarship,[5] and the aim of this inquiry is
to deal in specific terms with a number of key aspects
of the religion and history issue.

In order to give a general characterization to the
nexus of problems I plan to deal with, I have chosen
the phrase, "the historical dimensions of a rational
faith." By this phrase, I mean to convey two key problems. First, there is the problem of the relationship
between Kant's rational moral religion and the revealed
historical religion embodied by traditional Christianity. Put otherwise, this is the problem of determining
Kant's role in the Enlightenment's debate concerning
natural and revealed religion. I draw on Kant's historical context, not in order to pursue an historical
point, but in order to suggest the uniqueness of his
understanding of the relation between natural and revealed religion. Accordingly, Chapter II specifies
the reasons why Kant escapes easy categorization with
regard to the natural-revealed issue. This is because there is, as I shall demonstrate, a <u>constructive</u>
as well as a <u>reductionistic</u> element in his theory of
historical or revealed religion. This constructive
element is the pedagogically important role that an
historical faith plays in representing and thereby
mediating supersensuous moral ideas to a sensuous humanity. In other words, what I am calling the constructive aspect of Kant's theory of historical religion has a primarily epistemological, rather than ontological, function; it is, nevertheless, a crucial
function. In Chapter III, I shall clarify and investigate the manner in which this constructive aspect
operates, devoting special attention to the role of
the "schematism of analogy" in Kant's theory of historical religion. In a very real way, the mediating
function performed by historical religion is the practical parallel of the schematization process in the
theoretical realm.

The second key problem implied by the title of this
inquiry involves the complex relationship between moral and religious ends and temporality. By the end of
Chapter III, I shall have shown that Kant's own metaphor of historical religion as a "vehicle" for pure
moral faith courts the danger of undermining one of
the critical philosophy's most basic principles. This
is the principle that man's moral and religious life

is to be lived out in the noumenal realm only. If
this principle means anything, it means that the temporal span represented by history can have no influence on moral and religious "progress," given the radically a-temporal nature of the noumenal. Indeed, it
means that the very notion of moral and religious progress is potentially unintelligible. But, as I shall
show, there is a distinct theory of religious progress
embodied in the constructive aspect of Kant's theory
of historical religion: on the personal and individualistic side, this is reflected in his theory of conversion; and on the social and communal side, it is
reflected in his theory of the visible church. This
progressive strand in Kant's religious thought paral-
lels the teleological component in his philosophy of
history, and this parallel helps to shed light on what
Kant has in mind when he speaks of moral and religious
progress. In Chapter IV, then, I shall specify how
the problem regarding temporality and the noumenal
realm comes about for Kant and will inquire into possible means of solving this problem.

Much of my interpretation of Kant's religious philosophy relies on the systematic examination of certain points of contact between the theoretical and
practical sides of Kant's thought. This, for example,
is what lies behind the claim that historical religion
serves an important mediating role in Kant's understanding of religion. In particular, I am relying
heavily on what I shall call Kant's "principle of human limitations." This principle and its implications
will be examined momentarily. For now, it is important simply to stress the importance of the interplay
between theoretical and practical concerns in Kant's
thinking. Kant's freedom of intellectual movement is
severely restricted by this interplay. At the same
time, however, it is perhaps this very interplay which
constitutes the genius of his system.

Accordingly, the Introduction and first chapter of
this inquiry are intended to justify the angle of vision on which the actual interpretation of Kant's religious views relies. The remainder of the Introduction is devoted to introducing Kant's principle of
human limitations and to examining the problem of the
history of Kant-interpretation, in the hopes of making
my own sympathies clear. And Chapter I is devoted to
an examination of the basic vocabulary and ground
rules of Kant's critical philosophy, something which
is necessary, given my emphasis on the relation be-

tween the theoretical and practical sides of Kant's
thinking. Thus, just as my interest in the relation
of history to religion supersedes certain recent inquiries into Kant's religious thought,[6] my grounding
of the history and religion issue in a specifically
epistemological context is an improvement, I feel,
over a recent valuable study of Kant's views on history and religion.[7] This grounding is the purpose of
what I am calling Kant's principle of human limitations. In order to offer a clearer summary of the aims
of this inquiry, then, it will be helpful to set these
aims in the context of this principle.

Kant's Principle of Human Limitations

It would initially seem that the historical aspects
of religions--such as revelation, scripture, church,
and tradition--could hold little or no philosophical
interest for Kant, since they are firmly tied to the
phenomenal world. Not only does the phenomenal character of history conflict with the noumenal basis of morality and religion; the phenomenal world can only reflect what is contingent and never what is necessary
and universal. And necessity and universality, the
marks of the genuinely rational, characterize true moral religion for Kant.

Provisionally, then, it is important to suggest how
it is that historical states of affairs impinge upon
Kant's religious teachings. The point of contact, in
my view, arises on the basis of a systematic principle
which implicitly operates throughout the critical philosophy. I am calling this principle Kant's principle
of human limitations: it stipulates that, whenever a
claim about man's innate rational capacity is proposed,
that claim must always be balanced by a keen sensitivity
toward the finite situation within which man finds himself actually living.[8] Put otherwise, this principle
is what mediates between the rational and the empirical elements in Kant's philosophy; to allow the rational side to become completely autonomous would be
to give up the transcendental method and to fall into
the trap exposed by Kant's antinomies. Among other
things, then, the principle of human limitations is
what keeps Kant from joining contrasting elements in
his philosophy--such as sensibility and understanding--
into a higher metaphysical synthesis.[9] It is this re-
fusal to overstep the bounds of human limitations in

6

order to satisfy the apparent demands of reason which underlies the Dialectic of the first <u>Critique</u>. And, more to the point, it is Kant's sensitivity toward the limitations imposed on man by his sensuous condition which insures that there will be an important role in his philosophy for historical religion.

Accordingly, the principle of human limitations is what makes intelligible any inquiry into the relationship between history and religion in Kant's writings. The principle itself is a kind of connecting thread which runs through Kant's philosophy and illuminates the linkage between elements of his thought which otherwise seem quite disparate--yet the relationship among these various elements remains one of "linkage" and not "union." Kant is constantly aware that, although man is a rational being, he is nevertheless a being who lives under bounded, sensuous conditions. Thus, a kind of tension is intrinsic to Kant's theory of the human situation, and the very effort to balance the components of this tension is what makes Kant's philosophy "critical" rather than "rationalistic" in the purest sense. This effort to balance finitude and rationality is evident in Kant's epistemology, ethics, and religious thought. Instances of how the principle of human limitations affects these various areas of Kant's philosophy will suggest how it serves as the interpretive key I claim it to be.

From the standpoint of epistemological concerns, the principle of human limitations is suggested by Kant's doctrine of sensibility. The essence of this doctrine implies that what human beings can know is strictly limited by who they are. It so happens that "rational" beings are at the same time "sensuous" beings, so that human cognitive capacities are radically conditioned by the sensuous mode of human existence. The sensuous mode constitutes the passive or receptive side of being human in the Kantian sense; it is not something we can elect to have or not to have but is an inescapable condition which cannot be intellectually transcended. From this standpoint, the role of sensibility in authentic human cognition is not only a <u>thesis</u> in a Kantian epistemological claim but also an <u>effect</u> of a Kantian anthropological insight. In other words, Kant's doctrine of sensibility has ontological as well as epistemological implications.[10] This is the result of our possessing a sensible rather than intellectual form of intuition. The fact that only a <u>divine</u>

7

being could have an intellectual intuition clearly suggests the implications of finitude attending Kant's theory of sensibility.[11]

The key epistemological result of the principle of human limitations is that the capacity of human reason to establish points of contact with anything not reliant on either experience itself or on the conditions of experience is always characterized by Kant as being of a merely regulative nature. The notion of a constitutively all-powerful rational capacity is interdicted by Kant on the basis of the sensuous, finite situation in which man finds himself and which mediates all knowledge. Any temptation on Kant's part to propose an extravagant claim regarding human cognition is quickly tempered by his sensitivity toward the principle of human limitations. Consequently, it is not at all accidental that Kant's doctrine of reason as such (as distinguished from his doctrine of the understanding) appears in the Dialectic section of the Critique of Pure Reason. Here, human intellectual pretensions are kept in strict perspective.

An analogous situation arises within Kant's ethical theory. Kant everywhere takes for granted practical reason's innate sense of unconditioned moral obligation. This ineradicable "ought," however contentless, is the source of all of Kant's ethical concerns, the formal basis of the categorical imperative, and the distinguishing characteristic of rational beings. It distinguishes rational beings because of the implication of freedom in Kant's concept of ought; only in the case of a free and rational creature is the vocabulary of "ought" meaningful. What is most noteworthy about Kant's theory of moral obligation is the way something wholly unconditioned is an innate aspect of human reason; what was impossible on a theoretical level is postulated by Kant on a practical level. The fact that our awareness of the moral law is altogether mysterious epistemologically does not, for Kant, alter the sheer fact of that awareness. Thus, Kant's ethical theory is based upon the human apprehension of something inherently immutable, fixed, and limitless, in the strongest rationalistic sense. This is the whole point behind an imperative that is "categorical."

At the same time, however, the doctrine of an innate sense of moral obligation is balanced by Kant's systematic concession to human limitations. Never is the juxtaposition of "pure" and "impure" elements so apparent in Kant's thinking as in the case of his ethical writings. His postulation of our awareness of an unconditioned moral law, far from leading to a typically optimistic Enlightenment anthropology, is balanced by Kant's sense that there may never have been a morally "good" act performed by anyone at any time.[12] While such a complaint has a merely formal and hypothetical tone in the Foundations of the Metaphysics of Morals, it echoes with a particularly jarring ring in Kant's doctrine of radical evil, that most un-Enlightenment of Enlightenment doctrines.[13] Consequently, the impingement of something unconditioned upon human reason does not lead, as one might expect, to a positive claim about human capacities. Rather, it is balanced by what Kant calls man's "natural propensity" toward evil, an inescapable perversion of will linked to the conditions of human finitude.[14] Just as an intellectual intuition is what contrasts with man's sensible intuition, the notion of a completely "holy will" is what contrasts with man's weak and corruptible will.[15]

Thus, as in the case of his epistemology, the limitations imposed upon Kant's ethical thought derive from his awareness of who man is and his systematic inclusion of that awareness in his philosophical teachings. Accordingly, what seems in principle to be an optimistic and progressive ethical theory turns out to be carefully explicated within the context of human limitations. What has been called Kant's principle of human limitations is in effect a kind of reality principle, for its effect is to relate the world of formal philosophical reflection to the concrete world of finite human habitation.

Most important for our present purposes is the way the principle of human limitations affects Kant's religious philosophy. It is here that the link between religion and history is established in a crucial way, and it is on the basis of this principle that a treatment of the historical dimensions of Kant's rational faith becomes something more than merely arbitrary and artificial. Kant's theory of religion is rational in the sense that it is based upon what he believes to be an innate human capacity and not upon certain supernatural effects or ecclesiastical authority. At the same time, however, Kant's claims about the prospects for a "pure moral faith" are no more optimistic or ambitious than his claims about the worldly realization of morally good acts. Kant's Religion is as much a book about the universal tendency to fall into a religion of illusion and fanaticism as it is a treatise on

9

pure moral faith. Awareness of this leads to a tendency among commentators on Kant's religious philosophy to lump all the empirical elements of religion together with the objects of Kant's diatribe against perverse religious practices. But such a view ignores the balance provided by Kant's principle of human limitations, and it neglects the positive and constructive claims Kant makes with regard to historical religion. In particular, the traditional stereotype of Kant's religion ignores the fact that, for Kant, the empirical, historical, and representative side of religion, far from being automatically illicit, is an important mediator of a pure moral religion to a finite and sensuous humanity.

In examining this area of Kant's religious thought, the problem is essentially one of distinguishing the authentic source of Kantian religious faith from the means by which that faith is made humanly meaningful. In principle, practical reason is the sole source of authentic religion, and history has nothing to teach us; in practice, history assumes the status of a useful "illustrator"--perhaps even a "necessary" illustrator-- of what we could, in principle, know through reason alone. History has nothing "new" to tell, but--as phenomenal--history is the medium which is most accessible to human understanding. In an ideally rational world, the Critique of Practical Reason would be the only religious writing necessary for human life. But in the world as it is, concessions must be made, and it is at this point that Kant expresses a religiously positive and not merely reductionistic concern for history. Interpreting Kant in this way is not to alter the traditional view so much as it is to round out and balance that view through a systematic concern for what is entailed by Kant's principle of human limitations.

So far, these very general claims regarding Kant's view of the historical side of religion touch mainly on his view of historical revelation and historical religion itself, particularly as his view is expressed in Religion. Kant's concern for history at this point can be characterized as positive insofar as history becomes a medium--a "vehicle," in Kant's own words-- for moral truths that can, in principle at least, be known by reason alone. Detailed examination of this issue will focus heavily on Kant's notion of an historical vehicle and on the epistemological relationship

between this vehicle and Kant's concessions to human
limitations. Within this context, the ultimate question to confront is whether history as a religious
vehicle remains for Kant at the level of a kind of
heuristic aid, or if it becomes a genuinely necessary
medium for man's religious development, necessitated
by human limitations. There is an ambiguity in Kant
at this point, an ambiguity which will need to be
explored carefully if Kant's true position is to be
clarified.

Clearly, then, Kant's principle of human limitations leads directly to the first component of the
historical dimensions of a rational faith, namely, the
idea of historical religion as the <u>mediator</u> of supersensuous ideas to an inescapably sensuous humanity.
But as I indicated at the outset, there is a second
aspect of the historical dimensions of Kant's theory
of religion which I intend to explore. In my view,
the question of the mediating, pedagogical function of
historical religion implicates Kant in the problem
concerning the relationship between religion and temporality. In <u>Religion</u>, as I shall argue in Chapters
II and III, Kant clearly suggests that the historical
side of religion, particularly in the form of the
visible church, is becoming increasingly rational. By
this he means that maxims of belief--such as belief in
certain historical events of supposedly religious sig-
nificance--are increasingly giving way to maxims of
action. In other words, historical religion becomes
increasingly rational to the extent that theoretical
concerns (such as one's understanding of historical
events) become subservient to practical concerns
(deriving from the moral law). The traditional problem with historical religion has been the tendency on
the part of the ecclesiastical establishment to impose
certain maxims of belief as soteriologically necessary.
But with the Enlightenment, a more genuine understanding of the purely moral dimensions of a rational faith
was, in Kant's view, becoming increasingly dominant.
Kant is thereby inclined to be optimistic about the
progress of religion.

> If now one asks, What period in the entire
> known history of the church up to now is
> the best? I have no scruple in answering,
> <u>the present</u>.[16]

The historical side of religion is truly beneficial

only when it is instrumental toward moral ends. In Kant's view, these moral ends are being increasingly realized within the religious life of Western man.

Thus, it is clear that a vision of religious "progress" is implicit within the pages of Kant's Religion. The problem with this, as I have already suggested, is the apparent impossibility, by Kantian standards, of ever effecting the kind of rapprochement between religion and temporality that would make such a vision of religious progress intelligible. This impossibility stems from the obvious conflict between Kant's theory of time as a form of pure intuition and his theory of religion as based upon a wholly a-temporal noumenal realm. This conflict is related to Kant's principle of human limitations insofar as it necessarily arises out of a consideration of the mediating function of historical religion.

When this aspect of the historical dimensions of Kant's rational faith is examined in Chapter IV, I shall be particularly concerned to clarify the epistemological status of Kant's reflections on the progress of religion. For this, an important clue will be Kant's philosophy of history, with its strong teleological element. There are illuminating points of contact between Kant's views on religion and his views on history, a fact which supports the growing consensus that Kant's speculations on history are not the casual and philosophically disjointed products of his spare moments, but actually form a systematic and integral part of the critical philosophy.[17]

Furthermore, to take Kant's views on history seriously is to discover a potential solution to the religion-temporality conflict. There is the possibility that the teleological principle evident in both Religion and the writings on history ultimately yields a systematic portrayal of the phenomenal, real-world aspects of the summum bonum, the ultimate moral and religious goal in Kant's system.[18] A phenomenal expression of Kant's "highest good" may in fact be the point behind his theory of the visible, historical church as the "kingdom of God on earth so far as it can be brought to pass by men."[19] That is, it appears possible that the full meaning of the doctrine of the highest good ultimately yields a convergence of the teleological and moral currents pervading all of Kant's thinking. This would require Kant to suggest how the

12

increasing realization of morality--and thereby of free-
dom--might be reflected in the phenomenal world. Otherwise, the increase in man's moral responsiveness would
be a meaningless notion, totally detached from man's
worldly concerns.

Thus, the impetus behind such a view of Kant's doctrine of the highest good is the desire to salvage the
doctrine as a genuinely meaningful possibility rather
than let it remain a high abstraction. Such a salvag-
ing operation, permitting the worldly "exhibition" of
morality, requires a kind of splice between the worlds
of freedom and nature. And obviously, such a splice is
precisely what is called for by the confrontation between religion and temporality. An interpretation of
Kant involving this splice would include the claim that
the doctrine of the highest good is not simply a principle of personal morality (i.e., the correct proportioning of virtue and happiness), but is also the regulative idea of history, insofar as it promotes the totalization and realization "of morality in the realm of
nature and, in general, the reshaping of given empirical orders to fit moral demands."[20]

Such a doctrine of the highest good would be the
ultimate expression of Kant's implicit trust in the inherent rationality of the universe. In a rational universe, moral endeavor may suffer momentary frustrations,
but on the whole, it would continually increase, however slowly. Gradually, this process builds to the
point where the phenomenal world shows clear signs of
man's moral endeavor--for example, in the form of religion man embraces or in the ordering of his political
institutions. This is what would constitute the phenomenal dimensions of the highest good and would be
evidence of the splice between freedom and nature
which Kant needs. Morality does have an effect on the
phenomenal realm, if this viewpoint is correct. There
would seem to be partial justification for pushing Kant
in this direction, given his desire to balance a concern for man's rational capacity with an equal concern
for man's phenomenal situation. The principle of human limitations, in other words, seems to support an
interpretation of Kant based on a splice between freedom and nature, religion and history.

A major aim of this project, however, is to demonstrate that the doctrine of the highest good does not
offer the splice or bridge that Kant needs. I shall
argue that the so-called "historical dimensions of a
rational faith" ultimately betray a fundamental impasse

13

in Kant's religious thought. Kant saddles himself with a certain epistemological problem which requires a metaphysical solution; but such a solution is interdicted by his own epistemology. The impasse itself, then, is simply a reflection of the conflict between freedom and nature--the world of morality and Newton's world of appearances--within Kant's philosophy. It is brought about by an irremediable tension between certain demands imposed by practical reason and certain limitations set by theoretical reason. The parallel tracks represented by Kant's unshakable desire to have both science and religion reflect the one characteristic common to all parallel lines--they never intersect. To offer the doctrine of the highest good as the "regulative idea of history" as the solution to Kant's impasse is to distort the purely regulative status of Kant's "ideas of reason" (such as teleology) and to implicate him in the kind of metaphysical synthesis which he so strongly resisted in the Critique of Pure Reason. Accordingly, this inquiry into the historical dimensions of a rational faith ultimately betrays one of the basic flaws in Kant's system--namely, his metaphysical dualism.

Thus, the aim of what is to follow is to suggest how a genuinely complete account of Kant's religious thought requires more than a description of his strictures against natural theology and an explication of his theory of moral concepts. The fact that the eventual result reveals a serious shortcoming in the critical philosophy should not obscure several important lessons learned along the way; Kant's failures, it is generally agreed, are more instructive than the successes of most other philosophers. For one thing, Kant is not a crude reductionist with regard to the historical side of religion. Certain stereotypes of his position are apparently based on what the commentator expects to find in Kant, rather than on a clear reading of what Kant actually says. For another thing, the constructive aspect of Kant's theory of historical or revealed religion reflects an interesting theory of the social context of religion, a theory which is largely unaccounted for by the traditional emphasis on the individualistic, personal dimensions of Kant's moral and religious thought. And, as I have been suggesting and will eventually argue in greater detail, Kant's concern for these historical and social elements arises systematically from his epistemology, in which he continually strives to strike a balance between our cognitive capacities and limitations. Consequently, it is not alto-

gether inaccurate to suggest that the aim of this inquiry is simply to read <u>Religion within the Limits of
Reason Alone</u> in the light of the <u>Critique of Pure Rea-
son</u>.

A Note on Kant Interpretation

This inquiry into Kant, based on what I have called
his principle of human limitations, will require for its
justification the close analysis of certain key features
of Kant's epistemology. This, in turn, means that a
general interpretive framework, within which Kant's philosophical project can be placed, will have to be specified and defended. For the history of the interpretation of Kant has shown that one's estimation of Kant's
philosophy as a whole--the theoretical and practical
sides together--relies heavily on one's evaluation of
the meaning and purpose of the <u>Critique of Pure Reason</u>.
Yet the <u>Critique</u>, it goes without saying, can be taken
in a variety of very different ways.

My own stake in a particular view of the <u>Critique</u>
should be obvious. This is because the notion of a
Kantian principle of human limitations immediately connotes a view of that work in which epistemological and
metaphysical considerations meet in ways which have important consequences for one's philosophical anthropology. To emphasize, as I have, the dominance in the
first <u>Critique</u> of Kant's doctrine of sensibility is to
attribute to Kant a particular view of man: as I phrased
it earlier, the doctrine of sensibility implies that
what man can know is strictly limited by who he is.
And to place one's emphasis here is implicitly to al-
lign oneself with the controversial view of the <u>Cri-
tique</u> endorsed by Heidegger and his followers.[21] Thus,
certain problems of Kant interpretation need to be
sorted out and clarified if the substantive parts of
this inquiry are to seem justified.

I do not intend this examination of Kant to suggest
an apologia for the highly idiosyncratic, Heideggerian
interpretation of Kant. Indeed, as any reader of his
investigation of Kant knows, it is somewhat unclear
whether Heidegger in fact <u>has</u> an interpretation of Kant,
or if perhaps Kant simply serves as a springboard for
the promotion of Heideggerian categories, revolving
around his own emphasis on human finitude.[22] Yet by
the end of my inquiry, it will be readily apparent that

15

two themes in particular play central roles in my interpretation of Kant: the doctrines of sensibility and of the schematism. And these, it is important to note, are the foci of Heidegger's interpretation of Kant. Heidegger considers the notion of sensibility to be the clue to the finitude of the human situation, and he claims the schematism doctrine (which for him is "the heart of the whole Critique")[23] reinforces this insight by establishing the priority for Kant of time, or inner sense. Although I do not wish to be implicated in Heidegger's ultimate "ontologization" of Kant's epistemology,[24] I share his sense of the absolute importance of the themes of sensibility and schematization. Both themes suggest the dominant role played in Kant's thought by limiting concepts.[25] Perhaps the best way to characterize my agreement with the Heideggerian approach is to suggest that, in my view, Kant's epistemological strategy rests on certain metaphysical assumptions. This seems a terrible commonplace, but it is a point which is consistently neglected in the recent analytic investigations of Kant.[26] I will explicate further my understanding of the Kantian link between epistemology and metaphysics in Chapter I. I underscore the claim now in order to emphasize that the limiting concepts in Kant's epistemology betray a fundamental limitation of man, the "limitation of knowledge is but the manifestation of man's fundamental limitation, that is, man's finitude."[27] And it is this specific insight which is the basis of my effort to show a positive concern on Kant's part for the historical dimensions of a rational faith.

Nathan Rotenstreich has suggested that all interpretive approaches to the Critique of Pure Reason--and, by implication, to Kant's philosophy as a whole--share two important features. They take a certain trend or principle in Kant's thinking and make it the basis of a constructive and independent philosophical program; and they attempt a "winnowing of the wheat from the chaff" in Kant's system, in an effort to show what is of lasting importance in his philosophy.[28] Thus arises the dialectic, clearly evident in the history of modern philosophy, between constructive philosophy and the interpretation of Kant.[29] One might add to Rotenstreich's assessment that commentators on Kant normally give emphasis to one or the other of these two interpretive features.

Thus, whereas a Hegel or a Heidegger utilizes Kant as a means of promoting an original constructive philosophical effort, other philosophers self-consciously set out to "bring Kant up to date" by showing what remains of philosophical worth and interest in his thought. Modern analytic approaches to Kant are typical of this latter strategy. The idea of "winnowing the wheat from the chaff," for example, is clearly evident in P.F. Strawson's preface to his work on the first Critique.

> I have tried to show how certain
> great parts of the [Critique's]
> structure can be held apart from
> each other, while showing also
> how, within the system itself,
> they are conceived of as related;
> I have tried to give decisive rea-
> sons for rejecting some parts al-
> together; and I have tried to in-
> dicate, though no more than indi-
> cate, how the arguments and con-
> clusions of other parts might be
> so modified or reconstructed as
> to be made more acceptable.[30]

To borrow Jonathan Bennett's phrase, the analytic approach to Kant typically begins with the assumption that "the Critique still has much to teach us, but it is wrong on nearly every page."[31] Though this standpoint in itself does not effectively distinguish the contemporary analytic view of Kant from the traditional Continental view, it does result in a less ambitious and more stringent reading of Kant, with the primary focus on epistemology rather than on ontology and metaphysics. In this connection, J.N. Findlay's characterization is most apt.

> Anyone who enters into the living
> web of contradiction in which the
> Kantian writings consist must nec-
> essarily follow the illumination
> shed by some of its glinting fac-
> ets and ignore that which gleams
> from others...[Certain] Anglo-
> Saxon thinkers, in virtue of their
> very critical attitude towards
> certain central doctrines and as-
> sumptions of Kant, have in fact
> purged Kant's thought of much that
> is merely peripheral and overlaying,
> and have so released Hermes in the
> block, the philosopher in the pic-

17

ture-thinker and model-maker,
to a much greater extent than
would otherwise have been possible.[32]

What seems most desirable is an approach to Kant
which is more historical in intention than an analytic
"updating" of his epistemological concerns, but which
avoids the speculative excesses of the Continental preoccupation with metaphysics. The great virtue of works
by thinkers like Strawson and Bennett is the way they
cut through the obscurities of an extremely turgid
book and offer remarkably lucid accounts of the actual
arguments lurking in Kant's prose. This is no small
achievement and stands in contrast to those works on
Kant which are harder to understand than Kant's original. But the exclusive concern for individual arguments and their importance for contemporary epistemology runs the risk of distorting the point of Kant's
epistemology by removing it from the broader context
within which it is but a single part. To be sure,
Kant's epistemology has an integrity of its own, but
to impute to Kant an essentially epistemological interest is to take only a part of his philosophical project and mistake it for the whole.[33] The aim of Kant's
epistemology, in other words, is not only to salvage
respectability for philosophy, but to provide a framework within which moral and religious concerns might be
promoted in a philosophically legitimate way. This
fact is either ignored or belittled by most analytic
commentators, as exemplified by Strawson's query as to
why Kant finds it necessary to think "both sides" of
the bounds of coherent thinking, instead of finding it
sufficient simply "to think up to them."[34] For Kant,
to think "both sides" is to establish the possibility
of morality and religion. One senses that Strawson
judges this maneuver to be the unfortunate lapse of an
otherwise good epistemologist.

The point is that, given the complexities of the
Critique of Pure Reason, as well as the lasting importance of the epistemological issues raised there by
Kant, it is easy to lose sight of the broader critical
program which is at stake. This is easily understand-
able, for reading the Critique is somewhat like approaching a buffet at an exclusive restaurant--one
could stop virtually anywhere and make a complete meal
out of whatever happened to be at hand. But it is important to emphasize that of the three questions in the

back of Kant's mind--What can I know? What ought I to do? What may I hope?--the epistemological question is the first, not the last.[35] Especially when judging Kant's religious views, the purpose of the epistemology needs to be kept clearly in view. To fail to maintain the proper perspective is, to borrow R.G. Collingwood's warning, to court the risk of accusing Kant of a discrepancy or contradiction which is actually of the critic's own making.

> The contradiction of which the
> critic complains never existed
> in his victim's philosophy at
> all, until the critic planted
> it upon him, as he might have
> planted treasonable correspond-
> ence in his coat pockets; and
> with an equally laudable in-
> tention, to obtain a reward
> for denouncing him.[36]

Kant's specific arguments and reflections concerning epistemology, however interesting they may be to the analytic frame of mind, do not float in a vacuum, free from the influence of other Kantian concerns. As even a contemporary philosopher of science has admitted,

> the ultimate intentions embed-
> ded in the eventual 'critical'
> standpoint were deeply influ-
> enced by [Kant's] ideas in the
> field of the foundations of
> ethics and the nature of reli-
> gious thought.[37]

In contrast to the ambitions of certain Continental approaches to Kant, and the potential reductions of the analytic approach, it seems worthwhile to promote what might be called a "Weltanschauung approach." The term, of course, stems from the title of Richard Kroner's short but valuable book on Kant.[38] Obviously, to invoke the term, Weltanschauung, is to raise new questions as well as to settle others; the very vagueness of the term creates suspicions. But it seems possible to dismiss the metaphysical connotations of the term and utilize the idea of a Weltanschauung as a way of stressing the wholeness or totality of Kant's philosophy, however imperfect that philosophy may be. As Kroner himself suggests, all interpreters of Kant who believe Kant's

19

views on epistemology constitute the "center" or the "very essence" of his philosophy "ignore the inner structure of the whole."[39] One may disagree with Kroner's own interpretation, particularly his extreme emphasis on the primacy of the practical in Kant's thought, but the idea of having a balanced overview of Kant in mind whenever one explores a particular Kantian theme seems entirely defensible. This is not to say that any work on Kant needs to attempt the impossible task of dealing with all areas of the critical philosophy. Rather, it simply means that any authentic account of a particular strand in Kant's thinking must at least indicate that each strand is part of a larger, interlocking whole and is ultimately unintelligible without reference to the whole.

Kant himself made this same basic point in the Critique of Practical Reason.

> When it is a question of determining the origin, contents, and limits of a particular faculty of the human mind, the nature of human knowledge makes it impossible to do otherwise than begin with an exact and...complete delineation of its parts. But still another thing must be attended to which is of a more philosophical and architectonic character. It is to grasp correctly the idea of the whole, and then to see all those parts in their reciprocal interrelations, in the light of their derivation from the concept of the whole, and as united in a pure rational faculty.[40]

It is to see the "reciprocal interrelations" of the varied elements in Kant's own thinking which constitutes the key to the Weltanschauung approach. As John Smith has said in the foreword to Kroner's book, we have today "an overemphasis upon the details of Kant's system, particularly on the early part of the first Critique, and the consequent loss of a total perspective upon the Kantian philosophy."[41] Elsewhere, Smith develops this idea further.

> [It] is essential that we come to some understanding of the depth of [Kant's] struggle with the nature of perennial philosophical problems, especially their bearing upon the

20

religious concern...We have filled
our heads with arguments about forms
of intuition and categories, and
reams of paper have been consumed in
discussions of the things in themselves, but we invariably fail to
understand the dominant reasons and
motives behind the critical philosophy as such. We consistently fail
to understand Kant's philosophy as
a whole.[42]

If the special virtue of the Weltanschauung approach
is its recognition of the interdependence of the various
elements in Kant's philosophy, its drawback may be a
tendency to impute to Kant a systematic achievement which
Kant in fact never accomplished.[43] One may end up looking
for a "system" where there are only loose ends. The only
way to confront this problem is to work out an interpretation of an aspect of Kant's thought with the Weltanschauung notion in mind and see if it is illuminating in
ways that other approaches are not. In a way, the aim of
the Weltanschauung view of Kant is identical with that of
the principle of human limitations: both are intended to
serve as correctives for excessively one-sided views of
Kant's position on various issues.

Thus, in what follows, I am not suggesting that the
idea of the historical dimensions of a rational faith
requires a radically new or revolutionary interpretation
of Kant's religious thought, but merely a more balanced
interpretation which is interesting for its own sake. In
other words, to ferret out the epistemological basis of
the principle of human limitations, to maintain a broad
perspective on Kant's philosophical program, and thereby
to suggest the importance of empirical, historical conditions for Kant's rational religion, does not change the
fact that the source of authentic religion for Kant remains the innate awareness of moral obligation. At its
genuinely essential points, religion is a rational and
not historical affair for Kant. Thus, I find it impossible to agree with Michel Despland's recent suggestion
that Kant's writings on history provide "a better interpretive key" to his religious views than the "traditional
approach" which begins with his ethical works.[44] Such a
view is an excessive reaction against the stereotype promoted by commentators like Greene. It is in contrast to
both the reductionistic approach of Greene and the excessively revisionist view of Despland that the interpretive
genre represented by Kroner seems most valuable--just as
Kroner serves also as a corrective for particular ap-

proaches to Kant's epistemology. Thus, the theoretical and the practical, the empirical and the rational, the historical and the moral all have to be brought together in a coherent pattern if a true understanding of Kant is to be achieved. In all of this, I am in agreement with Allen Wood's recent characterization of "the critical philosophy itself as a _religious_ outlook, a profound conception of the human condition as a whole, and of man's proper response to that condition."[45] To take the critical philosophy as anything less than this is to run the risk of never understanding why, above all, Kant was driven by the question, "What is man?"[46]

CHAPTER I

THE EPISTEMOLOGICAL CONTEXT OF

KANT'S RELIGIOUS PHILOSOPHY

To speak of the "epistemological context of Kant's religious philosophy" is, initially, simply to refer to the well-known fact that any route to Kant's religious thought must first pass through his theory of knowledge. The discussion to be carried on in the present chapter, then, is in many ways a familiar inquiry into Kantian basics. At the same time, however, this inquiry will be cast in a form calculated to substantiate the claim that a systematic concern for the empirical, representative side of religion grows naturally out of Kant's formulation of his epistemological stance. The key, as I have already suggested, is the Kantian claim that any inquiry into the nature of human experience necessarily involves the commitment to a doctrine of human finitude. This results particularly from Kant's theory of sensibility and its implications for the nature of experience and cognition. For Kant, human life without the capacity for sensible "receptivity" is human life disconnected from any conceivable "world." As I shall suggest, such a doctrine invariably leads to a concern for the way supersensuous moral and religious ideas might best be mediated to an inescapably sensuous humanity. In this chapter, then, I will be concerned with: (1) the general problem of Kant's revolution in philosophical method; (2) the more specific problem of the epistemological basis of his principle of human limitations; and (3) the consequences of this principle for Kant's religious thought.

The Problem of Philosophical Method

Perhaps more than any other religious viewpoint, Kant's understanding of religion is intentionally molded in the context of epistemological concerns. This fact results in what is perhaps Kant's most important contribution to religious thought: his theory of religion constitutes such a notable advance precisely because of the way it elevates the importance of the personal and subjective dimensions of belief without a corresponding loss of epistemological integrity.[1] To be sure, a distinctive tradition had long existed which stressed the priority of the "existential" side of belief--Augustine, Luther, and Pascal are perhaps the dominant figures in this line. But Kant's defense of the personal mode of faith, based on his notion of practical reason, is achieved in the context of a self-consciously "enlightened," scientific climate of opinion and on the basis of a remarkably sophisticated and complete epistemology. What makes Kant intrinsically interesting is that he is not promoting a theory of the personal dimensions of belief at the expense of science, but precisely at the same time that he is bolstering the philosophical underpinnings of science. When Kant says he is denying knowledge in order to make room for faith,[2] he knows exactly what he is saying, and he is saying it without assuming an irrational posture. This is no small achievement in any age. Thus, by distinguishing between the theoretical and practical aspects of reason, Kant firmly establishes a theory of the personal dimensions of religion without seeming to minimize various cognitive problems. In W.H. Walsh's felicitous phrase, Kant's philosophy "keeps the world safe for the scientist without showing the door to the moralist and the religious man."[3]

This achievement of Kant's, as I have already anticipated, is based on a curious strategy of making sense of human intellectual capacities in the light of human intellectual limitations. The resulting tension between capacities and limitations does not, for Kant, constitute an irresolvable antagonism. Instead, it simply reflects what Kant takes to be the requirement that we understand various epistemological terms in their proper context, rather than in isolation from one another. The resulting theory of knowledge is so difficult largely because this proper "context" is extremely broad. Kant, in Strawson's characterization, is attempting to determine "the fundamental general structure of any conception of experience such as we can make intelligible to ourselves"--an ambitious and in many ways peculiar undertaking.[4] It is this task which Kant supposes to be the first step toward making "progress" in philosophy, a goal with which philosophers have traditionally been obsessed. Furthermore, the achievement of this Kantian task results, not only in a new form of epistemology, but in a reconstruction of metaphysics and a new philosophical attitude toward mo-

24

rality and religion. Accordingly, Kant's ambition makes
life difficult for his reader, and the situation is not
at all helped by the fact that Kant's style, in Arthur
Schopenhauer's charitable phrase, is "brilliantly dry."[5]

The epistemological basis of all this, of course, is
worked out in the Critique of Pure Reason, a perversely
confusing and perhaps even confused work. Here we have
really come "up against a bureaucracy of the intellect in
which [we] can wander forever from one department to the
next."[6] Even Kant himself would refer to the Critique as
"dry, obscure, opposed to all ordinary notions, and moreover long-winded."[7] It is not surprising, then, that the
enormous influence of the Critique is matched by a wide
divergence of views regarding its purpose and meaning.

The general aim of the first Critique is to lay out
a theory of experience and cognition in such a way as to
place metaphysics on the same kind of firm footing en-
joyed by mathematics and natural science. Kant's employment of the term, "metaphysics," not surprisingly, is ambiguous. He would eventually speak confidently and in
praiseworthy terms of his own "transcendental" metaphysics. But when he complains about the traditional unreli-
ability of metaphysics, he has in mind the school metaphysics of his day, which was characterized by a total
lack of consideration directed toward the potential limits of man's reasoning powers. Such "transcendent" metaphysics is always referred to by Kant in perjorative tones.
Kant's celebrated comment in the Prolegomena accurately
summarizes the anxiety which led to the writing of the
Critique.

> If [metaphysics] be science, how
> is it that it cannot, like other
> sciences, obtain universal and
> lasting recognition? If not, how
> can it maintain its pretensions
> and keep the human mind in sus-
> pense with hopes never ceasing,
> yet never fulfilled? Whether
> then we demonstrate our knowledge
> or our ignorance in this field,
> we must come once for all to a
> definite conclusion respecting
> the nature of this so-called
> science, which cannot possibly
> remain in its present footing.[8]

Kant--for whom mathematics is "the good luck of human
reason"[9]--systematically defends the mathematical-scien-

tific paradigm whenever he dispenses cognitive certification. Accordingly, the disputes of the school metaphysicians of the period seemed ludicrous to him, insofar as they brought philosophical discourse down to the level of mere opinion and "random groping." Thus, a philosophical reform is required, the initial step of which must be the establishment of knowledge that is both universally and necessarily certain. On this basis, metaphysics might become something to be relied upon rather than something to be doubted, disputed, and ridiculed.

It is important to emphasize at the outset this metaphysical theme underlying the <u>Critique of Pure Reason</u>. The first <u>Critique</u> is not simply an "epistemology book," but is self-consciously proposed as a means of overcoming the metaphysical impasse created by the conflict between rationalistic and empiricistic schools. Kant's "stake," in other words, is the intellectual status of metaphysics. In many respects, then, he is issuing a philosophical corrective, in much the same way that later German philosophers like Husserl and Heidegger supposed their work to be a corrective for a Western philosophy gone astray. This fact is well-known, but the sheer breadth of Kant's corrective is often forgotten and reduced to the level of epistemology alone. Yet as Kant himself says, he is proposing a philosophical method on the basis of which we might "secure for human reason complete satisfaction in regard to that with which it has all along so eagerly occupied itself, though hitherto in vain."[10] With one eye on the school metaphysicians of his day, Kant quite intentionally means something more than epistemology when he speaks here of this "complete satisfaction." And to get this philosophical project going, a revolution in method--a whole new way of thinking philosophically--is required. To paraphrase Wittgenstein's metaphor, Kant proposes to call philosophy back from its holiday, and thereby enhance the status and importance of metaphysics.

In light of all this, it is not surprising to find Kant speaking of his epistemological approach as a kind of "Copernican revolution."[11] The point of the analogy is to suggest what occurs when we effect a total reversal or reorientation of our view of a conceptual problem. In Kant's case, the problem at hand is the validity of metaphysics; in other words, the starting point of Kant's Copernican revolution is a metaphysical, not epistemological, issue.[12] His solution to the problem is to propose a philosophical method that will yield the desired kind of knowledge--that is, knowledge that will make philosophy as respectable as mathematics and natural science. But philosophy must do something more than simply catalogue Hume's "relations of ideas"; philosophy must offer knowledge that is not only necessarily certain, but which is genuinely informative as well. This line of reasoning results mainly from the apparently "factual" nature of things Kant supposes to be indubitable--the truths of Newtonian science and the certainty of the moral law. Consequently, Kant finds himself in the philosophically odd position of wanting to claim we can know something a priori which is not simply analytic. This conclusion results particularly from his view of the putative truths of Newtonian physics--e.g., every event has a cause. Thus, an authentic metaphysics would be composed of synthetic judgments known a priori. But since this odd sort of judgment could not be accounted for by the "old" methods--whether rationalist or empiricist--Kant suggests a new method which he calls transcendental.

Launching philosophy on the basis of a transcendental methodology is what Kant's Copernican revolution is all about. In a famous passage in the preface to the second edition of the Critique, Kant suggests what is to be gained from this philosophical shift.

> Hitherto it has been assumed that all our knowledge must conform to objects. But all attempts to extend our knowledge of objects by establishing something in regard to them a priori, by means of concepts, have, on this assumption, ended in failure. We must therefore make trial whether we may not have more success in the tasks of metaphysics, if we suppose that objects must conform to our knowledge. This would agree better with what is desired, namely, that it should be possible to have knowledge of objects a priori, determining something in regard to them prior to their being given.[13]

Thus, Kant has two difficulties which his Copernican revolution is intended to ameliorate. On the one hand there is the status of philosophical knowledge and its traditional inability to achieve the universal validity of mathematics and science; and on the other hand there is a body of data (such as the truths of Newtonian science) the truth of which Kant takes for granted but the possibility of which still needs to be accounted for philosophically. Like the astronomer or physicist, Kant is abandoning an old and problematic conceptual scheme in favor of another which offers greater explanatory power. Unlike the astronomer or physicist, though, Kant is not trying to add to our store of factual knowledge, but is simply trying to account for the possibility of such certain knowledge as we have. This is the task he imagines to be the rightful preoccupation of philosophers.

Kant's transcendental method in philosophy is precisely that approach geared to solve the dilemma which Kant formulates in his Copernican revolution.

> I entitle transcendental all knowledge which is occupied not so much with objects as with the mode of our knowledge of objects in so far as this mode of knowledge is to be possible a priori.[14]

It is this inquiry into the "mode of our knowledge" of objects which makes Kant's transcendental philosophy unique and revolutionary. Such a methodology shifts the philosopher's concern from the object of knowledge to the knowing subject, from the material to the formal element in cognition. By beginning with this inquiry into what the knower brings to cognition, Kant's transcendental philosophy involves a rigorous examination of the nature and limits of our reasoning capacity. This is what makes Kant's philosophy "critical"; critical philosophy is so-called because of the way "it turns back and examines itself."[15] The opposite of critical philosophy for Kant is what he calls "dogmatism," which tries to proceed "from concepts alone" and "is thus the dogmatic procedure of pure reason without previous criticism of its own powers."[16] As H.J. Paton has put it, Kant assumed that

> what was wrong with philosophy before his time was this--that philosophers blundered along trying to solve philosophical problems without ever asking themselves what it was they were doing and whether what they were doing was something that could be done.[17]

Kant's transcendental philosophy, then, begins with a kind of mental inventory, aimed toward curbing illicit speculative departures. This is what is meant when the

commentators speak of Kant's transcendental method as
the "inquiry into the conditions of the possibility of
experience." This somewhat cumbersome characterization
at least makes it obvious that the knowing process as
such will be the focus of Kant's attention.

The Critique of Pure Reason, then, can be read as a
kind of guidebook in reason's methodological progression
from a transcendent to a transcendental employment, from
a dogmatic and skeptical to a critical outlook.[18] It is
initially important to be clear about what Kant's inquiry into the formal rather than material side of cognition entails. This distinction does not coincide with
the simple dichotomy between reason and experience or
between the necessary and the contingent. The uniqueness of Kant's inquiry lies precisely in the way it is
probing that odd ground where the strict traditional
dichotomies no longer apply. A "transcendental" inquiry,
in other words, is poised to unravel the riddle posed by
Kant's opening observation that "though all our knowledge begins with experience, it does not follow that it
all arises out of experience."[19] John Smith has observed that to apply traditional dichotomies to Kant's
epistemology necessarily leads to a misunderstanding of
the essential point of doing transcendental philosophy.

> The idea that experience may have a
> necessary structure to be possible at
> all is not something which occurred to
> Kant's predecessors and it has been
> persistently misunderstood by many of
> his successors because they have tried
> to understand the purport of the 'tran-
> scendental' in terms of some dyadic
> distinction between the 'logical' and
> the 'empirical,' or even worse, between
> the 'factual' and the 'linguistic.'
> The mark of this confusion coincides
> with the conflation of 'a priori' and
> 'analytic' which at once reduces to
> nonsense Kant's fundamental question.[20]

The point is that to speak of the "formal" side of cognition is misleading if it simply connotes the canons of
formal logic. Kant himself carefully and continually
emphasizes the distinction between formal and transcendental logic,[21] and it is the very possibility of this
distinction which underlies certain key doctrines, such
as the metaphysical deduction of the categories. For
now, it is simply important to note the originality of

Kant's method and to avoid translating uniquely Kantian terms into more familiar but potentially distorting ones.

Epistemology and the Principle of Human Limitations

Kant's revolution in philosophical method, focusing on the knowing subject, leads to a lengthy consideration of our cognitive faculties. As I have suggested, epistemological and metaphysical concerns are never strictly divorced in the first Critique; one need not embrace the potential distortions of a Heideggerian "ontologization" of Kant's epistemology to agree with this claim. Indeed, I have pointed out that the very starting point of Kant's Copernican revolution is an explicitly metaphysical problem. This metaphysical motive is often obscured by the dramatic effect of Kant's self-conscious demolition of traditional transcendent metaphysics--by the time the reader of the first Critique reaches the Dialectic, it is easy to forget the heady Kantian claim in the opening pages of the first preface.

> In this enquiry I have made com-
> pleteness my chief aim, and I ven-
> ture to assert that there is not a
> single metaphysical problem which has
> not been solved, or for the solution
> of which the key at least has not
> been supplied.[22]

The point of contact between epistemology and metaphysics is guaranteed by the fact that the same Kantian "facul-ties" which constitute experience also constitute a par-ticular view of human life and of our capacity to com-prehend reality as such. After all, the very idea of a necessary "structure" imposed on human experience sug-gests that rational beings are at the same time limited beings, limited by that same structure which constitutes experience.

This point of contact between epistemology and meta-physics is helpful for the way it draws our attention to the predominance of "limiting concepts" in Kant's pro-gram. Metaphysics in the old style is outlawed because of certain limitations Kant is imposing. It is not too much to say that the point of a "critique" of theoreti-cal reason is, for Kant, the systematic mapping of lim-its to our cognitive activities. Thus, a dominant theme in the first Critique is the claim that rationality as such has certain strictures which limit any human being. Indeed, were it not for Kant's eventual appeal to the phenomenal-noumenal split, a dichotomy which provides us with a kind of dual citizenship, the doctrines of the first Critique would constitute a radically mechanistic outlook with highly restrictive consequences for our place in the world. It is only through the dual citizenship afforded by the noumenal realm that Kant avoids succumbing to a purely mechanistic form of naturalism.

The predominance of limiting concepts in the first Critique results in what I have earlier referred to as Kant's principle of human limitations. This principle states that Kant's concern for human intellectual capacities is always kept in balance with considerable sensitivity for human intellectual limitations. The best way to justify this principle is to focus on those doctrines of the first Critique in which the importance of limiting concepts is most forcefully maintained by Kant. Any number of Kantian themes might be selected for this task, but--keeping in mind the primary aims of this inquiry--two in particular would seem most relevant: the doctrine of sensibility, resulting in Kant's theory of intuition and the corresponding claim that an "intellectual intuition" is an impossibility for rational beings; and the Kantian claim that the noumenal realm is simply to be thought of as a limiting concept. These two themes need to be explored in some detail.

Kant defines human sensibility as the "capacity (receptivity) for receiving representations through the mode in which we are affected by objects."[23] Sensibility is the passive side of being human, through which objects are "given" to us. Furthermore, sensibility yields intuitions, which actually effect the connection between us and the external world and which provide the raw data to be synthesized by the concepts of the understanding. Sensibility is the sheer capacity to be affected by the external world, while intuitions are the most primitive form of "taking account" of that world. The whole complex doctrine of sensibility and intuitions is a theory of the epistemological "given," in the bedrock, foundational sense of that term.[24]

This well-known doctrine is the starting point of Kant's account of the cognitive process. It leads to the uniquely Kantian claim that space and time themselves are forms of pure intuition. Space and time are a priori for Kant, in the sense that they can never be thought away.[25] And anything that is known a priori must be brought by the knower, since the point of Kant's Copernican revolution is that we can know a priori of things only what we ourselves put into them.[26] This strategy guarantees for Kant that the notion of "necessary truth" will have some connection with human experience.

Since the theory of space and time as pure intuitions necessarily constitutes the point of greatest interest in the Transcendental Aesthetic, it is easy to lose sight of Kant's starting point. This is the notion that cognition is ultimately reliant on the human capacity to be affected by the external world, a capacity which Kant himself refers to as "receptivity."[27] This essentially empiricist claim remains, as it were, in the driver's seat as Kant subsequently works out his full epistemological program. Though the "blindness" of mere intuitions is in no way superior to the "emptiness" of mere concepts, it seems fair to say that there is something "foundational"--in the sense alluded to above--about the theory of sensibility which cannot quite be said of the faculty of understanding.

This is important because, whatever else it may be, the doctrine of sensibility is a doctrine of limitations. This is because the whole point of the doctrine is a theory of what must obtain experientially if genuine knowledge is to be secure. Kant's doctrine of sensibility, in other words, is the anchor that guarantees that his philosophy will not, like those of some of his predecessors, proceed by concepts alone. The anchor itself is embedded in finite, experiential conditions, the limitations of which cannot be legitimately traversed. The empiricistic strand implicit in the doctrine of sensibility must, of course, be kept in the perspective of the overriding transcendental method at work in Kant's thinking. But the fact remains that the starting point of Kant's epistemological inquiry, because of its link to human experience, effectively makes genuinely cognitive claims dependent upon the conditions of human finitude. This is the crucial ontological implication of an apparently epistemological claim and the natural result of Kant's focus on the knowing subject, rather than on the object known. What we can know is always conditioned by who we are.[28] This result is automatic, once Kant poses the epistemological problem in terms of the necessary conditions for the possibility of experience.

The implications of Kant's doctrine of sensibility are clearer still when we consider his abandonment of the notion of an "intellectual intuition." Prior to the publication of the first Critique, Kant had entertained the idea of an intellectual intuition or cognition,

32

as exemplified in his Inaugural Dissertation of 1770.[29]
By the time of the publication of the Critique of Pure
Reason, however, Kant was convinced that such a doctrine
was indefensible. As Kant emphasizes at the close of
the Transcendental Aesthetic, our "mode of intuition is
dependent upon the existence of the object, and is therefore possible only if the subject's faculty of representation is affected by that object."[30] Kant's subsequent
discussion of the noumenal affords him the opportunity
of saying that, were the noumenal to be taken in the
"positive" sense as "an object of a non-sensible intuition," we would thereby

> presuppose a special mode of intui-
> tion, namely, the intellectual, which
> is not that which we possess, and of
> which we cannot comprehend even the
> possibility.[31]

The key seems to be Kant's insistence that genuine cognition involves the knower's capacity to be "affected"
by the object, and this is precisely what the doctrine
of sensibility is all about.

> Even if we were willing to assume a
> kind of intuition other than this our
> sensible kind, the functions of our
> thought would still be without meaning
> in respect to it.[32]

Now the point of Kant's rejection of the notion of an
intellectual intuition has often been thought to be the
claim that categories cannot be legitimately applied to
what is not given in sense experience. This characterization, of course, is not incorrect, but the emphasis
is misplaced; rather, Kant's point is that sense experience is the necessary prerequisite for the application
of the categories. In other words, the genuine source
of human finitude in Kant's epistemology is not the categorial structure of the understanding, but the sensible
conditions which must obtain before the categories can
be employed.[33] The force of Kant's rejection of the
idea of an intellectual intuition does not derive from
his idea of the rightful employment of the categories,
but from his theory of the human capacity of receptivity.
This is the point of rejecting an "intellectual" intuition in favor of a "sensible" one.

Kant's eventual espousal of a sensible intuition--
the transition from the viewpoint of the Inaugural Dissertation to that of the first Critique--betrays a

33

peculiar undercurrent running through Kant's philosophical method. Assuming that one can be content with an epistemological vocabulary containing "intuitions" and "concepts" in the first place, it obviously seems preferable to adopt the claim that man possesses only a sensible intuition. The standpoint of the Critique is, in fact, a genuine advance over that of the Inaugural Dissertation for just those reasons Kant himself offers.

But what is odd about Kant's procedure is the lack of any argumentative basis for ascribing "intuitions" to us at all. To speak of a "sensible intuition," or to claim that sensibility is a "receptive" capacity, or the understanding a "spontaneous" capacity, are all comparable to what W.H. Walsh has said about Kant's claim that ours is a "discursive" intellect: they are all instances of "primitive truths" which have nothing as their basis except the fact that Kant claims them.[34] Kant's transcendental method yields certain interesting results which are compelling for the way they seem clearly derived from his premises. But Kant "says next to nothing about the premises from which he deduces" his results, or about the "type of argument he appeals to in reaching" them.[35] For example, what kind of knowledge is "knowledge" of our intellectual capacities and limitations? What kind of argument can be offered in support of the claim that man has both receptive and spontaneous capacities? Such questions, of course, touch on the perennial issue of how the critical philosophy itself is possible. One can grant that Kant arrives at certain truths which--arguably--can be called synthetic a priori, and which thereby seem to fulfill the aims of the first Critique. But what is troubling is the foundational claims--Kant's "primitive truths"-- which cannot possibly pass the transcendental test Kant applies to mathematics, natural science, and metaphysics. This result is, in an odd way, parallel to the fact that the logical positivists' verificationist principle could not itself be verified. In both cases, what we have is a philosophical method which can account for everything but itself.[36]

If one were to be mesmerized by the "problem of accountability," of course, it would be impossible to take seriously the central issues in this inquiry. I mention the problem at this point only because it seems to affect Kant's theory of sensibility so directly. One is not really convinced or left unconvinced by Kant's theory of sensibility as a crucial limiting concept. Rather, one either follows the theory along to see what

34

it entails, or one rejects it at the outset. To discern some other course would be to discover a form of philosophical argument which is certainly absent from Kant's own philosophy.

So far, then, we have seen how the doctrine of sensibility suggests an important aspect of human limitations. The Kantian linkage between bona fide knowledge and sensible conditions results in a certain vision of our standing in the world, considered from the standpoint of our cognitive capacities. The relevance of this point will eventually be clarified in the discussion of the manner in which supersensuous moral and religious ideas are communicated to a sensuous humanity. Kant's constructive theory of historical religion, in other words, stems directly from his doctrine of human sensibility. History is the medium which ameliorates this aspect of the principle of human limitations.

A second Kantian theme which substantiates the idea of a principle of human limitations is the theory of phenomena and noumena. The distinction between a phenomenal and noumenal realm arises for Kant on the basis of an implication regarding his theory of appearances, but its importance for the entire critical philosophy far outweighs the seemingly obscure point which serves as its basis. For without providing for the possibility of a noumenal realm, Kant could not introduce a theory of morality and religion, and this would undermine one of the fundamental purposes of doing "critical" philosophy in the first place. Thus, since the phenomena-noumena distinction is a key element in a broadly-based Kantian strategy, correctly understanding the distinction involves the inquiry into a number of seemingly discrete concerns which eventually coalesce in a single philosophical principle. Accordingly, correctly understanding the phenomena-noumena split is a classic instance of the need to assume a Weltanschauung approach to Kant, rather than reduce all Kantian principles to their lowest epistemological denominator. It is necessary, then, to preface a direct consideration of the phenomena-noumena problem with an examination of the difficulty it helps Kant resolve.

It is commonly recognized that the Critique of Pure Reason was written in large part to defend the orderly workings of a Newtonian universe from the nagging claims of a skeptical empiricism, especially Hume's.[37] In particular, the validity of the causality principle was at stake, a principle which seemed to undergird the whole complex network of Newtonian physics. A crucial result of Kant's formulation of synthetic judgments known a priori is the establishment of links between the necessary conditions of the possibility of experience-- arrived at transcendentally--and the central claims of Newtonian science. By this method, Kant creates a means of defending what Hume had found cause to question.

The basis of this Kantian achievement is Kant's assumption (and that is all it seems to be) that the analytic unities of thought have corresponding synthetic unities. This is the point of the metaphysical deduction, in which the classifications of formal logic suggest to Kant the classifications brought by the understanding to experience.[38] This correspondence between the classifications of formal and transcendental logic is what Kant calls "the clue to the discovery of all pure concepts of the understanding."[39] To oversimplify, Kant is merely claiming that the logical forms of judgment tell us what the categories are. The details of this procedure have ceased to be of major philosophical interest, given the type of formal logic Kant utilizes as his basis.[40] But whatever else one might feel inclined to say about Kant's strategy, it serves as an ingenious way of overcoming Humean skepticism without falling into a purely rationalistic philosophical framework.[41] Thus, for example, the principle of causality assumes the status of a category within Kant's system, thereby enjoying the peculiarly conceived objectivity with which Kant's categories are all endowed; what had for Hume been a mental "habit" becomes for Kant a necessary "rule."[42] Without this rule and others, experience itself is simply impossible. By way of this transcendental strategy, then, Kant lays down a philosophical foundation on which the claims of Newtonian science can securely rest.

Now all of this is important for our purposes because of the way it implicates Kant in a thoroughly deterministic world view. Because of his commitment to Newtonian science, Kant must defend the universality of causal connections, a principle which, in Kant's own words, "allows of no exception" whatsoever.[43] Insofar as man himself is part of the natural world described by Newtonian science, all his actions "must admit of explanation in accordance with the laws of nature."[44] In other words, from the theoretical standpoint established in the first Critique, we are completely determined beings;[45] we may "think" ourselves free, but we "know" ourselves as phenomena under the laws of nature.[46] To deny that we are fully determined would be to disrupt the regularity of the laws posited by natural science, a regularity which is the very basis of the prestige of science. Any other conclusion on Kant's part would undermine one of the basic purposes of writing the Critique in the first place.

The difficult problem posed by determinism is resolved by Kant on the basis of his phenomena-noumena distinction. The distinction itself arises from an epistemological consideration, but this origin appears suspiciously like a Kantian excuse to provide the means to salvage human life from a purely mechanistic world. The theory of appearances which dominates the first Critique is tempered by Kant with a distinction between what we can know about objects as appearances, and what we can think about them as things in themselves.[47] The language of "things in themselves" spares Kant the difficulties inherent in Berkeley-type conclusions and is introduced on the precarious basis of Kant's claim that "otherwise we should be landed in the absurd conclusion that there can be appearance without anything that appears."[48] The phenomena-noumena distinction, then, rests in turn on the distinction Kant draws between knowing and thinking. To "know" something by the standards of the first Critique is to be in a position to have sensible experience of something, to state an analytic truth, or to offer a piece of transcendental knowledge. These conditions impose important limits, whereas to "think" something merely requires that I not defy the rules of logical contradiction.[49] Thus, although it is impossible either to know or to think a square circle, it is quite conceivable that we can "think" the numenal reality of objects which we "know" only in their phenomenal aspect.

Kant's introduction of the notion of the noumenal seems at first to be a kind of speculative departure rather than an aspect of his principle of human limitations. But Kant is careful to broach the idea of the noumenal in cautious terms. He warns that the sheer "thinking" of something, such as the thing in itself which appears phenomenally, has a strictly limited result. That is, to be able to "think" something does not impart "real" possibility to that object, but only a "logical" possibility.[50] Put otherwise, to "think" the thing in itself is to deny that we could every disprove its reality at the same time it is to deny we could every prove it. To "think" the noumenal is to prove nothing. Rather, it is to preserve for Kant a form of logical possibility that will be important for his ethical and religious theory.

In his most explicit consideration of the phenomenal-noumenal dichotomy, Kant explicitly speaks of the noumenal as a "limiting concept."[51] He raises the question as to whether we might use the term noumenon in a positive or negative sense.

> If by 'noumenon' we mean a thing so far as it is <u>not an object of our sensible intuition</u>, and so abstract from our mode of intuiting it, this is a noumenon in the <u>negative</u> sense of the term. But if we understand by it an <u>object</u> of a <u>nonsensible intuition</u>, we thereby presuppose a special mode of intuition, namely, the intellectual, which is not that which we possess, and of which we cannot comprehend even the possibility. This would be 'noumenon' in the positive sense of the term.[52]

It is significant for our purposes that the adjudication of the proper sense of noumenon is conducted in the context of Kant's theory of intuition. Again we see that our cognitive limitations do not derive from the categorial structure of the understanding so much as from the doctrine of sensible receptivity which is the starting point of Kant's epistemology. When it comes to the task of fully accounting for the doctrine of the noumenal, in other words, Kant reverts to a foundational claim—intuition must be <u>sensible</u> and <u>passive</u> rather than intellectual and active. Thus, the sense in which the theory of the noumenal is a limiting concept dovetails with the sense in which the doctrine of sensibility is itself a limiting concept.

An important difficulty with Kant's requirement that the noumenal be understood only as a limiting concept is the way it conflicts with the epistemological basis on which the phenomena-noumena split was originally introduced. As we have seen, Kant introduces the notion of noumenon as the source of appearances, but this is something quite different than a limiting concept. George Schrader has suggested that Kant's twofold view of the thing in itself betrays Kant's status as "a confirmed realist throughout the critical period" and that Kant's private metaphysical views need to be distinguished from a consistently critical position.[53]

What is worse, Kant is implicated in the discrepancy between claiming we can "think" things in themselves--which, of course, requires the use of the categories--and claiming that the categories "are absolutely without meaning when applied beyond the realm of appearances."[54]

Despite these difficulties with Kant's doctrine, it is obvious that the genuine _critical_ function of the noumenal is as a limiting concept. Even Schrader thinks it possible to demarcate a genuinely critical form of the doctrine of the noumenal.[55] As Kant himself states, the noumenal is "limiting" in the sense that its function "is to curb the pretensions of sensibility"[56]--pretensions that would lead sensibility toward an intellectual, rather than purely sensible, intuition. (This "curbing of pretensions," as Bennett has noted, is "likely work for a 'limiting concept.'")[57] The manner in which the limitations suggested by the theory of the noumenal link up with those suggested by the doctrine of sensibility nicely illustrates the key feature of the principle of human limitations--what we can know is strictly limited by who we are. That Kant himself links the idea of an intellectual intuition with God merely reinforces this insight.[58] To be a rational being, capable of authentic cognition, is to be implicated in the finite conditions imposed by sensibility.[59]

Even though the phenomena-noumena distinction arises out of epistemological concerns, its chief importance lies in the way it helps Kant solve the determinism problem. Kant's phenomenal world of appearances, grasped through theoretical reason, can admit of no exceptions to the causal nexus. But by providing for the sheer logical possibility of a noumenal realm, Kant supposes he has provided at least the logical possibility of human freedom. From Kant's standpoint, to be able to view man from a dual perspective--noumenally as well as phenomenally--means that the theoretical realm of scientific cognition and description does not necessarily have an exclusive hold on the way we can describe human life. There is no hint in Kant of a theoretical _proof_ of the reality of freedom. Rather, Kant's only aim is to provide a stereoscopic perspective which will itself not be logically contradictory.[60] Accordingly, Kant is careful to emphasize that he has demonstrated neither the reality nor even the real possibility of freedom, but that his demonstration has merely a logical import. He has simply asked

whether freedom and natural necessity

can exist without conflict in one and
the same action; and this we have suf-
ficiently answered. We have shown that
since freedom may stand in relation to
a quite different kind of conditions
from those of natural necessity, the
law of the latter does not affect the
former, and that both may exist, independently of one another and without
interfering with each other.[61]

· Kant's approach to the determinism problem reveals
an interesting agnostic strand in his thinking which,
in turn, reflects his concern for human intellectual
limitations. The force of the demonstration of the logical possibility of the noumenal, and thereby of freedom,
is not the claim that freedom may exist. Rather, it is
the claim that the reality of freedom may not legitimately be disproved on theoretical grounds. Put otherwise, Kant's principle of human limitations cuts both
ways--it applies equally to what we can dismiss as to
what we can admit. This agnosticism bears important
results for Kant's ethical and religious theories, since
it opens the way for practical reason to postulate what
theoretical reason can never prove. The important point
is that practical reason is not defeated before it
begins--Kant's epistemological strictures offer no more
comfort to the atheist than to the theist.[62]

From Theory to Practice

The preceding considerations suggest the rather
ironic sub-plot of the Critique of Pure Reason. It
would seem that limitations placed on human cognitive
capacities would have negative or destructive consequences for speculation about religious affairs. But in
Kant's hands, these limitations have an essentially positive effect. The first Critique is often characterized
as destructive of religious concerns, but it is really
destructive of only a particular kind of metaphysically-
based natural theology. The broadest possible view of
the Critique suggests that Kant is implicitly attempting
to establish a theory of knowledge that will outlaw those
forms of religious thought which can be victimized by the
vagaries of philosophical disputes. At the same time he
does this, Kant is laying the groundwork for a religion
which, to him, possesses absolute certainty and universality. This is the whole point of his celebrated desire

"to deny <u>knowledge</u>, in order to make room for <u>faith</u>."[63]
The irony is that Kant should think that depriving theoretical reason of its speculative pretensions should
have a religiously efficacious result. The thrust of
this result is not so much the providing for the possibility of religious realities, such as God, freedom,
and immortality. Rather, it is the interdiction of the
theoretical demonstration of their impossibility, which
is quite a different thing.[64] The contours of this
Kantian insight suggest the close connection in the
critical philosophy between religious concerns and the
principle of human limitations: the constructive consideration of religious themes is in fact enhanced by
Kant's epistemological strictures.

All of this is made possible, of course, by Kant's
shift from theoretical to practical reason. The first
<u>Critique</u> really would be destructive of religious con-
cerns if theoretical reason were the only mode of human
reflection within the critical philosophy. But Kant's
introduction of the theory of practical reason changes,
so to speak, the ground rules and allows him to give
back with the left hand what he seemed to be taking
away with the right. Put otherwise, the so-called agnostic strand in Kant's thinking, evidenced in the
severe limitations placed on our theoretical capacities,
disappears dramatically when the same issues are considered from the practical point of view.

The distinction between theoretical and practical
reason is essentially the distinction between knowing
and acting. The foundation for the transition from a
philosophy of theory to a philosophy of practice was
originally laid down in the "Canon of Pure Reason" in
the first <u>Critique</u>.[65] The stake involved in this tran-
sition--the creation of a stereoscopic view of man which
can endorse both Newtonian science and the freedom of
the will--becomes increasingly explicit in works composed after the first <u>Critique</u>.

> [It] is an inescapable task of specula-
> tive [i.e., theoretical] philosophy to
> show...that we (do not) think of man in
> a different sense and relationship when
> we call him free from that in which we
> consider him as a part of nature and
> subject to its laws. It must show not
> only that they can very well co-exist
> but also that they must be thought of
> as necessarily united in one and the

41

same subject...This duty is imposed
only on speculative philosophy, so
that it may clear the way for practical philosophy.[66]

The point of such a "practical philosophy" is to clarify
and answer the "What ought I to do?" question in the way
speculative or theoretical philosophy treats the "What
can I know?" question.

Whereas theoretical reason is aimed at describing
and determining its object, practical reason is concerned with "making actual" its object.[67] Practical
reason, in other words, has to do with objects of the
will: it "is not a reason by which we know anything;
its reality is shown by an act."[68] Given this meaning
of practical reason, it is not surprising that it provides the context in which Kant discusses human freedom.
The sheer logical possibility of doing this is provided
theoretically, through the phenomena-noumena distinction. And the actual fulfillment of this chance to
speak of man stereoscopically occurs within the Kantian
theories of morality and religion, based on the notion
of practical reason. Significantly, Kant insists that
"in the final analysis there can be but one and the same
reason which must be differentiated only in application,"[69] and he assumes that in his Critique of Practical Reason he has shown how this can be so.

At the same time, however, Kant self-consciously
provides for the "primacy" of practical reason, making
possible the critical establishment of moral and religious themes and thereby fulfilling the promise of the
first Critique.[70] By the "primacy" of practical reason,
Kant simply means that, of the human "interests" involved in theoretical and practical reason, the interests of the practical remain paramount.[71] This suggests
that practical reason is free to pursue its own satisfaction, but only as long as its employment does not
openly contradict the mandates of theoretical reason.
Hence, the relation between theoretical and practical
concerns is quite intimate: practical reason, due to
its primacy, has the right to "postulate" where theoretical reason must remain silent; but theoretical reason
has the right to lay down certain limitations within
which such postulation must occur. The important point
is that practical reason can proceed in directions which
are closed off to theoretical reason. In this sense, as
Kant himself boasts, the second Critique "very satisfy-
ingly" completes and reveals "the highly consistent

42

structure of the <u>Critique of Pure Reason</u>."[72] Theoretical and practical reason are in no way in competition with one another, but are complementary and mutually beneficial, as long as the appropriate boundary lines are observed.[73]

Kant's turn from the theoretical mode of descriptions and demonstrations to the practical mode of actions and aims is meant to demonstrate that making a moral judgment or believing in God are of a unique epistemological order. They are not matters of theory but of practice, and a major part of the critical philosophy is devoted to showing that the latter carries a kind of certainty not provided for by the former. The transition from the practical as such to the practical insofar as it is freighted with moral implications is guaranteed by Kant's assumption of the universal sense of oughtness or moral obligation characteristic of rational beings.[74] This sense of duty is just that--a "sense" of duty which carries no content with it whatsoever. Practical reason can guarantee moral and religious certainties because of the indubitable quality of this innate sense of duty or obligation. A good example of the way Kant simply assumes, rather than argues for, the sense of duty is the structure of his <u>Foundations of the Metaphysics of Morals</u>. He proceeds, as he puts it, "analytically"

> from <u>common knowledge</u> to the determination of its supreme principle, and then synthetically from the examination of this principle and its sources back to common knowledge where it finds its application.[75]

The title of the first section of the <u>Foundations</u> is highly revealing in this respect: "Transition from the Common Rational Knowledge of Morals to the Philosophical."[76]

Kant's readiness to begin his ethical theory with this putative "common knowledge" of morals betrays a significant convergence of philosophical and psychological factors. Since there is no real argumentation on Kant's part for the validity of his starting point, one must look elsewhere for its source. And this source, it is generally agreed, is the enormous influence exerted on the young Kant by his parents' religious pietism, and on the mature Kant by Rousseau.[77] The impact of Rousseau on Kant was particularly profound and dramatic, resulting in an "awakening" in the practical sphere which in many ways is analogous to the awakening in the theoretical sphere produced by Hume.[78]

> I feel a consuming thirst for
> knowledge and a restless pas-
> sion to advance in it, as well
> as satisfaction in every forward
> step. There was a time when I
> thought that this alone could
> constitute the honor of mankind,
> and I despised the common man who
> knows nothing. Rousseau set me
> right. This blind prejudice
> vanished; I learned to respect
> human nature, and I should con-
> sider myself far more useless
> than the ordinary workingman if
> I did not believe that this view
> could give worth to all others
> to establish the rights of man.[79]

The peculiar juxtaposition of Rousseau and Newton in a single world view accounts for much of the character of the critical philosophy.

The specific contours of Kant's theory of practical reason, the notions of freedom and autonomy, and his determination of the supreme principle of morality through the categorical imperative, are not of direct relevance to the present inquiry. What is important, however, is the Kantian emphasis on the innateness of the moral law and the fact that all subsequent moral and religious claims on Kant's part rely upon this doctrine of moral obligation. The formative influence of this doctrine on Kant's understanding of man and his unique place in the world is crucial, but it is impossible to explain the origin of such a doctrine.

> [We] cannot answer the question,
> what is the source of the moral
> law? If we assigned a ground for
> it beyond the obligation itself,
> we should have destroyed the obli-
> gation as such. Moral obligation
> for Kant is as ultimate a fact as
> the existence of what is presented
> to us through our senses, and as
> inexplicable. We can explain the
> order and sequence of sense-pres-
> entations in terms of natural laws,
> we can use our knowledge of natural

laws to anticipate further sense-
experience, but we cannot explain
why we have sense-experience at
all. Neither can we explain why
there is moral obligation. We
must simply recognize it.[80]

It is this sense of moral obligation which distinguishes
"rational" beings from all other sorts of beings in the
world. Within the critical philosophy, it is an indeli-
ble mark signifying that human life is genuinely fulfilled only in moral and religious terms.

Because all of Kant's religious teachings stem from
his principle of the innateness of moral obligation, the
token of genuine Kantian religious belief is a kind of
personal certainty rather than theoretical possibility
or demonstration. Reason in its practical aspect, and
the unconditioned sense of oughtness, combine in Kant's
writings to yield what could only be a logical possibility within the realm of theoretical reason. Our religious life, then, becomes a matter of the subjective
apprehension of something of which we are implicitly
certain, rather than an external demonstration of something regarding which we need to be convinced. In this
sense, Kant's theory of morality and religion ultimately
rests on a form of moral intuitionism--exactly what
form, however, it is hard to say, given Kant's mere assumption of, rather than argument for, an innate moral
sense. What makes the issue especially complex is that
the intuitionism characteristic of Kant's ethical theory is _rational_ (i.e., to apprehend the moral law is a
necessary mark of a rational being) and thereby stands
in contrast to the theory of _sensible_ intuitions contained in his epistemology. Consequently, Kant's
blatant use of the vocabulary of the "subjective" and
"internal" dimensions of moral and religious certainty
can only raise eyebrows in the context of modern epistemological concerns. But there can be no question that
he self-consciously desires to draw the line between the
approximations of theoretical cognition and the absolute
assurance provided by the "internal" source of moral
awareness. When he alludes to his "admiration and awe"
for "the starry heavens above me and the moral law within me," Kant feels no need to translate the sense of his
"within."[81] Religious certainties, in turn, are not
really based upon "knowledge," but simply upon that universally given "sentiment of unconditional obligation
experienced in a context where action is called for."[82]

The forbidding epistemological doctrines of the Critique of Pure Reason, then, go hand in hand with a theory of the personal dimensions of religious belief. In this, Kant is not so much the great destroyer of religious belief as he is the precursor of those who--like Schleiermacher, Ritschl, and the religious existentialists--would attempt to establish a form of religious or moral "consciousness" which, at the level of theoretical reason, is non-cognitive. The formal link between Kant's innate sense of moral obligation and his religious teaching is located in his discussion of the postulates of practical reason.[83] Here, God, freedom, and immortality are not only elevated to a level of personal, practical certainty but "acquire objective reality" in a seemingly very strong sense.[84] The actual epistemological status of the postulates is nowhere satisfactorily explained by Kant, but what is noteworthy is the level of certainty practical reason can attain with regard to that about which theoretical reason must remain agnostic. The preservation of the moral and religious sphere from the theoretical criteria of a strictly cognitive mode of thought is the strategic result of Kant's move toward what amounts to a "two-level theory of truth."[85]

I have said that the formal link between the innateness of moral experience and the certainty of religious themes is established by Kant in his postulates. God, freedom, and immortality are just that--postulates. According to Kant, a postulate is "a theoretical proposition which is not as such demonstrable, but which is an inseparable corollary of an a priori unconditionally valid practical law."[86] Kant's arguments in favor of the postulates follow the form, "this must be so if something else is to be so." Such argumentation is characteristic of Kant and suggests the manner in which his position quickly becomes invulnerable once his premises are accepted. Consequently, the real threat to Kant's vision of the religious life is not so much the chance of a logical inconsistency as it is the possibility that the universe is intrinsically absurd and unwilling to abide by the mandates of Kant's various "must be so's." This possibility, quite simply, is one Kant never even considered.[87] His trust in the inherent rationality of things distinguishes him as a true child of the Enlightenment, regardless of his seeming idiosyncracies in other matters. Thus, God, freedom, and immortality are not tacked on as additions to Kant's moral theory; rather, they turn out to be the necessary and rational consequences of that theory--indeed, they are

46

the guarantors of the intelligibility of that theory--
once the notion of oughtness and the rationality of the
universe are both assumed. This "moral grounding" of
the idea of God guarantees that authentic religion, in
Kant's scheme, will be founded upon the "personal discovery of the involvement of God in [one's] own moral
situation," rather than upon metaphysical speculation or
theoretical proof.[88] Again, the apparent limitations
imposed by the first Critique turn out to be genuinely
beneficial for what Kant takes to be the authentically
religious life. The "utter insufficiency" of theoretical reason to solve the weightiest human problems does
not mean that these problems are irresolvable.[89]
Rather, it is a hint that our moral and religious lives
need to be thought out on a level different from the
level of mathematics and science.

The obvious result of Kant's view of religion is
that religious terms find their rightful employment and
genuine meaningfulness within a moral, not scientific,
context. This is the thrust of the opening lines of the
first preface to Religion within the Limits of Reason
Alone, where Kant makes religion dependent upon morality, reversing the traditional ordering.[90] This is a
good example of Kant's principle that "so much depends,
when we wish to unite two good things, upon the order in
which they are united."[91] Kantian religious discourse,
as Walsh has said, "is legitimate and meaningful because
it is internal to moral discourse, whose propriety and
significance no one would dispute"--no one, that is,
with a Kantian cast of mind.[92] In other words, the
meaningfulness of religious discourse is tied to the
"adoption of a practical attitude" and not to the demonstration of a theoretical claim.[93] In Kant's own words,
religious conviction

> is not logical, but moral certainty;
> and since it rests on subjective
> grounds (of the moral sentiment), I
> must not even say 'It is morally cer-
> tain that there is a God, etc.,' but
> 'I am morally certain, etc.' In
> other words, belief in a God and in
> another world is so interwoven with
> my moral sentiment that as there is
> little danger of my losing the latter,
> there is equally little cause for fear
> that the former can ever be taken from
> me.[94]

47

Because of the formalistic nature of Kant's writings, his emphasis on the personal, subjective mode of our appropriation of the moral law and religious reality is often underestimated. "Religion" as such is for Kant a matter of personal attitude, to be carefully distinguished from philosophy of religion and theology.[95] (Again, the influences of pietism and of Rousseau should be emphasized at this point.) Religion in terms of this personal attitude is the logical consequence of the distinction between the theoretical and practical, and the necessary condition of the formal definition of religion as the recognition of all duties as divine commands. Probably not by accident, this definition, once introduced in the second Critique, is amended in Religion within the Limits of Reason Alone to read, "religion is (subjectively regarded) the recognition of all duties as divine commands."[96] A distinction needs to be made regarding the sense in which "religion" for Kant refers to the traditional and institutional phenomena of "organized" religion, and the sense in which--subjectively regarded--religion is a form of "recognition" or level of awareness. The subjective nature of religious certainty is guaranteed, once Kant understands religion to derive from morality, rather than to depend upon theoretical demonstrations.[97]

Summary

It is time to consider the ground we have covered and to determine where we are headed. The predominance of limiting concepts in the first Critique has been attributed mainly to Kant's theory of sensibility. Our sensuous nature acts as a necessary filtering process through which the data of the external world must pass before we have earned the right to make cognitive claims. This epistemological standpoint results naturally from transcendental philosophy's insistence that thought must "turn back on itself" in order that we might inquire into the scope and nature of our reflective capacities. The way Kant's discussions of his theories of sensibility and of the noumenal as a limiting concept converge in his rejection of an "intellectual intuition" helpfully illustrates the consistent manner in which his principle of human limitations operates. Examples of the effects of this principle could have been multiplied, but the cases studied will prove to be most relevant for the ensuing discussion.

48

Secondly, we have seen how Kant's limiting concepts shape and condition the way he sets up his theory of religion. Although, as David Pears has said, "it is the negative aspect of critical philosophy which makes the first, and sometimes the most lasting, impression" on us,[98] a full and fair reading of Kant suggests the way the negative connotations of his limiting concepts are translated by him to effect a positive result. This result, as I have emphasized, is the preservation of moral and religious claims from the uncertainties of philosophical disputes by means of the establishment of the primacy of practical reason. By beginning with an innate and unquestioned dimension of human awareness which he takes to be rooted in reason itself, Kant is able to transcend the boundaries posed by theoretical limitations and postulate a type of religious discourse which is consistent and coherent, given his initial premise. Read in the context of the critical philosophy as a whole, the <u>Critique of Pure Reason</u> is the foundational step in a religious philosophy, rather than a self-contained epistemological program.

Thirdly, we have seen that the Kantian link between religion and practical reason guarantees a kind of non-cognitive, personal mode of religious faith. Kant's demolition of the proofs for the existence of God is not only an exposé of the pretensions of metaphysical theology; it is also the demonstration that the realm of theoretical proofs and disproofs is totally alien from the world of genuine religious certainty. The demolition of the proofs, in other words, is not only a revelation of the illegitimate employment of concepts beyond their proper scope. It is a gloss on the commonly known fact that no one is ever personally swayed one way or the other by such proofs.

Now all of this would seem to constitute an inauspicious beginning for any consideration of the <u>constructive</u> role that historical religion might play in Kant's religious philosophy. Authentic Kantian religion is based on an innate sense of moral obligation rather than upon the historical occurrences associated with historical religions. Furthermore, insofar as Kant's doctrine of moral obligation is rooted in our rationality (practical reason), his view seems to entail the <u>universality</u> of his brand of religion. What is genuinely rational necessarily transcends the local, empirical variations of time and place characteristic of historical religions. And, additionally, the doctrine of the noumenal which allows Kant to generate a theory of morality and religion in the first place would seem to imply a devaluation of the everyday phenomenal world, considered from a religious standpoint. As an aspect of this phenomenal world of appearances, history itself would be implicated in this potential devaluation. To speak, then, of the "historical dimensions of a rational faith" would appear to be shorthand for something Kant wants to be rid of instead of utilize.

Kant's view of religion unquestionably carries connotations of this sort. But, to repeat a central theme, our religious life—however rational its basis—must be expressed and communicated in a manner suitable to a life lived within the confines of sensuous limitations. The source of authentic religion may be rational, but to expect an unproblematic human appreciation of a genuinely rational religion is, for Kant himself, to expect too much. The crux of the problem, as Kant points out, is our need for a visible representation of inherently supersensible religious ideas.[99] That we should need the aid of some tangible representation does not impugn the essentially rational nature either of religion or of ourselves but simply reflects the limits of the human situation. Any consideration of even a rational religion needs to take the contours of this limited situation into account. In a way, Kant's entire career—and certainly his "critical" career—consisted of the struggle to overcome the gap between our reach and our grasp. And late in his career, by the time of the publication of Religion within the Limits, it was unquestionably clear to him that human limitations needed to be fully incorporated into any coherent critical philosophy of religion. The status of these limitations can only be ascertained through an examination of the theory of historical religion proposed in that work. It is time, then, to turn to a direct consideration of the problem of an historical religion and its relation to Kant's philosophy.

CHAPTER II

KANT'S THEORY OF HISTORICAL RELIGION

Kant's view of an historical faith is given its fullest expression in Religion within the Limits of Reason Alone.[1] This work is especially interesting for the way in which Kant brings his formal insights concerning rational religion into close relation with examples of the worldly and empirical aspects of traditional religion. This concern for traditional religious topics and "real world" manifestations of religious devotion is in marked contrast to the formalistic and philosophically "pure" style of works like the Critique of Practical Reason. This fact leads to the temptation to view Religion as simply the application to real world situations of Kant's rationalistic, morally-based religious concepts. To be sure, there is a grain of truth in such an interpretation, but this view does not allow sufficient room for the possibility that Religion involves certain creative departures as well as the application of lessons already learned. Thus, there is also a grain of truth in Michel Despland's suggestion that

> we find in Kant's authorship a series
> of fresh starts in which his mind...
> takes up new problems and lets its
> thinking arise from a consideration
> of these problems. Religion, a late
> work, and the only major one which
> was completed after the Critiques,
> is another one of these fresh starts
> (the last one to lead to a perfected
> work), which takes up a new problem,
> re-examines problems previously in-
> vestigated, and thus builds upon pre-
> vious work...Religion is thus a vast,
> new and vigorous undertaking which
> draws upon new sources and is prompted
> by a new problem.[2]

51

In approaching Kant's Religion, then, it is best to remain open-minded about what we might find there. Given the aims of the present inquiry, it is especially important not to assume automatically that the notion of an historical or revealed religion will be reduced away or dismissed outright by Kant. To claim, as some have done, that "Kant himself made no use of any concept of revelation"[3] or that his treatment of historical religion is essentially "polemical"[4] smacks of treating Religion on the basis of the interpreter's own expectations rather than on the basis of the subtleties of the work itself. Thus, although Despland may overstate his case, his interpretive framework has the merit of leaving open the possibility that everything we find in Kant's Religion may not simply be accounted for on the basis of his earlier works. At the very least, we should take into account Philonenko's suggestion that the purpose of Kant's Religion is to demonstrate that the religion of reason is not necessarily opposed to historical religion.[5]

Any interpretation of Religion within the Limits of Reason Alone faces certain difficulties posed by Kant's intentions and his historical climate. Although the main purpose of my inquiry is analytical rather than historical, it is worth noting at least a few of these difficulties before proceeding further.

In the first place, there is the simple fact that Religion was not written all at once, but actually represents the amalgamation of four separate essays. Furthermore, one of the essays or "books" met with difficulties at the hands of the censor when it appeared by itself in 1792.[6] Indeed, it was in connection with the publication of all the books comprising Religion that Kant had the most severe conflict of his career with the state censors and was forced to tell the government that

> in order not to fall under suspi-
> cion, it will be the surest course
> for me to abstain entirely from all
> public lectures on religious topics,
> whether on natural or revealed reli-
> gion, and not only from lectures
> but also from publications. I here-
> by promise this.[7]

The combination of the differentiation of the four books comprising Religion and Kant's troubles with the censor have led some to ask whether the work ought to be taken as a whole and whether it can be relied upon as a genuine and sincere expression of Kant's true position.

It seems safe to trust Kant on both counts. Regarding the essential unity of Religion, it is important to note that, despite the fact that Kant worked out the four books separately, he himself thought of Religion as a unity, just as we think of it today. This is made clear by a comment of Kant's in his first edition preface.

> In order to make apparent the relation of religion to human nature... I represent, in the following essays, the relationship of the good and evil principles as that of two self-subsistent active causes influencing men. The first essay has already been printed in the Berlinische Monatschrift of April, 1792, but could not be omitted here, because of the close coherence of the subject-matter in this work, which contains, in the three essays now added, the complete development of the first (p. 10).

In other words, Kant thinks of the essays comprising Religion as the development of a single theme; the interconnection of their treatment of this theme is so close that he cannot bring himself to omit a section which has already been published. We can add to this the fact that Kant, in his correspondence, would refer to Religion as a single and apparently unified work.[9] In a later chapter, I shall offer a further reason for viewing Religion as a unified and even systematic work, but for now, Kant's own reasons certainly suffice.

The problem of the relative sincerity of Religion is more important than the difficulties surrounding the unity of the work. Particularly if our aim is to evaluate Kant's view of an historical faith, it is crucial that we be able to rely on what he says on that issue in Religion. Those, like Troeltsch, who view Religion as being filled with diplomatic concessions to orthodoxy and utterances of prudence,[10] threaten to make interpreting the work an impossibility. But on the very surface of it, such a view seems contradicted by Kant's pride and self-consciousness as an "enlightened" man, which, of course, is for him synonymous with "autono-

mous." Despland proposes a number of reasons for dis-
agreeing with Troeltsch's view, based largely on the
coincidence of Kant's public and private statements
regarding religion.[11] An important clue comes from Kant
himself, as early as 1766, in his correspondence with
Moses Mendelssohn.

> [I] shall certainly never become a
> fickle or fraudulent person, after
> having devoted the largest part of
> my life to studying how to despise
> those things that tend to corrupt
> one's character. Losing the self-
> respect that stems from a sense of
> honesty would therefore be the great-
> est evil that could, but most cer-
> tainly shall not, befall me. Al-
> though I am absolutely convinced of
> many things that I shall never have
> the courage to say, I shall never
> say anything I do not believe.[12]

One is hard-pressed to discover anything in the critical
philosophy which runs counter to this Kantian standard.
It would be odd if Religion were somehow an exception to
this general characterization. One suspects that interpreters like Troeltsch rely on an "utterances of prudence" view of Religion because the work somehow fails
to conform to their expectations. At any rate, we can
feel safe in taking Kant at his word, even in Religion.

A third and final difficulty with regard to interpreting Kant's Religion is the place within that work of
Christianity. Theoretically, when Kant raises the conceptual issue of "historical" religion, he means any
historical religion; this is in keeping with his perception of a genuinely philosophical approach to a problem.
And, interestingly enough, Kant makes reference (usually
in footnotes) to various non-Western and seemingly exot-
ic historical religions as a means of illustrating various points. This results largely from the fact that
through

> a well-planned reading program, Kant
> brought himself fully abreast of the
> translations from Eastern religious
> sources and the best scholarly studies
> in comparative religion made during
> the seventeenth and eighteenth cen-
> turies. From these materials he came

to a vivid awareness of the actual
pluralism of religions of revelation.[13]

And in the text itself, Kant briefly deals with Judaism
and with what he calls the "Mohammedan type of belief."

But despite the appearance of comprehensiveness, it
is obvious that Kant is primarily concerned with Christianity as an historical religion. Whenever Kant wants
to utilize an actual historical example of one of his
themes, he draws upon Christianity; and when he wants to
examine an historical religion in both its "natural" and
"learned" aspects, he again draws upon Christianity. In
Religion, Kant offers what amounts to his doctrine of
original sin, his Christology, his doctrine of the
church, and his theory of grace--he is guided, in other
words, by traditionally Christian categories. Consequently, it is clear that in the working out of Religion, "historical" faith comes close to being synonymous
with "Christian" faith. Whether this fact violates the
philosophical stance he is bringing to the study of historical religion is a very real question. In any event,
the overriding aim of Religion is revealed by Kant himself when, in a letter to C.F. Stäudlin, he says that in
Religion he has attempted to demonstrate how "a possible
union of Christianity with the purest practical reason
is possible."[14] In my own examination of Religion, then,
I shall not hesitate to follow Kant's example and use
Christianity as the key instance of an historical religion. It should be kept in mind, however, that--in prin-
ciple--any instance of an historical religion would be
suitable for Kant's analysis.

Problems such as these lie in the background of any
inquiry into Kant's Religion. Their proper resolution
has a great deal to do with how we view this work.
Hopefully, this brief summary provides a sense of the
bearing these problems have on the question of an historical religion and an indication of what a complete
resolution of such problems might look like.

Natural and Revealed Religion

Kant's actual view of revealed or historical reli-
ligion, as it is proposed in Religion, must be understood against the background of the Enlightenment's
debate over natural and revealed religion. The Enlight-

enment's critical sense, of course, undermined the orthodox notion of a unique and specific revelation embodying a set of truths not attainable by reason alone.[15]
Such a notion was scandalous on at least two counts: on
the one hand, there was the problem of a divine miraculous intervention in the regular natural order, an order
which Newtonian science had shown to be altogether consistent and dependable in its workings; and on the other
hand, there was the "offense of particularity," the
difficulty of the historical and geographical "specificity" of revelation, which seemed in principle to exclude countless persons from the hope of salvation.[16]
Problems of this sort gradually led to a devaluation
of the idea of revelation and to a corresponding increase in the number of those adhering to some form or
other of natural religion or deism. For these thinkers,
the touchstone of true religion must necessarily be universal, something which is accessible to all men, everywhere. If the truths of religion are discoverable by
reason alone, without the aid of a specific divine communication, then religion must be a matter of what all
reasonable men are capable of knowing.

From the standpoint of the "reasonable" men of the
late seventeenth and eighteenth centuries, only morality
seemed to meet this criterion--only on the basis of
morality could any claim of religious truth be properly
made.[17] This insight, of course, gradually led to the
primacy of morality, over against religion, since now
true religion was tested by moral standards, rather
than the other way around. This turnabout was a classic
instance of what Cassirer has called "an exchange of
index symbols."

> That which formerly had established
> other concepts, now moves into the
> position of that which is to be es-
> tablished, and that which hitherto
> had justified other concepts, now
> finds itself in the position of a
> concept which requires justification.[18]

A genuinely "natural" religion, then, paring away all
supernatural and ecclesiastical embellishments, would
become a more simple and reasonable matter of the
awareness of moral duties as divine commands. When
Kant proposed his definition of religion along these
lines, he was not breaking new ground but culminating
an already existing trend.[19] Morality was already the
cornerstone of "enlightened" religion.

Consequently, it would at first appear as though Kant were a natural bedfellow of the proponents of natural religion and the critics of revelation. But Kant's own theory of theoretical reason makes this easy categorizing impossible. For the critical edge of Kant's theory of reason cuts as much against what he can reject as against what he can accept, and the same agnostic strand evidenced in his view of theistic proofs is at work in his approach to the problem of revelation. Thus, because of the effects of his principle of human limitations, Kant views the outright rejection of the idea of revelation as involving an illegitimate employment of theoretical reason. At the same time, it goes without saying that Kant could never feel at home with the orthodox proponents of a genuinely revealed religion. But to refuse to incorporate belief in a supernatural complement into a religion of reason does not, for Kant, necessarily require that he impugn the possibility or even the reality of that complement (pp. 48, 83).

Kant's position, then, is somewhat unique. He cannot establish his religious philosophy on the basis of a particular miraculous revelatory occurrence, lest he disrupt the universality characteristic of practical reason; yet he cannot simplistically affirm the unreality of revelation at the outset, lest he traverse the legitimate limits of theoretical reason. Here, as elsewhere, limiting concepts strictly determine Kant's freedom of philosophical movement. Thus, instead of launching a critique of revelation, Kant advocates what he calls "the principle of reasonable modesty in pronouncements regarding all that goes by the name of revelation" (p. 122). Such intellectual modesty affects Kant's treatment of all supposedly supernatural aspects of religion. His definition of miracle, for example, is not the implicitly perjorative Humean one which identifies miracle with an interruption of natural law. Rather, Kant simply suggests that miracles are "events in the world the operating laws of whose causes are, and must remain, absolutely unknown to us" (p. 81). Furthermore, Kant takes special pains to distinguish his rationalist approach to religion from a purely "naturalist" approach: the former maintains that natural religion alone is morally necessary, but without denying outright the possibility of revelation; the latter maintains both the moral necessity of natural religion and the impossibility of a divine revelation (p. 144). Thus, from the outset, the agnostic strand in Kant's thinking not only shapes his view of an historical religion, but guarantees that he will in fact _have_ a view on this issue.

The flexibility inherent in Kant's approach to the problem of historical religion is reflected in the ambiguity of the title of his book. In the context of the age of Enlightenment, and with a view of Kant as the great rationalist in religious matters, a religion "within the limits of reason alone" (_innerhalb der grenzen der blossen Vernunft_) connotes a religious philosophy suitably reduced to conform to the mandates of philosophical reason. The elements characteristic of an historical or positive religion would, it seems safe to assume, receive short shrift if this were indeed the point of Kant's title. But Kant is not developing a theory of religion "from" or "of" reason alone; rather, he intentionally speaks of a religion "within the limits of" reason alone to demarcate the specific task he is undertaking.[20] His title, in other words, is the setting of certain parameters rather than a claim about the nature of religion. In Jean-Louis Bruch's phrase, Kant's title implicitly admits the existence of a religion _outside_ the limits of reason alone.[21] If it seems odd that the author of the three _Critiques_ should write a book dealing with historical religion, it would be odder still if he had chosen as his title religion "from" or "of" reason alone. As it is, a religion "within the limits of" reason alone opens the door to the philosophical treatment of themes which seem at first to be wholly discontinuous with a religion of practical reason.

The clue to the correct understanding of _Religion_ is provided by Kant himself in his preface to the second edition. Here, he speaks of two concentric circles, the inner one representing the pure rational faith based upon practical reason, the outer one corresponding to historical religion based upon revelation.

> The philosopher, as a teacher of
> pure reason (from unassisted prin-
> ciples a priori), must confine him-
> self within the narrower circle,
> and, in so doing, must waive con-
> sideration of all experience (p. 11).

Kant's comment here simply echoes a common and consistent theme in the critical philosophy regarding the nature of the specifically "philosophical" task. This point is clear enough, especially given the fact that revelation "can certainly embrace the pure religion of reason, while, conversely, the second cannot include what is

58

historical in the first..." (p. 11).

Kant's initial step, then, is to distinguish carefully between a religion arrived at a priori, as exemplified by the second Critique, and a religion based upon empirical determinants. Were he to remain satisfied with this distinction, it seems obvious that he could sustain little interest in the trappings of an historical religion. This starting point, in other words, would lead easily to a morally-based theory of natural religion and a potential rejection of revealed religion as morally indifferent or perhaps even harmful. But Kant does not take this route. Following his example of the two concentric circles, he proposes a sort of experiment (Versuch) on the basis of which, even as a philosopher, he might deal with the historical side of religion. Thus, Kant proposes to

> start from some alleged revelation
> or other and, leaving out of con-
> sideration the pure religion of
> reason (so far as it constitutes
> a self-sufficient system), to exam-
> ine in a fragmentary manner this
> revelation, as an historical system,
> in the light of moral concepts; and
> then to see whether it does not lead
> back to the very same pure rational
> system of religion (p. 11).

This proposed experiment tells us a number of things. Implicit in Kant's whole approach to the writing of Religion is his awareness that the essentials of a religion of pure reason were discussed in the Critique of Practical Reason; there is no need to re-write that book. Religion will genuinely add to the Kantian corpus by, in part, inquiring into the idea of an historical faith, based upon historical revelation, "in the light of moral concepts"--that is, in the light of what has been previously worked out in Kant's ethical writings, especially the second Critique.[22] Furthermore, this is not simply a philosophical exercise on Kant's part, but is done with the aim of seeing whether this procedure "does not lead back to the very same pure rational system of religion" produced by the critical philosophy. In effect, Kant is launching a search for potential points of contact between the historical manifestations of religious faith and his own rational moral faith. As he puts it, if his "experiment" is successful, "we shall be able to say that reason can be found to be not only compatible

with Scripture but also at one with it, so that he who
follows one (under the guidance of moral concepts) will
not fail to conform to the other" (p. 11).[23]

Granted all these considerations, there still remains the question of why Kant supposes this experiment
to be worth carrying out. The answer, it seems obvious,
has been foreshadowed in Chapter I. As rational beings,
we can rely on the authenticity of a religion based upon
practical reason; but as limited and sensuous beings,
we are unable consistently to appreciate the truth and
mandates of a pure moral faith and need heuristic aids
suited to our sensuous condition. Kant's theory of historical religion, developed in Religion, is precisely
that aid which will guarantee the fulfillment of our
religious life. Far from siding with the natural religionists in a wholesale rejection of revealed religion,
Kant will appropriate revealed religion and utilize it
for rational ends.

This aspect of Kant's religious philosophy has made
it appropriate to speak of Kant's "worldly theory of
religion."[24] Authentic Kantian religion must be "worldly" because of the inescapably sensuous nature of rational beings. That is, "worldly" here connotes the
sensuous form which religious ideas must assume before
they can be easily apprehended; this does not alter the
rational source of Kantian religion, but only its means
of mediation. For epistemological reasons, then, Kant's
theory of historical religion is a necessary concession
to man's conditioned situation as finite rational creature.[25] From this viewpoint, the sorts of topics found
discussed in Religion cease to be a surprise; Kant is
seeking out that Überschritt which will mediate between
pure moral concerns and man's worldly, sensuous life.[26]

The logic behind all of this becomes clearer still
once we examine the manner in which Kant handles the
terminology associated with the debate over natural and
revealed religion. Kant's extensive discussion of the
natural-revealed problem can be reduced to two key claims:

> 1) an historical religion, based
> upon an historical revelation,
> can never legitimately claim to
> be necessarily valid or universal;
>
> 2) but because of human weakness and
> ignorance, an historical religion
> has the important task of serving

as the sensuous and tenable
"vehicle" for pure moral religion.

The first claim derives from the unalterable rational
basis of Kant's view of religion; the second derives
from the demands of the principle of human limitations.
Major sections of Religion are devoted to mediating between the different requirements posed by these two
insights.

In distinguishing historical from rational religion,
Kant is obviously sorting out the empirical from the
a priori elements. An "historical faith" is defined by
Kant as a religion based upon an historical revelation.
(p. 95). By definition, all religion consists for Kant
of the recognition of our duties as divine commands.
Accordingly, whereas a pure rational faith consists of
obedience to purely moral laws, an historical faith is
based upon what Kant calls merely "statutory laws" (p. 95).
Purely moral laws, being ingrained in practical reason,
can be known through reason alone; statutory laws, however, presuppose some kind of historical revelation and
therefore need to be "propagated among men by tradition
or writ" (p 95). This means that an historically revealed religion requires that "I must know in advance
that something is a divine command in order to recognize
it as my duty," whereas a natural or rational religion
simply requires that "I must first know that something
is my duty before I can accept it as a divine injunction"
(pp. 142-3). Consequently, what Kant is calling an historical faith is at the same time an "ecclesiastical
faith" (p. 96). This is because an historical faith,
based upon a revelation not universally accessible, requires a learned, priestly class to preserve, study, and
promulgate the revelatory information on which the faith
is based (pp. 151ff.), information which is normally
preserved in scripture (pp. 97-8). Furthermore, the
statutory laws founding an historical faith constitute
the basis of a visible church, insofar as they suggest
or imply certain institutional arrangements necessary
for achieving ecclesiastical ends (pp. 91ff.).[27]

This cluster of terms--historical faith, statutory
laws, ecclesiastical faith, visible church--is sugges-
tive of the empirical thread which links whatever Kant
associates with historical revelation. On one level,
this simply suggests the sorts of connotations the idea
of "historical revelation" evoked in Kant's time. But
more importantly, Kant's delineation of what necessarily

follows from the concept of an historical revelation
clearly reflects the reasons why such a revelation could
not be the ultimate basis of his own notion of authentic
religion. The clue here, of course, is the empirical
aspect; the kind of knowledge associated with an historical revelation is "impure" and, as such, cannot serve
as the ground of a genuinely rational faith. Seen from
this angle, Kant's theory of revelation appears in its
negative aspect, the idea of revelation having an apparently limited validity due to its association with the
empirical.

The sense in which this side of Kant's view is in
fact negative becomes clearer when we analyze Kant's
understanding of "historical knowledge." By its very
nature, the concept of an historical revelation is tied
to conditions of historical knowledge, since the "content" of a revelation is an historical event (or series
of events) which needs to be recorded, preserved, and
reported. This aspect of revelation would become genuinely problematical only in the nineteenth century, when
thinkers like Kierkegaard and Kähler would become aware
of the discontinuity between faith claims and historical
judgments. But even though Kant did not live to witness
this crucial development, his own epistemology[28] led him
to conclude that historical knowledge, to borrow Kierkegaard's term, could only be an "approximation."[29]
Even the most certain historical proof must, in Kant's
view, remain subject to "the absolute possibility of
error" (p. 175). Like "all empirical knowledge," historical knowledge carries with it the "consciousness not
that the object believed in must be so and not otherwise, but merely that it is so; hence it involves as
well the consciousness of its contingency" (p. 105). At
this point, Kant has implicitly grasped and formulated
the crucial aspect of Lessing's "ugly ditch," the tension between contingent matters of fact and necessary
truths of reason. Consequently, due to the very nature
of historical knowledge, the potential importance of an
historical revelation is, for Kant strictly limited.

The concept of an historical faith, then, based on
an historical revelation and preserved in scripture, is
undercut by the contingency of historical knowledge. At
this point--indeed, at any point at which he is deline-
ating the "negative" side of historical revelation--
Kant is very close to the viewpoint of the natural religionists. The "offense of particularity" is as offen-
sive to Kant as to a Reimarus. Scriptural testimony
requires some form of validation external to itself,

such as the security provided by learned exegetes who can vouch for the validity of the events recorded. "The pure faith of reason, in contrast, stands in need of no such documentary authentication, but proves itself" (p. 120). The "self-evidence" of pure religion implies an adverse judgment on the wholly contingent aspects of a religious tradition which is always in need of scholarly confirmation. In his own way, Kant is suggesting that man's religious life is too important to be left at the mercy of the fluctuating researches emanating from the biblical scholar's study.

All of this means that Kant's qualms regarding the nature of historical knowledge are joined by more systematic considerations regarding the religious function of historical knowledge. It should be recalled that, as philosopher, Kant feels licensed to investigate the empirical aspects of religion only "in the light of moral concepts" (p. 11). This is in keeping with his general aim of determining whether any historical manifestation of religion coincides with a pure moral religion. Accordingly, historical knowledge--no matter how sacred such putative "knowledge" may be within a particular religious tradition--must be considered by Kant from the standpoint of its moral use.

> We must not quarrel unnecessarily
> over a question or over its histor-
> ical aspect, when, however it is
> understood, it in no way helps us
> to be better men, and when that which
> can afford such help is discovered
> without historical proof, and indeed
> must be apprehended without it. That
> historical knowledge which has no
> inner bearing valid for all men be-
> longs to the class of adiaphora,
> which each man is free to hold as he
> finds edifying (p. 39n.).

What makes the difference, then, is the degree of moral edification which is either promoted or impeded by the historical aspect. Historical knowledge can attain religious efficacy only when it is considered in the light of moral concerns (p. 170).

There is a further difficulty with regard to the efficacy and importance of an historical revelation, a problem which Kant treats more by implication than through a frontal attack. This difficulty stems from

63

Kant's phenomenal-noumenal distinction, and the subsequent fact that anything implicated in the "historical" must of necessity be phenomenal as well. I emphasized in the previous chapter that the moral emphases of Kant's view of religion are rooted in the noumenal realm. The key concept which generates the possibility of a moral and religious life--namely, human freedom-- is postulated by Kant precisely on the grounds provided by the phenomenal-noumenal distinction. Building upon this strategy, Kant details a theory of the religious life which he claims is valid despite the fact that its manifestations never genuinely "appear" in the world of public experience. Just as there is no way to detect whether a man is acting freely, there is no way to claim that he is acting morally or religiously either. As Kant himself puts it, pure moral faith "has no public status, and each man can become aware only in and for himself of the advances which he has made in it" (p. 115).

Given the context provided by the phenomenal-noumenal distinction, it obviously becomes problematic to speak of the "appearance," through revelation, of a divine or religious truth. Even granting the sheer possibility that a revelation may occur (and Kant nowhere denies this possibility), it is impossible from a Kantian viewpoint ever to concede that the appropriate epistemological conditions might obtain such that we could genuinely "know" a divine revelation were we to witness one. Quite simply, whatever could "appear" would be subject to human sensibility and the application of the categories; furthermore, whatever could "appear" could never be self-validating in the way a moral claim, based on practical reason, can be. Consequently, the whole procedure by which Kant, after embracing the Newtonian world view, generates a theory of religion (i.e., his establishment of the phenomenal-noumenal dichotomy) works against the possibility that a divine revelation could ever be a meaningful or recognizable part of that theory. What it might mean for God himself, or a divine communication, ever to "appear" historically is something that is simply unaccounted for by Kant's epistemology. But, here as elsewhere, the double-edged nature of Kant's cognitive limitations plays an important role. For the fact that we are not in a position to recognize a revelation means that we are not entitled simply to reject the notion either. This is the net result of Kant's "principle of reasonable modesty" regarding what we claim about the concept of revelation--and this principle, in turn, is implicitly derived from Kant's principle of human limitations.

Thus, Kant's inquiry into the terminology of revealed religion suggests a distinction between religion as natural and universal and religion as supernatural and particular. In the latter case, religion is implicated in the vagaries of historical knowledge, as serious a difficulty as the reliance of religion on school metaphysics. But most crucially, the geographical and chronological specificity of an historical religion means that it "dispenses with the most important mark of truth, namely, a rightful claim to universality" (p. 100). Kant's rationalist commitment is best illustrated by this criterion of universality. Genuine religion requires "no assertorial knowledge" (p. 143) but is based upon that "practical knowledge" which needs "no historical doctrine" (p. 169), since it is inherently universal. Contrary to the character of an historical religion, this practical knowledge

> lies as close to every man, even the
> most simple, as though it were engraved
> upon his heart--a law, which we need
> but name to find ourselves at once in
> agreement with everyone else regarding
> its authority, and which carries with it
> in everyone's consciousness uncondition-
> ed binding force, to wit, the law of
> morality (p. 169).

This claim ties in illuminatingly with Kant's specific comments on revelation. As we have seen, Kant--as a matter of principle--remains agnostic regarding the question of a genuinely "historical" revelation. But he is willing to say that "the pure religion of reason is a continually occurring divine (though not empirical) revelation for all men" (p. 113). Kant seems willing, then, to speak of a revelation "engraved upon" man's heart--that is, rooted in practical reason. This point is clarified somewhat by Kant's distinction, in his Vorlesungen über philosophische Religionslehre, between an "inner" and an "outer" revelation.[30] Whereas an outer revelation is a specific historical occurrence, an inner revelation is simply our awareness of the moral law. As Kant says in Religion, "God has indeed revealed His will through the moral law in us" (p. 135).

Obviously, Kant is seeking a way of retaining the idea of revelation in a form which will carry his coveted mark of universality. His agnosticism with regard to a traditional historical revelation is balanced by his belief that our sense of moral obligation has a divine source. Accordingly, a "revelation" for Kant can be either an external occurrence, embodied in "works" and "words,"[31] or it can be the conscious apprehension of God's implication in our moral awareness.[32] The first kind of revelation is genuinely informative, adds to our knowledge, but is particular and wholly contingent; it is the object of Kant's agnosticism. The second or inner form of revelation is simply a gloss on what we, as rational beings, are already aware of through practical reason; it fulfills the demand for universality. "Inner" revelation, then, is a way of speaking about those implicit, rational connections which guarantee the validity of postulating the existence of God on the basis of our moral awareness. Ideally, these two senses of revelation converge in our religious life, and a major part of the intention behind the writing of Religion is Kant's desire to show that the outer revelation on which Christianity is based is ultimately compatible with the inner revelation rooted in practical reason. The possibility of this project is assured by Kant's theoretical agnosticism; the realization of the project is promised by the method of applying a moral hermeneutics to the historical elements of Christianity.

Thus, Kant's criterion of universality promotes a variety of reductionism with regard to his inquiry into historical religion. Only the religion of reason, expressed through moral concepts, can attain the universality characteristic of Kant's form of philosophical truth. Insofar as any historical faith fails to agree "with the universal practical rules of a religion of pure reason," it simply cannot be of any philosophical interest to us (pp. 100-1). This moral test, based on the criterion of universality, echoes the principle embraced by natural religionists when they sought to explain what was "natural" about their religion: the search for what is "natural" involves the search for what is "universal," and morality alone seems to meet this requirement. For Kant, only a morally-based, pure religious faith

> can be believed in and shared by everyone, whereas an historical faith, grounded solely on facts, can extend its influence no further than tidings of it can reach, subject to circumstances of time and place and dependent upon the capacity [of men]

> to judge the credibility of such
> tidings (p. 94).

Genuine Kantian religion is rooted in practical reason
and not reliant on the contingencies of historical
circumstances.

In the course of my impending inquiry into what I
have called the constructive aspect of Kant's theory
of historical religion, this reductionistic side must
never be lost from view. Kant's criterion of universality results in his adamant insistence that no empirical
truth can ever be soteriologically necessary (pp. 80,
102, 166, 169-70). From Kant's viewpoint, perhaps the
greatest danger to religion is the possibility that
"the knowing, believing, and professing of [historical
accounts] are themselves means whereby we can render
ourselves well-pleasing to God" (p. 80). The ultimate
perversion of a faith based on practical reason would be
this elevation of contingent matters of fact to the
status of religiously necessary truths.

The Utility of Revealed Religion

There is unquestionably evident in Kant a reductionistic view of historical religion, a view which attracts
the most attention because of its obvious compatibility
with the teachings of other familiar Kantian writings.
But alongside this implicit reductionism is an important
constructive aspect. The need for such a constructive
aspect, as I shall explain momentarily, stems from the
principle of human limitations; the possibility of such
an aspect is provided for by Kant's claim that there are
countless manifestations of historical religion which
contain a rational core surrounded by contingent empirical elements.

> Yet in part at least every religion,
> even if revealed, must contain cer-
> tain principles of the natural reli-
> gion (p. 144).

> We can say further that even in the
> various churches, severed from one
> another by reason of the diversity
> of their modes of belief, one and the
> same true religion can yet be found
> (p. 98).

67

> [Pure] moral faith...alone consti-
> tutes the element of genuine religion
> in each ecclesiastical faith (p. 103).

Just how we are to take this Kantian claim is not altogether clear. It seems based upon an implicit conclusion on Kant's part that, given the universality of practical reason, an element of pure moral faith must, in principle, be present in any historical religion embraced by rational beings--that is, simply by virtue of the nature of the "beings" involved. If this is so, there immediately arise questions regarding the possible artificiality of the "experiment," mentioned in Kant's second preface, on which his inquiry into historical religion is justified. If Kant knows that every religion, "even if revealed," contains at least an element of pure moral faith, then it becomes circular to ask whether an examination of an historical religion, in the light of moral concepts, might not "lead back to the very same pure rational system of religion" (p. 11). Kant seems wholly oblivious to this potential circularity.

Yet although this problem regarding the basis of Kant's claim may arise, the utility of the claim is fairly obvious. By holding out the possibility that there may be a rational, moral core within an historical faith, Kant can justify what he will have to say about the heuristic value of historical religions. But before pursuing this important point in depth, it is crucial to specify the manner in which Kant generates a philosophically constructive view of historical religion in the first place.

Kant's basic distinction between a natural and revealed religion is, in his own words, a classification of religion "with reference to its first origin and its inner possibility" (p. 143). But there is a further classification, the classification of religion "with respect to its characteristics which make it capable of being shared widely with others" (p. 143). This type of classification leads to the distinction between, again, natural religion (of which "everyone can be convinced through his own reason") and what Kant calls "learned" religion ("of which one can convince others only through the agency of learning") (p. 143). In effect, this is still simply to distinguish between natural and revealed religion, but it is the type of classification here which is important for Kant. For the distinction between these two types of classification allows Kant to claim that

> no inference regarding a religion's
> qualification or disqualification to
> be the universal religion of mankind
> can be drawn merely from its origin,
> whereas such an inference is possible
> from its capacity or incapacity for
> general dissemination, and it is this
> capacity which constitutes the essen-
> tial character of that religion which
> ought to be binding upon every man
> (p. 143).

Kant's strategy here is clear. He wants to establish without equivocation that the mark of authentic
religion is its communicability (and thereby its universality). This is necessitated by his derivation of
religion from the universally given sense of duty which
all rational beings possess. If genuine religion were
not universally communicable, then Kant's theory of
practical reason would be undercut.

At the same time, however, Kant wants to rely on his
criterion of universality without eliminating the potential efficacy of a revealed religion. The distinction
between classification according to origin, and classification according to the capacity to be widely shared,
enables Kant to do this. As a result--and this is the
key point--"that religion which ought to be binding
upon every man"

> can be natural, and at the same time
> revealed, when it is so constituted
> that men could and ought to have dis-
> covered it of themselves merely
> through the use of their reason, al-
> though they would not have come upon
> it so early...Hence a revelation...
> might well be wise and very advanta-
> geous to the human race, in that,
> when once the religion thus introduced
> is here, and has been made known pub-
> licly, everyone can henceforth by
> himself and with his own reason convince
> himself of its truth. In this event
> the religion is objectively a natural
> religion, though subjectively one that
> has been revealed; hence it is really
> entitled to the former name. For in-
> deed, the occurrence of such a super-
> natural revelation might subsequently

be entirely forgotten without the
slightest loss to that religion...
(pp. 143-4).

A number of important themes are coming together in
this remarkable comment. By remaining agnostic, on
theoretical grounds, about the sheer possibility of a
revelation, Kant can incorporate this notion in his religious speculations, at least in the form of an "experiment." By actually incorporating it, Kant can give an
account of pure rational religion which will tie in with
the actual history of revealed religion. And by reserv-
ing the idea of a revealed religion for an account of
the method of dissemination of a religion, Kant can protect the natural (i.e., rational) basis of religion.
One of the great ironies implicit in Kant's <u>Religion</u> is
the fact that the <u>absolute validity</u> of an <u>historical</u> religion is rejected by Kant on the grounds that such a
religion can never be universal, yet the <u>real utility</u> of
an historical religion arises precisely because of its
geographical and chronological particularity. A revealed religion is suited to the particular situations of
real people, and thereby teaches us what we "<u>could and
ought to have discovered</u>" by ourselves through reason
alone. It becomes clear, then, that Kant balances his
rejection of a revealed religion as soteriologically
efficacious with an endorsement of such a religion as an
important instrument for rational religious ends.

The fact that a religion can be both objectively
natural and subjectively revealed helps explain Kant's
claim that historical faiths can contain a rational
core. In particular, it explains the Kantian claim that
there is only one true "religion" but there can be
"faiths" of several kinds (p. 98). Clearly, what Kant
refers to as the one "true" religion is "objectively
natural"; but as we have seen, an objectively natural
religion can also be "subjectively revealed." As we
might expect, it is with regard to a religion which is
both objectively natural (and thereby derived ultimately
from practical reason) and subjectively revealed (and
thereby expressed in representative, historical forms)
that the genuinely constructive aspect of Kant's theory
of historical religion comes to the fore. On the basis,
both of his "experiment" launched in the second edition
preface to <u>Religion</u>, <u>and</u> of his trust in the rational
element lurking within instances of historical religion,
it is precisely this area of "overlap" which Kant is
looking for and finds philosophically interesting.

A key contention of this whole inquiry is that Kant's principle of human limitations lies at the source of the constructive aspect of his doctrine of historical religion. Whether this amounts to saying that the objectively natural and universally valid religion of the second _Critique_ actually requires, for its dissemination, an historical aspect reflecting the moral aspect is a question to be faced in the following chapter. For now, it suffices to say that the connection between historical religion and Kant's principle of human limitations arises naturally from the manner in which I have explicated that principle. That is, the basis of the principle, on my interpretation, is Kant's doctrine of sensibility. An inescapable aspect of being a rational creature is the mediating role played by our sensuous nature in any situation which can be called "experience," by Kantian standards. Kant's postulates of practical reason, which constitute the core of his religious doctrine, are rooted in the noumenal realm. But the noumenal, as Kant unmistakably argues, is not subject to our experience; it is a "limiting concept" only, and the force of this term is precisely to reemphasize our sensuous, as opposed to intellectual, mode of intuition. Consequently, any fully coherent Kantian religious philosophy needs some form of mediation between the noumenal nature of God, freedom, and immortality and our unalterably sensuous nature—if, that is, the common man is to have some tangible aid by which to help him apprehend what he innately already knows. None of this affects the ultimate source of Kant's rational religion, but only its mode of mediation. The arguments of _Religion_ suggest that historical religion plays this mediating role.

On this view, it is not accidental that: (1) the same work which contains Kant's definitive statement regarding historical religion also contains his doctrine of radical evil; and (2) Kant's suggestions regarding the utility of historical religion always arise in the context of a claim about human limitations. By "reason of a peculiar weakness of human nature," says Kant, "pure faith can never be relied on as much as it deserves" (p. 94).

> [For] man the invisible needs to be
> represented through the visible (the
> sensuous); yea, what is more, it needs
> to be accompanied by the visible in
> the interest of practicability and,
> though it is intellectual, must be

made, as it were (according to a
certain analogy) perceptual (p. 180).

Human life being what it is, an historical religion can
be religiously efficacious in a key way. Whatever
Kant's attitude toward the truth and superiority of a
pure moral faith, he emphasizes the "natural need and
desire of all men for something sensibly tenable, and
for a confirmation of some sort from experience of the
highest concepts and grounds of reason" (p. 100). Because of this need, "some historical ecclesiastical
faith or other, usually to be found at hand, must be
utilized" (p. 100).

Nowhere is the contingency of the historical side
of religion denied by Kant, and nowhere does he claim
that any particular historical event or set of events is
soteriologically necessary. At the same time, however,
the status of historical religion as a beneficial--and
perhaps necessary--stage in mankind's journey toward a
pure moral faith is confirmed by Kant, on the grounds
that the sensual and finite limitations of human nature
require this historical element. Kant specifically invokes the themes of human sensibility--the "natural need
and desire of all men for something sensibly tenable"
(p. 100)--when he justifies the utility of historical
religion. The implication is that the proliferation of
limiting concepts in Kant's epistemology leads to results in his religious philosophy other than simply the
demolition of the theistic proofs.

Summary

The relationship between the principle of human limitations and Kant's theory of historical religion adds
a new dimension to his religious thought. Traditionally, interpreters of Kant have emphasized the specifically cognitive strictures which Kant places on our religious life. The stringent epistemology of the first
Critique undermines the existing, metaphysically-based
natural theology which presumed to offer religious
"knowledge." The turn to practical reason demonstrates
to Kant's satisfaction that, whatever else it may be,
religious certainty is not reliant on theoretical
claims. All of this is familiar. But what the new departures of Religion suggest is that, however innate the
truths of a rational, moral religion may be, human
awareness of those truths is often distorted, perverted,

72

or absent altogether. An historical religion, then, precisely because it affects man sensibly, where man is most "receptive," assumes the role of a maieutic force in Kant's scheme. Ideally, historical religion exerts a kind of obstetric pull, bringing into the light of day man's hidden awareness of something he already knows.

The actual constructive aspect of an historical religion, then, is the role it plays as a visible representation of moral ideas. In view of this result, it is not surprising to find Kant speak of historical religion as a "vehicle" for promoting the ends of pure moral religion.[33] An "historical faith attaches itself to pure religion [as] its vehicle," Kant says, in "conformity with the unavoidable limitation of human reason" --i.e., in conformity with our inability to envision moral ideas without a tangible representation of those ideas (p. 106). Despite the necessary agnosticism regarding the revealed basis of an historical faith, an account of that revelation can be a vivid and valuable means of "furthering the vitality of [one's] pure religious disposition" (p. 170). An historical faith, then, based on historical revelation, is "merely a means, but a most precious means" of furthering religious ends (p. 152).

It is obvious, then, that the relation between an historical religion and a pure moral faith is a means-end relation. Historical religion, as a vehicle, is the "husk" carrying the kernel of pure moral religion. But there is a serious ambiguity in Kant's distinction, an ambiguity implicit in the very term, "vehicle." If we place our emphasis on the moral source and nature of authentic Kantian religion, then an historical faith as a vehicle or visible representation appears genuinely contingent and dispensable. But if we place our emphasis on how we come to believe, then there is the clear possibility implicit in Kant's treatment that an historical faith is a necessary and indispensable part of man's religious life.[34] Its necessity would derive from the worldly, sensuous conditions in which we live and the corresponding requirement that our link to the authentically religious be mediated by what is recognizable and tangible. Thus, although any intelligent reading of Kant must yield the conclusion that we can apprehend religious truth through reason alone, it is perhaps necessary to qualify this as an "in principle" claim only. For "in fact," our worldly situation is such that our access to rational religion seems to require an

73

historical mediator.

In effect, two competing lines of thought appear in Kant's Religion, and the contradiction never seems to be clearly resolved. As Kant himself says rather ambiguously, "ecclesiastical faith...naturally precedes pure religious faith," adding in a footnote that "morally, this order ought to be reversed" (p. 97). This is at once a claim of the superiority of a moral over an historical faith, and a perhaps reluctant admission that historical religion is in fact necessary as well as inevitable--precisely because human failing is inevitable though not necessary. We are not helped much by a comment, toward the end of Religion, which is an odd mixture of agnosticism and rational religion.

> Whatever, as the means or the condition
> of salvation, I can know not through
> my own reason but only through revela-
> tion, and can incorporate into my con-
> fession only through the agency of an
> historical faith, and which, in addi-
> tion, does not contradict pure moral
> principles--this I cannot, indeed, be-
> lieve and profess as certain, but I can
> as little reject it as being surely
> false; nevertheless, without determin-
> ing anything on this score, I may ex-
> pect that whatever therein is salutary
> will stand me in good stead so far as
> I do not render myself unworthy of it
> through defect of the moral disposition
> in good life-conduct (p. 177).

In answering the question, "What is Kant's theory of historical religion?," we find ourselves left wondering how strongly we are to take his theory. In particular, we are left wondering if the "utility" of the histori-cal vehicle in fact becomes a "necessity," due to the principle of human limitations. As we shall see, the answer to this question arises only in the light of the examination of a number of seemingly diverse issues.

CHAPTER III

THE STRUCTURE OF KANT'S THEORY

OF HISTORICAL RELIGION

The previous chapters have indicated that, because
of certain cognitive strictures on the one hand, and the
demands of practical reason on the other, an historical
faith assumes a type of mediating role in Kant's religious philosophy. No historical religion is "true" in
the normal Kantian sense, since every such religion
fails to meet Kant's criterion of universality. Yet
the very idea of an historical religion is in certain
ways appealing to Kant, since it is that form or mode
of religion which is most readily and concretely accessible to human life. It is, as I have shown, the human
need for something "sensibly tenable"[1] which inclines
Kant to claim that a revealed religion is "merely a
means, but a most precious means" of promoting authentic
religious ends (p. 152). All of this suggests that, for
Kant, the philosophical adjudication of the natural-
revealed distinction is not as simple as one might have
wished. Indeed, the very fact that Kant is particularly
concerned to inquire into the case of a religion that is
"objectively" natural yet "subjectively" revealed (p.
144) represents the middle way he is seeking between the
extreme positions characteristic of his own century.
What emerges from this philosophical balancing act is a
serious interpretative problem, insofar as Kant never
clearly resolves the exact relation he endorses between
a pure moral faith and a revealed historical one. It is
toward the clarification of this issue that the present
chapter is directed.

Before proceeding further, it may be helpful to indicate, in outline form, the general structure of Kant's
position as I have examined it so far:

> 1) authentic religion is, for Kant,
>   based upon the universal demands

of practical reason;

2) the principle of human limitations enforces a theoretical agnosticism with regard to the problem of revelation;

3) an historical religion or faith, based (by Kant's definition) on an historical revelation, can never meet practical reason's criterion of universality;

4) yet because it assumes tangible, representative forms, an historical religion is well-suited to the needs of a sensuous humanity;

5) an historical religion can therefore be useful as a "vehicle" for a pure moral faith.

Hopefully, this is a fair and accurate rendering of Kant's position. Assuming that it is, it becomes immediately apparent that the interpreter of Kant is left with certain difficulties. I can perhaps summarize these difficulties by suggesting that the interpreter's main task in connection with Kant's theory of an historical religion is to:

1) identify the method by which Kant determines that an historical religion is in fact serving as a vehicle for pure moral faith;

2) determine what, in such cases, the actual relationship between the historical and the moral aspects is;

3) and determine what happens to the specifically historical aspect, once the moral core has been discovered and appreciated.

All of this is a way of asking what the specific value of an historical religion is for Kant. The ultimate issue at stake, as I have suggested earlier, is the possibility that the heuristic value of an historical faith becomes either soteriologically or pedagogically necessary. If this could be demonstrated, then the traditional view of Kant would certainly have to be altered. My concern, then, is to determine how strongly Kant wants us to take his doctrine of an historical faith.

By way of anticipation, I might point out that, in my view, Kant's thinking ultimately reaches an impasse on the issue of religion and history. This is because his commitment to the universal mandates of practical reason is severely conditioned by the preponderance of limiting concepts in his thinking. Thus, on the one hand, Kant's rationalistic predilections keep him from ever conceding that any particular historical aspect is soteriologically or pedagogically necessary for our religious life; but on the other hand, his principle of human limitations militates against the worldly satisfaction of those very same rationalistic predilections. This results, as I shall show, in an unresolved tension within Kant's Religion and reflects a certain discontinuity between that work and Kant's earlier writings.

For the purposes of dealing with the three problems specified above, the present chapter is divided into three sections. In a rough way, each section is intended to deal with the corresponding problem laid out above. Although there may seem to be little continuity among the topics treated in these three sections, their incorporation into a single chapter seems justified, since they are all derived from the single question of how strongly Kant wants us to take his theory of an historical faith.

Thus, in order to determine Kant's method of ferreting out the moral meanings implicit in an historical faith, the first part of this chapter will deal with his approach to the problem of scriptural interpretation. This inquiry will illustrate the way Kant rather self-consciously sets out to prove that pure moral concepts can be clothed in seemingly contingent historical examples, the life of Jesus being the paradigmatic instance. This demonstration by Kant is at least partly due to his desire to show the conformity existing between Christianity and a religion of practical reason. As I shall suggest, the case of Kant's theory of scriptural interpretation will betray the essential circularity of the main argument in Religion.

The second part of the chapter moves on to a consideration of an important epistemological issue raised by Kant. In order to clarify Kant's understanding of the relation existing between the moral and historical elements in a given faith, I shall examine the place of his theory of schematism within Religion. This will--perhaps to the reader's chagrin--require an extensive investigation of the schematism doctrine in the first Critique in order to give us a sense of what Kant has in mind whenever he invokes this doctrine. But this momentary digression is necessary if we are to appreciate Kant's suggestion in Religion that the role played by historical faith is analogous to the schematizing of the categories (pp. 58-9n.). I shall indicate how this amounts to the claim that an historical faith makes tenable, in time and therefore in concrete, sensible instances, what is inherently supersensuous. I hope to clarify the justification for this Kantian claim and to consider if this issue helps us understand the actual relationship between historical and moral faith which Kant is endorsing.

The third and final part of this chapter will be addressed to the question of the fate of the historical aspect of religion, once the moral core has been located and appreciated. It will be important here to specify the sense in which Kant wants us to understand his suggestion that an historical faith serves as the "vehicle" for a pure moral religion. I shall suggest that Kant's theory of the visible church is an important clue for the adjudication of the "vehicle" issue. Quite naturally, this third part will engage us in a direct consideration of the problem of the potential necessity of an historical faith within Kant's system. On this issue, I shall contrast my own conclusions with those of Michel Despland, who offers a provocative but perhaps forced interpretation of Kant's views of such matters. And finally, this concluding section will indicate how the problems of this chapter are intimately related to the knotty issue of Kant's understanding of the relationship between nature and freedom, and this will serve as a natural transition to the fourth and final chapter.

Kant's Theory of Biblical Interpretation

A recent author has claimed that, with regard to the field of biblical interpretation, "Kant had the privilege of seeing almost everyone, no matter from what hermeneutical school, united against him."[2] Insofar as this claim is accurate, it nicely symbolizes something that I have been suggesting all along--namely, that

78

Kant's resolution of the natural-revealed distinction is unique, the product of the balance he wants to strike between the limitations of theoretical reason and the demands of the practical. Moreover, Kant's theory of interpretation is a prime example of what he has in mind when he speaks of the priority of the practical in religious matters.

In Book III of Religion, Kant makes the somewhat reckless claim that "history proves that it has never been possible to destroy a faith grounded in scripture" (p. 98). Given this assumption on his part, it is not surprising to find him saying "how fortunate" it is

> when such a book, fallen into men's hands, contains, along with its statutes, or laws of faith, the purest moral doctrine of religion in its completeness...(p. 98).

Thus, the moral element in a religious scripture becomes for Kant a specific instance of the general case of an historical faith which is serving as the vehicle for a pure moral religion. The problem simply becomes that of seeking out this moral element.

All of this leads naturally to Kant's claim that the intention of the exegete should be to seek the moral element in the text at hand (p. 103). To be sure, Kant is speaking here only of the philosophical (and not theological) approach to the text, a distinction important for the academic climate of his time. But even so, he is embracing a hermeneutical principle which, though it solves certain problems, immediately spawns a whole set of new ones: it is the principle that a religious text can "mean" something other than what it "says." This is in fact predetermined by the title of that section of Religion in which Kant deals with the interpretive problem: "Ecclesiastical Faith Has Pure Religious Faith as its Highest Interpreter" (p. 100). Indeed, Kant's theory of biblical interpretation is predetermined by that "experiment," posed in his second preface, which justifies the writing of Religion in the first place by allowing the philosopher to examine revealed religion "in the light of moral concepts" (p. 11).

Accordingly, if the moral meaning of a text is to be appreciated, the text must undergo an interpretation "in a sense agreeing with the universal practical rules of a religion of pure reason" (p. 100). Kant does not outlaw other sorts of interpretation, such as a genuinely historical approach, but simply claims that such theoretical enterprises can have no religious value.

> For the theoretical part of ecclesiastical faith cannot interest us morally if it does not conduce to the performance of all human duties as divine commands (that which constitutes the essence of all religion) (p. 100).

Kant readily admits that the "literal meaning" of the text may not seem to support his moral presuppostion, and indeed our interpretation "may often really be forced" (p. 101). But if the text can "possibly support" this moral approach, this form of interpretation "must be preferred to a literal interpretation" which often yields either "nothing at all [helpful] to morality or else actually works counter to moral incentives" (p. 101). Kant's moral approach to the text, then, assumes the form of a type of moral duty.

> [An] attempt such as the present... to discover in Scripture that sense which harmonizes with the most holy teachings of reason is not only allowable but must be deemed a duty (p. 78).

Revealingly enough, the phrase, "most holy," here modifies "teachings of reason" rather than scripture. And in fairness to Kant, it should be mentioned that he adds a note to this comment in which he concedes that "it may be admitted that [the 'moral sense'] is not the only one" (p. 78).

Kant's position on the biblical issue, then, is a classic instance of the meaning he gives the phrase, "the primacy of the practical." With regard to religion, the only object of Kant's interest is whatever might be morally advantageous, and not what happens to be theoretically interesting. Any theoretical (e.g., historical) "maxim of knowledge" must be in the service of a practical "maxim of action" (p. 109).[3] This mandate of practical reason means that the study

> of the Bible is for Kant antiquarian and devoid of value unless it serves

moral ends and reinforces the
will to realize them. As a
purely scientific object the
Bible is dead; its importance
lies only in its power to influence...[The] extrinsic (moral
and philosophical) interest...
should determine in each case
the proper mode of interpretation. We may therefore conclude
that Kant regards Biblical exe-
gesis only as a means for other
ends.[4]

Kant's view of a "correct" interpretation, then, is
clearly implied when he raises the question "as to
whether morality should be expounded according to the
Bible or whether the Bible should not rather be expounded according to morality" (p. 101n.).

This approach to the problem of interpretation, of
course, is altogether consistent with the general
framework of Kant's philosophy of religion. If religion has practical reason as its primary reference
point, then we are not concerned with the theoretical
and cognitive. After all, as Kant points out, religion itself, when correctly conceived, involves no
"assertorial knowledge," not even of God's existence
(p. 142). From this viewpoint, one ought not approach
a religious text seeking "proofs" or "facts" to be
believed. Rather, the Bible is for Kant a kind of
"psychological and educational auxiliary" which is of
value insofar as it is instrumental in promoting moral
ends.[5] For Kant, the question of what is historically
"true" gives way to a consideration of what is morally
advantageous.

In effect, then, Kant's divorce of what a text
means from what it says results in a total lack of
interest on his part for the author's original "intention."[6] Kant does not even require the original
author's awareness of the potential moral meaning of
his text in order for the moral meaning to be present.
This of course relieves Kant of a variety of potential
problems, since no distortion of a text can possibly
arise through his theory unless we assert that the
moral meaning is the one exactly intended by the original author (p. 102). Accordingly, we must allow the
question of the "intention" behind the text to drop
out, "to be left undecided and merely admit the

<u>possibility</u> that their authors may be so understood."

> For the final purpose even of reading these holy scriptures, or of investigating their content, is to make men better; the historical element, <u>which contributes nothing to this end</u>, is something which is in itself quite indifferent, and we can do with it what we like (p. 102, my emphasis).

Consequently, Kant is concerned neither for the literal, historical referent of a biblical text, nor for the original intention of the author. Instead, he is concerned solely for the text's moral meaning, since this alone can "make men better." Kant's theory of scriptural interpretation thereby assumes the nature of a theory of religious symbolism. That is, he is concerned for the <u>meanings</u> which a religious text embodies and represents in an expressive or narrative form--the form involved embodies the meanings without being identical to them. The fact that the text serves as a carrier, not of theoretical information but of moral meanings, has been anticipated by my earlier emphasis on the way Kant's principle of human limitations is derived from his doctrine of sensibility. Where a sensuous humanity is concerned, the appropriate bearer of supersensuous moral ideas is a symbolic, textual aid. Ideally, this aid captures the moral element in terms of vivid and picturesque narratives, which enliven the imagination of the common man and inspire his sense of moral duty.

Kant's advocacy of a "symbolic anthropomorphism" with regard to our conception of God is a fairly familiar theme.[7] What is not so well-known is his concern for biblical narratives as the symbolic expression of moral ideas.[8] What makes this aspect of his thought interesting is the fact that Kant is not simply stripping away the narrative or representative element as the unnecessary remnant of a superstitious era; rather, he is genuinely "interpreting" scriptural material, always with a view to the moral core but also with a sense that the representative aspect is worthy of respect. The underlying methodological assumption seems to be drawn directly from his principle of human limitations--it is religiously advantageous to have the supersensuous rendered into tangible form (p. 180). Thus, his principle of human limitations leads to

Kant's high regard for scripture precisely because scripture is the best means of bridging the gap between moral and religious ideas and the sensible conditions of our worldly lives. Kant, then, greatly respects the "personifications" and "vivid modes of representation" characteristic of biblical passages.

> He did not speak of them with the condescension of most enlightened deists who saw such 'fables' as useful for primitive Jews, old women, savages, peasants, and humble pious artisans, but who presumably did perfectly well without them themselves. Kant spoke of these stories with reverence and shared no urge to debunk them in the privacy of his circle of enlightened friends and readers.[9]

It is interesting to note that Kant's utilization of biblical narratives for moral purposes occurs in works besides Religion. An obvious instance of a narrative suitable for moral purposes is the Book of Job, and Kant does not forfeit the chance to appropriate this vivid and affecting drama. Significantly enough, it is in his essay entitled "On the Failure of All Theodicies" that Kant finds the example of Job most useful.[10] Kant's elucidation of the title of his essay--his description of the failure of all theodicies-- is followed by his invocation of Job as a moral example. The shortcoming of Job's friends is attributed by Kant to their efforts to offer "ratiocinations" regarding "things of which they should have confessed that they had no knowledge."[11] In contrast, Job is characterized by "free and sincere outspokenness," because he eventually confessed "that he had spoken unwisely about things that were above his reach and which he did not understand."[12] In case we have missed the point regarding the pretensions of theoretical reason, Kant embellishes his description of Job in terms which nicely summarize his religious philosophy as a whole.

> Thus, only the uprightness of the heart, not the merits of one's insights, the sincere and undisguised confessions of one's doubts, and the avoidance of feigned convictions which one does not really feel

> (especially before God, where dis-
> semblance would never work), these
> are the qualities which caused the
> upright man Job to be preferred in
> the eyes of the divine judge to the
> pious flatterers.[13]

Through Kant's eyes, the moral of the Job story is that
"Job proved that he did not base his morality on his
faith but his faith upon his morality."[14] Given Kant's
view of the relation between religion and morality,
this is a very convenient interpretive result.[15]

A more interesting example of Kant's appropriation
of a biblical narrative for moral ends is his use of
Genesis in his essay entitled, "Conjectural Beginning
of Human History."[16] This seemingly straightforward
essay, so different from the Critiques in style, implicitly deals with a variety of issues as complex as
those Kant dealt with in any of his writings. This is
because, from Kant's viewpoint, any account of the beginning of a specifically human history must account
for the origin of freedom, but without making "freedom"
appear to be "caused."[17] The problem of the essay, in
other words, is to speak of human freedom in terms of
its antecedent conditions, without seeming to "account
for" freedom on the basis of those same antecedent conditions. And, given Kant's commitment to the notion
of causality embraced by Newtonian science, his task
in this instance is a very difficult one.

It is not necessary to add anything to this brief
description of this essay to emphasize its relevance
to the heart of the critical philosophy. This makes
it all the more noteworthy that Kant should utilize
the Genesis narrative as, in his own words, "a map for
my trip."[18] Furthermore, Kant suggests that his trip
"may take the very route sketched out in" the Genesis
account.

> Let the reader consult it (Gen.
> 2-6) and check at every point
> whether the road which philoso-
> phy takes with the help of con-
> cepts coincides with the story
> told in Holy Writ.[19]

Needless to say, there is a neat coincidence between
the road taken by philosophical "concepts" and the
narrative provided in Genesis--at least by Kant's

reading. In effect, we have--seven years prior to the publication of Religion--an example of an inquiry into a revealed religion which shows that such a religion can be compatible with the religion of reason. And this sort of inquiry, as I have suggested, is the key aspect of the "experiment" which later helped legitimate the writing of Religion.

All of this suggests that Kant's use of biblical narratives is to be taken seriously. It seems fair to suggest that he is no more reductionistic in his view than the demythologizing movement of our own time, if by demythologizing we understand a theory of the interpretation of myths and not a technique for their demolition. Kant's definition of miracles guarantees that supposedly mythological elements in the Bible will not be rejected outright as the archaic remnants of a superstitious age; and his theory of human limitations provides him with a rationale for making an instrumental use of the mythological element. Thus, in the cases of Kant and the modern-day demythologizers, the interpretive presuppositions involved appear analogous if not identical: the meaning of the text is something other than the literal word; therefore, the interpreter needs a methodological tool by which to peer through the literal word and appreciate the latent meaning. It is, of course, with regard to the nature of this "latent meaning" that the comparison breaks down. Where the "understanding of existence" implicit in the text is the controlling factor for the demythologizers (at least of the existentialist, Bultmannian sort), the pedagogically important moral meaning is the controlling factor for Kant.

Kant's efforts to get at the moral meaning of scripture are especially evident in his treatment of Jesus. For Kant, Jesus is a kind of "teacher" of natural, moral religion. Kant selectively appropriates the so-called "teachings" of Jesus in order to demonstrate their essentially moral thrust. As a result, Jesus' teachings require no historical verification, since they "carry their own proof" (p. 147). By the very nature of his rationalistic presuppositions, then, Kant avoids the problems involved in any "quest" of the "historical Jesus." Because of his theoretical-practical distinction, Kant guarantees that the "historical" element--even if we could sketch it out in full detail-- would be of no religious interest to us. Thus, precisely in his account of Jesus, two important features of Kant's religious viewpoint are clarified: his view

of scriptural interpretation really does emanate in a
theory of religious symbolism, since the implicit moral idea and not the authentically historical element
in which the former is clothed is seen to be the controlling factor; and even in the case of an important
historical referent, like Jesus, it is the universally
valid moral ideas--and not the contingent, historical
"facts" involved--which are of central concern.

Thus, not surprisingly, Kant's treatment of Jesus
is geared, not to establishing the historical accuracy
of the biblical account, but toward molding the biblical account such that it blends smoothly with the mandates of practical reason. For example, Jesus' admoni-
tion to place the first Commandment above all others,
and his advocacy of the Golden Rule, appear--under Kant's
treatment--suspiciously like the categorical imperative.

> [Jesus] combines all duties (1)
> in one universal rule...namely:
> Perform your duty for no motive
> other than unconditioned esteem
> for duty itself, i.e., love God
> (the Legislator of all duties)
> above all else; and (2) in a
> particular rule, that, namely,
> which concerns man's external
> relation to other men as univer-
> sal duty: Love every one as your-
> self, i.e., further his welfare
> from good-will that is immediate
> and not derived from motives of
> self-advantage (p. 148).

All of this suggests what, for Kant, is particularly
advantageous about the Christian revelation in Jesus.
What comes "from the mouth of the first Teacher" is
not a statutory but a moral religion and is therefore
capable "of itself, without historical learning, to be
spread at all times and among all peoples with the
greatest trustworthiness" (p. 155). Because Kant can
fit Jesus into universalizable ethical categories, the
status of Jesus stands in no need of historical verification.

It is obvious that Kant's Jesus, like Kant's Bible,
is instrumental toward certain practical ends. What
is additionally noteworthy about this Jesus is Kant's
unambiguous characterization of him as not soteriologically necessary, in the sense that this Jesus introduces

nothing new but simply personifies certain truths.[21]
This is especially clear in Kant's comparison of Jesus
to what Kant calls the rationally-based "archetype"
of a person well-pleasing to God. Insofar as there is
a Christology evident in Religion, it is the doctrine
of a particular human life which exemplifies the archetype already present in practical reason--it is the
"personified idea of the good principle" (p. 54). The
archetype to which Jesus corresponds is the idea of a
disposition well-pleasing to God--in other words, a
person of complete moral perfection whose every act is
motivated by duty alone (pp. 54-6). The important
point is that this "idea" is genuinely rational; Jesus
does not effect it, but simply personifies it. We
need "no empirical example to make this idea of a person well-pleasing to God our archetype; this idea as
an archetype is already present in our reason" (p. 56).

Thus, all of this suggests the way Kant distinguishes between the moral and the historical aspects
of a given faith. It is important to emphasize at
this point that Kant is here discussing the appropriate
philosophical approach to biblical interpretation.
Kant's method of avoiding censorship troubles and quar-
rels consists of a scrupulous regard for the distinctions among professional tasks. This approach is
natural, given the divisions within German universi-
ties on the basis of "faculties." As Kant points out
in his first preface to Religion, the philosophical
theologian and the biblical theologian (a Kantian distinction which really amounts to that between philosopher and theologian) ought to respect each other's
respective tasks.

> So long as this philosophical
> theology remains within the lim-
> its of reason alone, and for the
> confirmation and exposition of
> its propositions makes use of his-
> tory, sayings, books of all peo-
> ples, even the Bible, but only
> for itself, without wishing to
> carry these propositions into
> Biblical theology to change the
> latter's public doctrines--a
> privilege of divines--it must
> have complete freedom to expand
> as far as its science reaches...
> [The] right of censorship of the
> theologian (regarded merely as

divine) cannot be impugned when
it has been shown that the philosopher has really overstepped his
limits and committed trespass upon
theology...(p. 8).

Kant's concern for distinctions among faculties, of
course, reaches its peak in his Der Streit der Fakultäten,[22] which, as Karl Barth has pointed out, is notable
for the way it is more or less limited to the debate
between the philosophical and theological faculties.[23]
In this work--published five years after the appearance
of Religion--Kant's comments regarding the distinction
between the philosopher and the theologian are more
aggressive and less diplomatic in tone than in Religion.
For our present purposes, what is most interesting
about Kant's Streit is the attention Kant gives there
to the problems of biblical interpretation.[24] In other
words, the problem of the theory of biblical interpretation arises for Kant just at that point where he
wants to establish the autonomy (within certain limits) of the philosopher who is concerned with religion.
This suggests the importance of Kant's own theory of
interpretation within his religious philosophy.

Given this summary of Kant's theory of interpretation, and particularly his view of the meaning of Jesus,
the method by which Kant isolates the moral core within
an historical faith gradually comes into focus. It is,
it seems safe to suggest, what we as rational beings
bring to the text which guarantees that the text will
yield a moral meaning. As I have shown, Kant unequivocally claims that our pinpointing of the moral meaning need not--and sometimes must not--be carried out
with any particular concern for the original author's
intention. Kant's position amounts to saying that
where the literal or apparently intended meaning of a
text does not support morality, the interpreter is justified in proposing a hidden moral meaning--even if
this "may often really be forced" (p. 101). In other
words, so much the worse for the literal meaning. In
the philosopher's hands, the text simply becomes instrumental toward the ends of Kant's practical philosophy. This is in distinct contrast to the theologian's
approach to biblical interpretation, since the theologian, in Kant's view, must rely on the literal meaning
of the biblical material.[25]

One is left wondering if the philosopher's presuppositions are the only thing guaranteeing a moral mean-

ing within a biblical passage. In other words, does
Kant's "method" of establishing the moral element in
an historical faith amount to nothing more than imposing the practical philosophy on an historical text?
The only conceivable Kantian reply to this question
goes to the heart of the potential coincidence of moral and historical faiths, but it is far from satisfactory. Kant feels justified in promoting his theory of
interpretation because of what he calls "the predisposition to the moral religion...hidden in human reason" (p. 102). One should recall, at this point, that
a continuous theme running through Religion is the
conflict between man's "original predisposition to
good" and his "natural propensity to evil." Kant's
efforts to distinguish and elucidate these two anthropological characteristics are not always successful,
but the "predisposition to good" would appear to
underlie what Kant calls the "predisposition to the
moral religion." The real object of Kant's interest,
underlying his predisposition talk, is no doubt practical reason. And because practical reason is a
universal aspect of all rational beings, any religious
text potentially contains elements of moral religion.
All that is needed is a willingness to seek these elements out (p. 98).

An advantage of this approach, of course, is that
it gives Kant good reason to be interested in any religious text. As James Collins has pointed out, Kant's
morally-based, experimental approach to Christianity
shows "that the philosophically ascertainable meaning
for religion is indeed present in the Christian revelational form."

> If the experiments are repeated for
> other religions, then the Kantian
> philosopher of religion can exhibit
> a universally valid meaning of reli-
> gion. It holds for men existing
> under all historical conditions, and
> hence is the common theme of reli-
> gious truth which is variously ren-
> dered concrete and human in all reve-
> lational developments.[26]

Thus, in its most extreme form, Kant's assumption of
a universal predisposition to moral religion antici-
pates--at least in conceptual form--the post-Kantian
achievements of thinkers like Otto and Troeltsch.
Kant's universal predisposition, rooted in practical

reason and legitimating his theory of scriptural
interpretation, amounts, quite simply, to a type of
religious a priori. And with regard to Christianity
alone, Kant's theory of a universal predisposition
to moral religion provides him with a means of establishing a unity of the biblical canon.[27] The original
and universal predisposition, in other words, makes
it possible for Kant to establish the mandates of
practical reason as the interpreter's guiding thread.
This, in turn, enables the interpreter to read a unity
into the Bible which overcomes the difficulties that
arise from the seeming discrepancies and discontinui-
ties characteristic of the biblical record. Thus, for
example, harmonizing of the Old and New Testaments becomes possible by means of Kant's method.

Consequently, any inquiry into Kant's rationale
for deriving a moral meaning from an historical text
comes full-circle back to the problem of the imposi-
tion of a potentially foreign meaning on to the text.
Kant's "method" of interpretation, it would seem, is
immune not only to conflicts within a given text, but
to conflicts among a variety of diverse religious
texts. But this seemingly beneficial result cuts both
ways. Precisely because his theory of interpretation
is based on a particular universal human predisposition, Kant has saddled himself with the problem of
justifying the moral merits of any religious text
whatsoever. It is, of course, convenient for his own
purposes that the Bible seems so amenable to his approach. But--in principle--Kant cannot claim any
privileged status for the biblical account, so that
regardless of the particular respect he might have for
Christianity, his theory of scriptural interpretation
requires that he be concerned with the moral element
embedded in the written traditions of any historical
faith. This, for example, is a direct result of Kant's
utilization of Jesus in an instrumental, rather than
soteriological, manner.

The reason Kant's method of interpretation proves
so unsatisfactory is that it betrays the circularity
of his philosophical approach in Religion. I anticipated this problem in the previous chapter, but now
the difficulty appears in its full form. If Kant is
committed to the presupposition that rational elements--
however few--reside implicitly in any historical faith
embraced by rational beings, then his experimental inquiry into revealed religion "in the light of moral
concepts," with the aim of seeing whether this "does

not lead back to the...pure rational system of religion," loses its innocent and experimental character. The result of such an experiment is a foregone conclusion, given Kant's theory of practical reason. There is of course the possibility that certain particular historical faiths, like Christianity, may more completely approximate the religion of pure reason, but Kant seems committed to the claim that any historical faith whatever must contain at least a minimal aspect of rational religion.

Religion within the Limits of Reason Alone, then, has a peculiar subterranean conflict infecting its pages: (1) on the one hand there is a free and rational inquiry into the potentially rational aspect of an historical faith; and (2) on the other hand there is a strong Kantian commitment to a rational core implicit in any human endeavor. A positive result is established for (1) on the basis of Kant's invocation of (2). But since (2) is simply an aspect of the philosophical anthropology to which Kant is committed, the so-called "experiment" posed by (1) and launched in the second preface of Religion turns out to be less an experiment than a deduction. Kant's theory of practical reason has drastically restricted his freedom of philosophical movement with regard to any inquiry into the religious life of rational beings. The result is a hermeneutical "circle" with a vengeance.

The Theory of Schematism within Kant's Religion

The previous section was aimed at determining the "method" by which Kant establishes that an historical religion really is serving as a vehicle for pure moral faith. The case of Kant's theory of scriptural interpretation was found to be illuminating for the way it revealed the prior commitments Kant brings to his inquiry into historical religion. Every interpreter carries presuppositions, but in Kant's case, the presuppositions involved tend to predetermine not only the questions he asks the text, but the answers he gets. Thus, the "method" by which Kant discovers the moral core of an historical faith is in fact an offshoot of his theory of practical reason, and this guarantees in advance the discovery of that same moral core. And this, as I have shown, amounts to saying that Kant discovers in historical religion precisely what he himself has already put there. That he can do

91

this is guaranteed by his systematic disregard for the
"intentions" of the original biblical authors; and
that he does do this is guaranteed by the question-
begging which his second preface "experiment" turns
out to be.

In this section, I will be concerned with another,
more theoretical aspect of Kant's method of inquiry
into historical religion. An investigation of the
role played in Religion by Kant's theory of schematism
should help illuminate the actual relationship between
the historical and the moral elements in an historical
faith by highlighting certain key epistemological considerations. This is because Kant invokes references
to schematization in Religion just at those points
where he is trying to elucidate how it is that an historical faith can concretize and represent moral ideas.
Thus, the schematism issue is important for the way it
helps us understand the Kantian link between the phenomenal-sensible and the moral-supersensible. Obviously, then, an inquiry into this issue not only clarifies
Kant's view of the relationship between the moral and
the historical; it suggests an epistemological strategy
by which Kant ameliorates the effects of his principle
of human limitations. If, as I suggested in Chapter I,
man's moral and religious reach exceeds his epistemological grasp, the theory of schematism plays a central
role in bridging the resulting gap.

It should come as no surprise that this inquiry
needs to be routed through a prior examination of
Kant's theory of schematism as such. This is one of
the least understood and most infrequently treated aspects of the first Critique, something for which Kant
himself is to blame, given his tortured discussion of
the issue. (Kant himself, in the Prolegomena, refers
to the first Critique's schematism chapter as "important and even indispensable, though very dry.")[28]
Coming as it does on the heels of the Transcendental
Deduction, Kant's theory of schematism might be neglected partly because the commentator's intellectual
strength has been drained by the preceding pages. But
it is not fair to claim, as some have, that the theory
of schematism is an unnecessary addendum which really
has no place in the Critique. It is quite true, as
Walsh has observed, that the details of Kant's argument
in the schematism section are "highly obscure" and that
"it is hard to say in plain terms what general point
or points Kant is seeking to establish."[29] But this
is not the same thing at all as saying that the theory

does not "fit" Kant's epistemology. Hopefully, the intelligibility (if not the validity) of the theory of schematism as such will be implicitly established in the course of the effort to show its relevance to Religion.

In what follows, then, I propose to do three things. First, I shall point out those passages in Religion where Kant invokes the schematism theme and briefly comment on the context of these passages. Secondly, I shall launch an extensive excursion into the murky epistemological waters of the first Critique in an effort to clarify what it is Kant has in mind when he invokes the schematism theme. Although this excursion will at times seem to take us far afield of our central concerns, I consider it to be justified on the grounds that it illustrates Kant's consistent desire to give sensible, empirical expression to our rationality, both in its theoretical and its practical aspects. As an epistemological mechanism, then, the theory of schematism symbolizes what I understand Kant to be doing with his theory of historical religion as a whole. Thirdly and finally, I shall return to Religion in order to apply to the interpretation of that work what we have learned from our analysis of Kant's theory of schematism.

1. References to Schematization in Religion. Kant alludes to his theory of schematism only briefly in Religion, but the allusions occur at key points and in significant contexts. In due course, I hope to show that this is by no means an arbitrary move on Kant's part, but a logical and predictable association for him to make, once the theory of schematism is correctly understood. In the early pages of Book II (pp. 54ff.), when Kant is endeavoring to give an account of the meaning of Jesus, he mentions the "schematism of analogy" as playing an important role in our understanding of Jesus. Kant is attempting to explain what he means by the "personified idea of the good principle," which, as I indicated in the previous section, is Kant's way of speaking about Jesus. He has claimed that this "idea" resides archetypally in practical reason, and that, in principle, no empirical representation is required for us to realize this idea. Given this starting point, Kant goes on to play out the Christian notion of revelation by way of speculating about what would obtain were a man to arrive on earth who was "as perfect an example of a man well-pleasing to God as one can expect to find in external experience"

93

(p. 57). He warns us against automatically assuming
that such a man would be of supernatural origin, for

> the presence of this archetype in
> the human soul is in itself suffi-
> ciently incomprehensible without
> our adding to its supernatural
> origin the assumption that it is
> hypostasized in a particular indi-
> vidual. The elevation of such a
> holy person above all the frailties
> of human nature would rather, so
> far as we can see, hinder the adop-
> tion of the idea of such a person
> for our imitation (p. 57).

Obviously, Kant wants to preserve a "personified
idea of the good principle" that human beings can
relate to and thereby use as an ethical example. To
exaggerate the distance between ourselves and a figure
such as Jesus is morally counter-productive, since it
tends to discourage us from trying to emulate such a
figure. In order to protect the practical utility of
a Jesus-like figure, Kant insists that he must be con-
strued along the lines of a fully human "godly-minded
teacher" and not as some kind of divine being (pp. 58-
9).

This is the context in which the schematism theme
is first invoked by Kant. Precisely where Kant wants
to speak of the intrinsically supersensuous (i.e., a
disposition morally well-pleasing to God) becoming
both visible and conducive to human imitation, Kant's
mind turns to a seemingly obscure theme drawn from
his epistemology. Not surprisingly, Kant's invocation
of the theory of schematism is couched in the idiom of
his principle of human limitations.

> It is indeed a limitation of human
> reason...that we can conceive of no
> considerable moral worth in the
> actions of a personal being without
> representing that person, or his
> manifestation, in human guise (p. 58.).

This is a gloss on Kant's claim that to exaggerate the
moral status of the personified version of the good
principle would discourage us from trying to approximate a similar level of moral worth. All of this is
not to assert that such moral worth is conditioned by

human limitations, but only

> that we must always resort to some
> analogy to natural existences to
> render supersensible qualities in-
> telligible to ourselves...Such is
> the schematism of analogy, with which
> (as a means of explanation) we cannot
> dispense. But to transform it into a
> schematism of objective determination
> (for the extension of our knowledge)
> is anthropomorphism, which has, from
> the moral point of view (in religion),
> most injurious consequences (p. 58n.).

Kant goes on to amplify this cautionary note by
claiming that

> while, in the ascent from the sensible
> to the supersensible, it is indeed
> allowable to schematize (that is, to
> render a concept intelligible by the
> help of an analogy to something sensi-
> ble), it is on no account permitted us
> to infer (and thus to extend our con-
> cept), by this analogy, that what holds
> of the former must also be attributed
> to the latter. Such an inference is
> impossible, for the simple reason that
> it would run directly counter to all
> analogy to conclude that, because we
> absolutely need a schema to render a
> concept intelligible to ourselves (to
> support it with an example), it there-
> fore follows that this schema must
> necessarily belong to the object itself
> as its predicate...[For] between the
> relation of a schema to its concept and
> the relation of this same schema of a
> concept to the objective fact itself
> there is no analogy, but rather a
> mighty chasm, the overleaping of which
> ...leads at once to anthropomorphism
> (p. 59n.).

Kant is telling us a lot in these notes, and the
central importance for this entire inquiry of the
point he is making should be readily apparent. The
notion of schematism, it would appear, affords Kant
the means of proposing a theory of analogy by which

he can bridge the gap between the phenomenal-sensible and the moral-supersensible. If this is true, then Kant's invocation of the theory of schematism lies at the heart of what I have called the constructive aspect of his theory of historical religion. Sustained analysis of Kant's remarks must await my investigation of his treatment of schematism in the first Critique. But before pursuing that issue, it is necessary to specify another, less significant, instance in Religion of Kant's reference to the schematism theme.

. Near the end of Book III, Kant asks the question, "What period in the entire known history of the church up to now is the best?"

> I have no scruple in answering, the present. And this, because, if the seed of the true religious faith, as it is now being publicly sown in Christendom, though only by a few, is allowed more and more to grow un-hindered, we may look for a continuous approximation to that church, eter-nally uniting all men, which consti-tutes the visible representation (the schema) of an invisible kingdom of God on earth (p. 122).

As in the earlier example, Kant here invokes the notion of schematism in order to offer a theoretical account of how we might render the invisible visible through some means of representation. The reference in this second instance is obviously brief and meant as a passing remark, and its full force will become apparent only in the light of my analysis of Kant's doctrine of the church. For the moment, the mere citing of this reference substantiates the insight offered with regard to the earlier reference: the theory of schematism, whatever it is, lies at the center of Kant's understanding of the beneficial and morally advantageous aspect of historical religion; the schema's role is signified by another passing reference by Kant, in which the term is used synony-mously with the word "representation" (p. 88). In order to appreciate the full impact of this claim, it is necessary to determine what the schematism theme connotes for Kant himself. It is time, then, to re-turn to the Critique of Pure Reason.

2. The Theory of Schematism Clarified. To understand Kant's theory of schematism, it is important to
keep in mind the overall purpose of the Transcendental
Analytic, that section of the Critique in which the
schematism chapter appears.[30] As the commentators
never tire of telling us, the Transcendental Analytic
is the heart of the Critique of Pure Reason. This is
because this section, more than any other, answers the
peculiar question which Kant is concerned to face: How
are synthetic a priori judgments possible? By posing
his question in just this way, Kant immediately makes
his revolutionary premise clear. He takes it as given
that there are synthetic a priori judgments (or, more
correctly, synthetic judgments known a priori[31]); his
question, then, is not whether such judgments are possible, but how they are possible. It is precisely
through addressing this "how" rather than "whether"
question that Kant fashions the distinctive (i.e.,
transcendental) style of the first Critique.

In the course of accounting for synthetic judgments
known a priori, Kant relies on his theory of the understanding, that cognitive faculty which stamps the human
intellect as a discursive, rather than intuitive, instrument. As a spontaneous or active faculty (in contrast to the receptive faculty of sensibility), the
understanding produces concepts which behave in the
manner of rules, shaping our experience in certain
necessary ways.[32] The Analytic of Concepts--the first
section of the Transcendental Analytic--justifies not
only the notion of concepts in general but also the
specifically Kantian claim that there are such things
as pure or a priori concepts, which are, of course,
Kant's categories. Showing what the categories are is
the task of the metaphysical deduction; showing how
the categories necessarily constitute human experience
is the task of the transcendental deduction. Kant's
aim throughout is to demonstrate that without a battery
of rule-like and necessary concepts which are derived
from no experience whatever, no intelligible account of
experience could be proposed.

The specific contours of Kant's deductions are not
of immediate importance here. But to appreciate the
role of the theory of schematism--not to mention the
implications of its particular location in the Cri-
tique--it is important to distinguish between what the
Analytic of Concepts achieves and what it leaves un-
done. Through the deductions, Kant demonstrates to
his own satisfaction the categorial structure of the

human mind and the necessary implication of the categories in any conception of experience that we might
make intelligible to ourselves.[33] Most importantly,
the Transcendental Deduction has established a crucial
link between the conditions of self-consciousness and
the conditions of objective knowledge; by getting to
the one (through the vocabulary of the "unity of apperception"), Kant feels he has gotten to the other as
well.[34] That is, the possibility of the self-ascription of connected experience, besides answering Hume's
troubling questions about the nature of the "self," is
demonstrated by Kant in such a way that the conditions
of that possibility establish the conditions of objective knowledge.

> [All] unification of representations
> demands unity of consciousness in the
> synthesis of them. Consequently it
> is the unity of consciousness that
> alone constitutes the relation of
> representations to an object, and
> therefore their objective validity
> and the fact that they are modes of
> knowledge; and upon it therefore
> rests the very possibility of the
> understanding...The synthetic unity
> of consciousness is, therefore, an
> objective condition of all knowledge.[35]

Crudely stated, the point of all this is to carve
out an epistemological foothold somewhere between
Hume and Berkeley. Kant simultaneously answers them
both through a strategy of using the necessary unity
of apperception (which tells me nothing more than
"that I am"[36]) as a premise which gets him to the
claim that all experience must be subject to the concepts. And this latter claim, given the Kantian view
of the relation between intuitions and concepts,
amounts to the further claim that all experience must
be of a world which, however much "shaped up" by man's
intellectual apparatus, is nonetheless objective.
This connection between the possibility of the self-
ascription of experiences and the objectivity of the
external world is helpfully summarized in two theses
proposed by Strawson.

> [There] must be such unity among
> the members of some temporally ex-
> tended series of experiences as is
> required for the possibility of self-

98

consciousness, or self-ascription
of experiences, on the part of a
subject of such experiences (the
thesis of the necessary unity of
consciousness)...

[Experience] must include awareness
of objects which are distinguishable
from experiences of them in the sense
that judgments about these objects
are judgments about what is the case
irrespective of the actual occurrence
of particular subjective experiences
of them (the thesis of objectivity)...[37]

Happily enough, it is not necessary for our purposes
to untangle all the arguments and pseudo-arguments
going into Kant's ambitious project. It is important
simply to notice that, by setting up his theories of
the categories and consciousness in the way he does,
Kant provides both for the connectedness of experience (contra Hume) and for the objective reality of
the external world (contra Berkeley).[38]

The problem with this result is the gap still remaining between the operation of the categories and
the putatively objective world. Put otherwise, granted
that the self-ascription of connected experience and
the objectivity of the external world are demonstrated
together, how does the Kantian philosopher propose to
bridge the gap between the categories and their particular instances of use or application? This difficulty is especially acute, given the fact that the
categories possess no empirical element whatever.
"The difficulty is, in effect, one of bringing [the
categories] down to earth."[39] It is this problem that
the chapter on schematism is meant to solve. As Kant
himself puts it at the start of the schematism chapter,
how "is the subsumption of intuitions under pure concepts, the application of a category to appearances,
possible?"[40] His answer to this question is peculiar.

Obviously there must be some third
thing, which is homogeneous on the
one hand with the category, and on
the other hand with the appearance,
and which thus makes the application of the former to the latter
possible. This mediating representation must be pure, that is, void

of all empirical content, and yet
at the same time, while it must
in one respect be _intellectual_, it
must in another be sensible. Such
a representation is the _transcenden-_
tal schema.[41]

This is a highly metaphorical passage, and the
idiom of a mediating "third thing" does not especially
help us understand just what a transcendental schema
is. It does, however, indicate the problem which the
schematism process is intended to overcome. Categories
and instances of perception (i.e., the manifold of intuition) are intrinsically heterogeneous. Thus, if
the categories are to have "real significance"--in the
sense that they are genuinely _referential_--rather than
mere "logical significance"--in the sense that we can
make up grammatically correct sentences about them--
then some "third thing" is needed which links categories and instances of perception.[42] This third
thing, moreover, in order to do its job, must share
features in common with both intuitions _and_ concepts.

The schemata of the pure concepts of
understanding are thus the true and
sole conditions under which these
concepts obtain relation to objects
and so possess significance.[43]

The significance spoken of here by Kant is the significance derived from empirical utility. The schematism
chapter is intended to guarantee this utility.

As a mediating "third thing" the schema operates
as a rule for synthesis--it is the "representation of
a universal procedure of imagination in providing an
image for a concept."[44] The very fact that the role
played by the schema is to link intuitions and concepts
buttresses Kant's epistemological stringency; it means
that categories can only be applied to intuitions, and
not to things in themselves. Thus, the theory of schematism marks a significant aspect of the difference
between the first _Critique_ and Kant's _Inaugural Disser-_
tation.[45] Kant emphasizes this when he claims that the

conditions of sensibility constitute
the universal condition under which
alone the category can be applied
to any object. This formal and pure
condition of sensibility to which

100

> the employment of the concept of
> understanding is restricted, we
> shall entitle the schema of the
> concept. The procedure of under-
> standing in these schemata we shall
> entitle the schematism of pure
> understanding.[46]

Thus, the theory of schematism guarantees that the
categories will be anchored to empirical states of
affairs. Like the doctrine of sensibility, the doctrine of schematism is a weapon in the Kantian battle
against speculative metaphysics.

The important thing to keep in mind about the
schema is its operation in a "rule-like" manner. This
has the effect of making the schema a sort of concept,
insofar as Kant speaks of concepts themselves in terms
of their rule-like behavior.[47] Whether or not Kant
makes good on his theory of schematism, he has at
least improved "on most theories which link concepts
with images."

> Instead of associating each concept
> with a single image, or with a set
> of exactly similar images, Kant's
> theory associates each concept with
> a rule for image-production.[48]

The importance of this rule feature is, as indicated
earlier, its referential aspect. The specific reason
that schemas as rules for creating images in fact do
overcome the categories' referential problem is that
schematization always occurs in terms of time. This
is one of the more puzzling features of the theory,
but it is that feature without which the categories
would never be "brought down to earth."

The fact that "time" is the clue to the nature of
the "third thing" mediating between intuitions and
categories suggests the predominant role played in
Kant's philosophy by the doctrine of inner sense.
Time, unlike space, is "the only feature which is
common to every object of experience, including the
empirical self."[49] Thus, time alone has the attributes
necessary for the mediating function between two heterogeneous entities--it is the clue to the "third
thing."

> [A] transcendental determination of

> time is so far homogeneous with
> the category, which constitutes
> its unity, in that it is univer-
> sal and rests upon an a priori
> rule. But, on the other hand,
> it is so far homogeneous with
> appearance, in that time is
> contained in every empirical
> representation of the manifold.
> Thus an application of the cate-
> gory to appearances becomes pos-
> sible by means of the transcen-
> dental determination of time,
> which, as the schema of the
> concepts of understanding, me-
> diates the subsumption of the
> appearances under the category...
> The schemata are thus nothing but
> a priori determinations of time
> in accordance with rules.[50]

It may well be that Kant's selection of time is somewhat arbitrary.[51] Even so, its role as homogeneous
with both categories and the manifold of intuition
helps to clarify just what it is Kant wants his theory of schematism to do.

The most mysterious aspect of Kant's theory is
what he says about the source of transcendental schemas. Precisely because Kant wants to (1) posit schemas as necessary for the application of the pure concepts of the understanding and (2) thereby distinguish
schemas from concepts, he cannot claim that schemas
arise out of the faculty of understanding. This
leaves him hard-pressed to account for their source,
just how much so being indicated by the obscurity of
what he does say on this issue.

> This schematism of our understand-
> ing, in its application to appear-
> ances and their mere form, is an
> art concealed in the depths of the
> human soul, whose real modes of
> activity nature is hardly likely
> ever to allow us to discover, and
> to have open to our gaze. This
> much only we can assert: the image
> is a product of the empirical facul-
> ty of reproductive imagination; the
> schema of sensible concepts, such
> as of figures in space, is a product

102

> and, as it were, a monogram, of
> pure a priori imagination, through
> which, and in accordance with which,
> images themselves first become pos-
> sible.[52]

So it is the "a priori imagination" which is the source
of the schema, and this imaginative capacity is an "art
concealed in the depths of the human soul." It is difficult to know what to say about this. As Bennett has
suggested, Kant's theory at this point amounts to the
claim that "there is something which we do but which
we cannot catch ourselves at because it lies too deep,"
which Bennett likens to "Locke's assurance that we do
not usually observe our conversions of raw into interpreted sense-data only because we perform them 'so
constantly and so quick.'"[53]

All of this suggests that to know the purpose of
the schematization process is not necessarily to know
its meaning. The theory seems to amount to a claim
about a rule-like procedure which produces images or
representations, which in turn link categories with
instances of perception. This process is produced by
the a priori imagination and always occurs in terms of
time. The net result is the ability, not only to "use
a word" correctly (i.e., grammatically), but

> to imagine the sorts of situation to
> which it applies, which means having
> the ability to produce a series of
> images. Having this ability is what
> Kant means by possessing the schema
> of the concept in question...[54]

Just on the face of it, Kant would seem to have
burdened himself with infinite regress-type problems.
If a schema is necessary for the correct application
of a particular category, do we not need some further
conceptual apparatus to guarantee the correct application of that particular schema? Furthermore, Kant's
discussion of the theory, besides being highly metaphorical, is permeated with serious ambiguities. It is
not at all clear, for example, whether Kant means the
theory to apply just to the categories, or to empirical
as well as pure concepts. The difference between the
two cases seems clear. There is, to borrow Bennett's
example, a great difference between relating the (empirical) concept "dog" to the specific instance of a
"loyal though bad-tempered borzoi with an off-white

coat and bad teeth," and relating the (pure) concept "substance" to something that is "spherical, orange-coloured, sweet-tasting, and rich in vitamin C."[55] There are problems attending the latter case which do not affect the former. And indeed Kant expressly begins his schematism chapter as though it is only pure concepts he is concerned with.

> But pure concepts of understanding
> being quite heterogeneous from
> empirical intuitions, and indeed
> from all sensible intuitions, can
> never be met with in any intuition.[56]

But he then goes on to speak in terms which unmistakably implicate empirical as well as pure concepts in what he is doing, as when he uses the concepts "triangle" and "dog" as examples for his discussion.[57] One gets the feeling that the validity of the schematism doctrine is undermined from the outset by Kant's own confusions regarding its purpose.

Furthermore, it is not at all clear what the schematism chapter genuinely adds to the transcendental deduction. If it really does add something, then its results would seem to be in potential conflict with the deduction. Norman Kemp Smith has gone so far as to conclude that the schematism chapter is an artificial and unnecessary aspect of Kant's argument which was included simply for the sake of the symmetry of Kant's beloved architectonic.[58] He understands Kant's schematism chapter to be the answer to the problem of subsumption, i.e., the subsumption of intuitions to categories. But, Smith argues, schematism (by Kant's own account) is not a process of subsumption at all, but a process of creative synthesis, "whereby contents are apprehended in terms of functional relations, not subsumption of particulars under universals that are homogeneous with them."[59] This is because the category can never be a "predicate" of a possible judgment, as though it is added to a judgment already formulated. Rather, the category (again, by Kant's own account) is intrinsic to the articulation of the judgment in the first place.[60] Smith's argument amounts to the claim that if we are forced to take the schematism chapter at face value, then Kant's original theory of categories falls through.

Smith's criticism is ultimately aimed at demonstrating that the schemata and the categories are identical.[61] Hence, on his reading, the metaphor of the "third thing"

mediating between the intuition and the category is
what is specifically misleading and artificial about
Kant's theory. He suggests that Kant is attempting
to establish a relation beween the data of sense and
the categories which is analogous to the relation between certain particulars and the class to which those
particulars belong.[62] But this analogy, Smith claims,
is incorrect, insofar as there can be no quality per-
taining to intuitional material which is common to a
category (in contrast to certain shared qualities of
a particular and its class). As it turns out, then,
it is precisely the _inappropriateness_ of the analogy
Kant is offering which is "ultimately the sole ground
which he is able to offer in support of his description of the schema as a 'third thing.'"[63] In other
words, there is no analogy existing between a subsumption that is _logical_ (a particular and its class)
and one that is _synthetic_ (the Kantian theory of judgments), yet it is the very failure of this analogy
which Kant invokes to prove the necessity of a "third
thing."[64]

Whatever its merits, Smith's criticism helps illuminate what it is that Kant is up to in his schematism chapter. The categories have transcendental
functions and, following the Analytic of Concepts,
Kant is obligated to state the conditions under which
these functions have empirical value. On Smith's
view, Kant is generating an unnecessary third term--
unnecessary because the function involved is suffi-
ciently provided for by the Kantian categories--for
reasons of architectonic symmetry. Warnock has proposed a criticism which combines Smith's complaint
with my own earlier suggestion that Kant's theory of
the schema falls victim to an infinite regress problem.[65] Like Smith, Warnock contends that the schematism chapter is in conflict with the results of the
Transcendental Deduction. He argues that the theory
of schematism itself is based on a false premise,
insofar as, on Warnock's view, it is impossible to
have a concept without also having the ability to
use that concept--a view which, Warnock admits, rests
on the additional claim that to have concepts presupposes knowing a language.[66] If, as Kant suggests, the
schema is a kind of rule, then for a particular schema
to do its job as a model _for_ a concept is no different
than using the concept itself. If so, then the schema is unnecessary as a third term; if not, then what
Kant proposes to do with the schema is impossible for
the same reason it is impossible for the categories

themselves. Warnock quotes approvingly Prichard's remark that the schematism process "said to be necessary because a certain other process is impossible is the very process said to be impossible."[67]

Given these confusions and criticisms, it is not surprising to find a recent commentator suggest that there are three possible readings of the schematism chapter. Moltke Gram has distinguished among: (1) the schema as a "third thing"; (2) the schema as a "rule"; and (3) the schema as a sort of intuition.[68] Considering that Smith's interpretation leads to the claim that the schema is really a way of speaking about the categories, we have at least four readings. Given these interpretive difficulties on the one hand, and the general aims of this present inquiry on the other, it is perhaps wise to distinguish between what Kant wants his theory to do, and what the theory really amounts to; we can remain concerned with the former, without being excessively hindered by the problems posed by the latter.

Consequently, it is important to utilize these various interpretations as a way of getting clear about Kant's intentions. Placed in the broadest possible context, the intention behind the schematism theory would seem to be Kant's desire to guarantee that rationality (in this case, the functioning of the categories) has reference points in the phenomenal sphere. Whatever its precise meaning, the transcendental schema is clearly understood by Kant in functionalist terms, its function having to do with some sort of bridge-building activity. The actual bridge-building involved in the schematism process is symptomatic of Kant's general aim to bring together the various dualities his philosophy establishes; it is also symptomatic of his aim to overcome the failures of both rationalism and empiricism. Whether this bridge-building is superfluous, or whether the bridge itself is a faulty structure, is not ultimately important. What is important is Kant's sensitivity to the potential abyss existing between rationality and empirical states of affairs. Whatever its faults, the theory of schematism is meant to neutralize the potential effects of this abyss. The theory of schematism, in other words, reflects what has been called Kant's "active searching for the means of mutual adaptation between pure general meanings and particular sensuous conditions."[69] As such, the schematism theory is itself an expression of Kant's principle of human limitations.

106

3. Schematization and Practical Reason. It does not take an extraordinary imaginative leap to see how the schematism issue dovetails with my inquiry into Kant's view of historical religion. Given the connotations which his theory of schematism evokes in the first Critique, Kant's allusions to the theory in Religion can mean only one thing: they refer, however obscurely, to a process by which rationality and sensible representations are brought together. But in this case, the rationality involved is not the categorial structure of the intellect, but the mandates of practical reason. However, to relate the schematism theory to the mandates of practical reason introduces a serious difficulty, since it is not altogether clear what, in this case, is to be schematized. Rotenstreich has put his finger on this problem by pointing out that, within the realm of practical reason, there can be no schematism in the proper sense of the word "since there is no structure on part of the given world which makes it subsumable under the moral law."

> Further still: the problem within the realm of ethics is not one of subsumption of given facts to the moral law, but one of the full realization of the moral law which amounts to a creation of a new reality in the spirit of the imperative inherent in the moral law.[70]

The Kantian distinction between theory and practice, in other words, makes the potential relevance of the schematism doctrine to practical reason highly problematic. Not only does practical reason have to do with actions rather than with judgments, but it relates to what is intrinsically supersensible (i.e., the moral law) rather than to empirical images.

Kant himself points out this problem in the Critique of Practical Reason. A "judgment under laws of the pure practical reason seems to be subject to special difficulties," since practical reason is dealing with the "supersensuous."[71] In other words,

> to the law of freedom (which is a causality not sensuously conditioned), and consequently to the concept of the absolutely good, no intuition and hence no schema can be supplied for the purpose of applying it in concreto. Thus the moral law has

no other cognitive faculty to mediate its application to objects
of nature than the understanding
(not the imagination); and the
understanding can supply to an
idea of reason not a schema of
sensibility but a law.[72]

Put otherwise, "the gap between the law and the sensuous world in the realm of ethics is wider and deeper
than in the realm of [theoretical] knowledge."[73]
Whereas a schema can overcome the gap between concept
and instance of perception, only a law can bridge the
gap between morality and instance of a moral act.

The difficulty, then, is that there are no empirical images corresponding to moral ideas. The moral
law, as an idea of pure practical reason, has no
matching schema which serves to "exhibit" that law.[74]
This is one of the reasons why we can never be certain that an act is a genuinely "moral" act.[75]

Now on the surface, it would seem that all of this
leaves little room for the theory of schematism understood from the practical point of view. Yet we already know that Kant makes allusions to the theory in
Religion and he does so in a context which suggests a
process by which intrinsically supersensuous moral
ideas are becoming visible. Thus, on the one hand,
we find Kant claiming that the gap between practical
reason and the phenomenal world is too wide to be
bridged by a schema; and on the other hand, we find
him invoking the schematism doctrine in the context
of practical reason. The solution to the discrepancy,
of course, is the fact that in Religion, Kant is not
referring to the schematism doctrine per se, but to
what he calls the "schematism of analogy" (pp. 58-9n.).
Schematism per se (which Kant calls "schematism of
objective determination" in Religion) has to do with
concepts and intuitions and results in an extension
of our knowledge. But the theory of schematism can
also have to do with ideas of reason--including moral
ideas.[76] In this case, however, the schematization
process must be altered slightly because, in the case
of "ideas" (in the Kantian sense), there is no corresponding intuition as in the case of concepts.[77]

It is this "slightly altered" sense of the schematizing process which is the schematism of analogy in
Religion. Since there is no possible intuition corresponding to moral ideas, no true schematization is pos-

sible. What is possible is a schematizing process which is based on an analogy between the moral idea in question and some intuitable representation. This process results in symbols--including religious symbols--and is touched on by Kant in the Critique of Judgment. All manner of "sensible illustration," says Kant, is one of two forms.

> It is either schematical, when to
> a concept comprehended by the under-
> standing the corresponding intuition
> is given, or it is symbolical. In
> the latter case, to a concept only
> thinkable by the reason, to which no
> sensible intuition can be adequate,
> an intuition is supplied with which
> accords a procedure of the judgment
> analogous to what it observes in
> schematism, i.e., merely analogous
> to the rule of this procedure, not
> to the intuition itself, consequent-
> ly to the form of reflection merely
> and not to its content...All intui-
> tions which we supply to concepts
> a priori are therefore either sche-
> mata or symbols, of which the former
> contain direct, the latter indirect,
> presentations of the concept. The
> former do this demonstratively; the
> latter by means of an analogy...[78]

And, in a passage which anticipates certain sections of Religion, Kant goes on to say that "all our knowledge of God is merely symbolical."

> [And] he who regards it as schematical,
> along with the properties of understand-
> ing, will, etc., which only establish
> their objective reality in beings of
> this world, falls into anthropomorphism...[79]

By the time of the writing of Religion, Kant did not rest so heavily on the term "symbol" as on the no- tion of schematism of analogy. But it seems clear that in both cases Kant is talking about the same thing. This is because Kant's definition of the "symbolical" manner of sensible illustration in the third Critique is virtually identical to his definition of the "sche- matism of analogy" in Religion. What is common to both is Kant's emphasis on proceeding by analogy rather than

109

by direct intuition. Whatever we call the process, it salvages the possibility of sensibly representing moral ideas, a possibility which seemed jeopardized by the sharp contrast between theory and practice drawn by Kant in the second _Critique_.

The schematism of analogy, then, is _like_ the original theory of schematism insofar as it serves the purpose of linking two heterogeneous entities; it is _different_ insofar as it relies on a type of analogy and not on an intuition. In the case of schematism proper, a concept can be schematized in one and only one way, whereas "the relationship between [a moral] idea and symbol is altogether less intimate," permitting a variety of possible analogies to be drawn.[80] Even so, the epistemological principle involved is the same, and it is not in the least an arbitrary move on Kant's part for him to draw on the schematization theme considering the job he wants done in _Religion_. Whereas in the first _Critique_ Kant wants to exhibit the referential status of the categories, in _Religion_ he wants to concretize and represent certain moral ideas. In both cases, something that is invisible is being made visible. It is just that, in the case of _Religion_, this representative process is carried out by a kind of proxy.

This rather extended theoretical journey tells us a number of things about Kant's references to schematism in _Religion_. For our purposes, two themes are especially important. First, it is obvious that Kant's invocation of the schematism theme within the practical context of _Religion_ buttresses his epistemological stringency in religious affairs. That is, the whole point of a schematism of _analogy_ is to reject the notion that we can have a direct intuition of religious truths. In effect, the schematism of analogy is a kind of "interpretation" rather than a kind of "knowledge"--the difference involved is that between a heuristic device and a genuinely cognitive tool. The fact that the schematism of analogy amounts to a kind of "interpretation" is reflected in the fact that we are free to draw whatever analogy seems appropriate in each given case. This difference between interpretation and knowledge is the reason Kant warns against transforming a "schematism of analogy" into a "schematism of objective determination"; whereas the former is a "means of explanation," the latter constitutes "the extension of our knowledge" which, religiously considered, can yield only "anthropomorphism" (p. 58n.).

110

Thus, the schematism theme touches on the heart of Kant's religious teaching, insofar as it implies the characteristic Kantian claim that there can be no theoretical knowledge of God. Furthermore, the fact that Kant utilizes his schematism idea to effect a theory of analogy suggests how our putative "knowledge" of God is to be understood. Accordingly, Kant's

> distinction between a knowledge-building schematism and a schematism designed for the analogical interpretation of man's situation in the world avoids confusion about the nature of religious statements and the cognitive implications of religious actions.[81]

Ironically enough, then, by drawing on one of his most theoretical of epistemological teachings, Kant has bolstered his religiously crucial distinction between the theoretical and the practical.

Secondly, Kant's appropriation of the schematism doctrine in Religion reflects his desire to make supersensuous religious truths relevant to the human situation. It is this theme which makes schematization an important component in what I have called the constructive aspect of Kant's theory of historical religion. We should perhaps recall that the question generating this section of this chapter is, "What is the actual relationship between the historical and moral elements in a given religion?" What we now know about the schematism doctrine suggests this relationship is to be understood in terms of the way the historical side exhibits and reflects the moral side--historical religion is to pure moral religion what the schema is to a particular category.

All of this helps to explain Kant's interpretation of Jesus as the "personified idea of the good principle." What Jesus essentially is--i.e., a disposition well-pleasing to God--is a moral idea which has complete objective reality regardless of whether it is ever personified (pp. 55-6). "We need...no empirical example," Kant points out, "to make the idea of a person morally well-pleasing to God our archetype; this idea as an archetype is already present in our reason" (p. 56). But Kant is keenly aware of the remaining gap between this idea--however real it may be--and the inclinations and moral blindness of the masses of

men. Jesus, then, becomes a vivid and concrete re-
minder of what, in principle, we already know but regarding which we perhaps need to be reminded. In his
own words, Kant simply wants to remind us that "we
must always resort to some analogy to natural exis-
tences to render supersensible qualities intelligible
to ourselves" (p. 58n.). Thus, from the standpoint of
Kant's moral hermeneutics, Jesus is simply symptomatic
of the way the Judeo-Christian tradition has expressed
moral ideas through an analogy drawn from experience
and oftentimes rooted in a particular personality.
The very notion of the moral law and the very idea of
a disposition well-pleasing to God are not the sorts
of things we could ever "see." But they are the sorts
of things that can be symbolized and personified, and
this is the point of the schematism of analogy. Consequently, whenever we are talking about Jesus, or
God's "love for the world," or the "fatherhood" of
God, we are doing two things: we are giving representative form to a moral idea; and we are doing so
by way of analogy, and not by way of an extension of
our theoretical knowledge. In no way is our store of
information increased.

It is important not only to emphasize the analog-
ical character of Kantian talk about God from the
framework of historical religion, but to specify just
what is analogous to what for Kant. If, for example,
we speak of God's love for humanity as analogous to
a father's love for his children, we are not--on Kantian
grounds--positing an analogy between God and the idea
of a father. Rather, we are positing an analogy between two relations: the relationship between God and
humanity is analogous to the relationship between father and children. This point comes through more
clearly in the third Critique, where Kant, as we have
already seen, speaks of the symbolic mode of representation. Kant's example there is of a despotic state
being represented by a machine, such as a hand mill.

> For between a despotic state and a
> hand mill there is, to be sure, no
> similarity; but there is a similari-
> ty in the rules according to which
> we reflect upon these two things and
> their causality.[82]

Keeping clearly in mind what we can legitimately do
with the concept of analogy, then, helps guard against
turning a justifiable schematizing process into an

illicit inference. To repeat Kant's warning in the
key part of Religion,

> between the relation of a schema
> to its concept and the relation
> of this same schema of a concept
> to the objective fact itself there
> is no analogy, but rather a mighty
> chasm, the overleaping of which...
> leads at once to anthropomorphism
> (p. 59n.).

The specific setting of the schematism doctrine
within Religion, then, suggests how it is that the
Kantian philosopher of religion is to bridge the gap
between supersensuous moral ideas and an inescapably
sensuous humanity. As in the case of its strictly
epistemological context, schematization in its practical context is intended to guarantee that rationality will have reference points in the phenomenal
sphere. Put otherwise, Kant's schematism of analogy
is meant to provide sensuous heuristic aids which will
awaken the religious man's awareness of what he intrinsically knows through practical reason. In effect,
then, what the schematism of analogy does within Religion is just what Kant's Religion does within the
Kantian religious philosophy as a whole. In both cases,
the historical, empirical representation of moral ideas
is being taken seriously by Kant because of its powerful mediating role. The Socratic motif here is readily apparent, and nowhere does Kant explicitly maintain
that the representative process performed by historical
religion is soteriologically necessary. Rather, what
is involved here is what James Collins has appropriately referred to as Kant's "humanizing" of theism and his
"proportioning" the moral ideal "to the actual world
of nature and culture."[83] None of this should be surprising, once the point of Kant's principle of human
limitations has been grasped. For there are, says Kant,
religious truths

> so mysterious that God can reveal
> [them] to us at best in a symbolic
> representation in which only what is
> practical is comprehensible to us,
> and that we, meanwhile, cannot at
> all grasp theoretically what the re-
> lation of God to man might be, or
> apply concepts to it, even did He
> desire to reveal such a mystery

113

to us (p. 159).

This examination of the schematism doctrine, then, helps us to understand how we are to view Kant's conception of the historical dimensions of a rational faith. In particular, the schematism of analogy, because of its mediating, representative role, reflects the way a revealed, historical faith for Kant is to be viewed as the "applied" aspect of an otherwise "pure" religion. Indeed, Kant's distinction between a "natural" and "revealed" religion is more appropriately rendered as the distinction between "pure" and "applied" religion.[84] A revealed, historical faith, in its ideal form, is a pure moral religion "applied" to the sensuous and communal aspects of human life as it is actually lived. This process of application and accommodation, typified by the schematism of analogy, is necessary if Kant's moral conception of religion is to be "brought down to our human soil [and] made relevant for the concrete world of human experience..."[85]

Consequently, it is altogether wrong to think of Kant as intrinsically opposed to the trappings of an historical faith, such as revelation, scripture, and church. The religion of pure practical reason has not "dehistoricized" Christianity so much as it has found a way of discovering the moral meaning embodied in Christian symbolism and imagery. The alternative is to have a religion of practical reason existing in a vacuum. The one question remaining is what becomes of this historical element once the moral meaning is perceived and appreciated. It is to this question that the final part of this chapter is devoted.

Historical Faith as a Vehicle
for Pure Moral Religion

In the first part of this chapter I inquired into Kant's theory of biblical interpretation as a means of identifying the method by which Kant discovers the moral element within an historical faith. Then, in the second part, I drew upon Kant's allusions to the doctrine of schematism in the pages of Religion as a way of determining how Kant construes the actual relationship between a pure moral religion and a revealed historical faith. Both inquiries made it clear that, from the Kantian standpoint, a moral religion and an historical faith are--in principle--compatible.

114

The former, of course, always has priority in Kant's view, but it is readily apparent that there is a valuable place for the latter as well. Consequently, it is impossible to agree with T.M. Greene's characterization of Religion as the "virtual reduction of religion to morality," the expression of Kant's

> comparative indifference to the
> unfolding of historical events
> and a certain lack of sympathetic
> understanding toward imaginative
> portrayals of life in secular and
> religious literature.[86]

Kant is not only deeply concerned about the moral meaning of history, but is--as we have seen--sufficiently sympathetic toward "imaginative portrayals of life in...religious literature" to appropriate various religious narratives as valuable expressions of moral and religious truths.

Thus, the correct way to appreciate the historical dimensions of Kant's rational faith is to inquire into the moral core which he seems to think is present in all faiths, given the universality of practical reason. The compatibility of a moral religion and an historical faith remains intact as long as we view the latter, not as an end in itself, but as the sensuous expression of the ideas contained in the former. The only thing that frightens Kant is the human tendency to make assent to the ecclesiastical and statutory aspects of religion the heart of religious faith. The whole of Book IV of Religion is Kant's effort to distinguish such "pseudo-service" to God from genuine moral service. The historical aspect is legitimate only as long as the maxim of moral action is never subordinated to the maxim of belief. Yet as long as the proper balance is maintained, an historical faith becomes a useful "vehicle" for a pure moral religion (p. 106).

The question which remains concerns the fate of this historical "vehicle" once the moral element has been located and appreciated. It is here that we begin to touch upon the extremely crucial issue of whether or not an historical faith is somehow religiously necessary for Kant. The question at stake seems to be this: on the one hand, even given the universality of practical reason, what is the net effect of that universality if an ignorant and corrupt humanity remains blinded to the mandates of the moral law; and on the other hand, even given the contingency of an historical faith, how can we dismiss the necessity of such a faith if it so effectively communicates moral ideas to an inescapably sensuous humanity? Put otherwise, can it be said that the heuristic value of an historical faith--which Kant clearly endorses--ever assumes the force of pedagogical or soteriological necessity?

At the start of this chapter, I anticipated this question by indicating that, in my view, Kant's rationalistic predilections in religious matters remain dominant. In other words, however strong a case one might make for the "constructive" aspect of Kant's view of an historical faith, it can never warrant replacing the religion of the second Critique with a religion of revelation. I shall buttress this claim further toward the end of this chapter, particularly with a view to the somewhat different view of Kant recently proposed by Michel Despland. First, however, it is necessary to point out an ambiguity in the very notion of the necessity of an historical faith. I briefly mentioned this ambiguity at the close of Chapter II and now is the time to examine this issue more closely.

On the one hand, the necessity of an historical faith might be understood to mean the reliance of human salvation upon a particular historical event or series of events. Thus, for example, orthodox Christianity has traditionally understood its reference to Jesus of Nazareth in terms of Jesus as some kind of "saving event" and not simply as a great religious teacher. The life, death, and resurrection of Jesus are all somehow constitutive of human salvation; something "happened" in that life which is qualitatively unique and which cannot be embodied in any set of universal truths that could be established independently of that event.[87]

But on the other hand, the necessity of an historical faith can be taken to mean the reliance of man upon revealed religion up until the time he is of sufficient intellectual maturity to appreciate a religion of pure reason. In this case, an historical faith assumes the role of a teacher in the course of man's religious development. But, contrary to the standpoint of orthodox Christianity, no particular historical event or series of events is soteriologically necessary; rather,

116

the historical expression of moral truths is simply
pedagogically necessary. And, once the "lesson" has
been learned, the historical aspect can be eliminated,
its purpose having been served. The religious development of man, in other words, goes hand in hand with the
full development of his rational capacities. Gradually,
man progresses to a "higher level" of religious devotion and no longer needs the heuristic aid provided by
the revelational and historical aspect. But he did
need that aspect in order to reach the higher, rational
level. In this sense, the historical faith was initially necessary, and the metaphor of a "vehicle" virtually means just what it says.

Given Kant's doctrine of practical reason and the
important role played in his religious thought by the
postulates, the first or soteriological sort of "necessity" would not seem to offer much promise for interesting discussion. Kant is, above all, concerned with
the universality of our moral awareness, he builds his
religious philosophy directly upon this moral awareness, and he is thereby not the least reliant on specific historical events which are, supposedly, religiously efficacious. Moreover, as he himself puts it,
"there exists absolutely no salvation for man apart
from the sincerest adoption of genuinely moral principles into his disposition" (p. 78). Kant is ultimately
committed, not to the soteriological efficacy of anything
contingent, but to the absolute reality and validity
of something universal. With this in mind, it does
not seem altogether odd to speak of Kant's religious
outlook as a synthesis of Platonism and Christianity.[88]
And once this is admitted, the notion of soteriology
in terms of specific historical events ceases to be
a fruitful topic of inquiry.

But the second kind of necessity is more interesting. Not only would the theme of pedagogical necessity seem to echo the Enlightenment's preoccupation with
a "progressive" view of human history; it would seem
to be implicated in certain comments Kant himself
makes in Religion.

> In man's strivings toward an ethi-
> cal commonwealth, ecclesiastical
> faith...naturally precedes pure
> religious faith...[H]istorical
> faith...as ecclesiastical...will
> itself cease and pass over into
> a pure religious faith equally

obvious to the whole world. To
this end we ought even now to labor
industriously, by way of continu-
ously setting free the pure religion
from its present shell, which as yet
cannot be spared. Not that it is to
cease (for as a vehicle it may perhaps
always be useful and necessary) but
that it be able to cease...(pp. 97,
126n., my emphasis).

Kant is here giving us the definite impression that
a genuinely moral religion is a goal for rational beings, the attainment of which is dependent upon certain historical and ecclesiastical forms. The exact
nature or content of these forms is immaterial; what
is important is that we go through the stage represented by historical religion in order to reach the
ultimately rational goal. Thus, Kant--like Lessing,
Herder, and Schiller[89]--is working out a scheme of
"moral education" within the theoretical confines of
the critical philosophy.

[When] a religion of mere rites and
observances has run its course, and
when one based on the spirit and the
truth (on the moral disposition) is
to be established in its stead, it is
wholly conformable to man's ordinary
ways of thought, though not strictly
necessary, for the historical introduction of the latter to be accompa-
nied and, as it were, adorned by
miracles, in order to announce the
termination of the earlier religion,
which without miracles would never
have had any authority. Indeed, in
order to win over the adherents of
the older religion to the new, the
new order is interpreted as the fulfillment, at last, of what was only
prefigured in the older religion and
has all along been the desire of
Providence (p. 79).

The best clue for determining the meaning of Kant's
hints at a theory of moral education is his doctrine
of the historical church. Indeed, his view of the
church, especially as it appears in Book III of Religion, is an important link among a number of concerns

118

which have dominated this inquiry. In particular,
Kant's doctrine of the church focuses the problem of
an historical faith serving as a "vehicle" for a purely moral religion (and thereby illuminates the question of the ultimate dispensability of the historical
aspect); it highlights Kant's very real concern for
the social context of the religious life (and thereby
balances the individualistic emphases of the second
Critique); and it suggests a teleological component
embedded in man's religious awareness and devotion
(and thereby establishes an important point of contact between Kant's religious thought and his philosophy of history). Thus, an inquiry into Kant's view
of the church not only helps to round out this investigation of Kant's theory of an historical faith, but
also anticipates some of the themes to be dealt with
in the concluding chapter.

To appreciate Kant's reflections on the visible,
historical church, it is perhaps helpful to step back
and attempt to consider the structure of Religion as
a whole. I suggested in the previous chapter that
there are certain interpretive difficulties connected
with the structure and style of Kant's Religion. The
work is often taken to be disjointed and loosely organized, and Kant's possible sensitivity toward the
state censors is for some an important consideration.
At the same time, however, it seems possible to suggest that the structure of the work--particularly the
connection of the first three books--has an integrity
of its own. The link connecting Books I through III
is partially evident in the Table of Contents of the
English translation (pp. iii-iv). Books I and II are
anthropological: they constitute a powerful statement
regarding Kant's optimistic view of the original nature of man, balanced (in accordance with his principle of human limitations) with his well-known commitment to a doctrine of radical evil. What in Book I
is simply a distinction between the "predisposition
to good" and the natural "propensity toward evil"
reaches the level of a conflict in Book II. The stake
involved in this "conflict" is what Kant calls the
"sovereignty over man" (e.g., p. 50).[90]

This conflict between the good and evil principles
remains crucial in Book III and is the connecting
thread holding the first three books together. In
Book III, however, Kant effects an important change
in idiom as he pursues his topic--he drops his concern for the highly abstract terminology of principles

and ideas and begins to deal with the conflict in more concrete and historical terms. Book III has to do with the actual "victory" of the good over the evil principle. And, significantly enough, this victory is conceived by Kant within the context of a rationally-based historical church, which serves as the foundation of what Kant calls the kingdom of God on earth (pp. 85ff.). In effect, the kingdom of God on earth is synonymous for Kant with an historically actualized religion of pure moral faith (p. 113). The idea of a kingdom of God, in other words, serves Kant as a symbol for the ideal moral community. As such, it is a refined version of what Kant spoke of in the Foundations of the Metaphysics of Morals as a kingdom of "ends."[91] The refinement in question consists of Kant's increasing sensitivity later in life toward the concrete social and historical dimensions of the lives of rational beings living together in community.[92]

This understanding of the church helps explain why, as I pointed out in the previous section of this chapter, Kant speaks of the visible church as the "visible representation (the schema) of an invisible kingdom of God on earth" (p. 122). The theory of the schematism of analogy operates in terms of the church in the same way it works in terms of Jesus. That is, the visible church is the worldly analogue for the moral idea of the kingdom of God. As such, the church not only serves as the visible representation of a supersensuous moral idea, but it also provides the concrete social context within which rational beings can actually strive to effect the ethical ideal represented by the kingdom of God. Given this dual role to play, the church, not surprisingly, occupies an important place in Kant's religious thought.

The progression from Book I to Book III, then, constitutes a movement from abstract anthropological speculations toward increasingly concrete empirical considerations. This movement represents a transition from the point of view of the individual to the point of view of the community.[93] Kant's aim is to specify those worldly conditions which would foster and promote the rational and thereby desirable outcome of the conflict in human life between man's predisposition to good and his propensity toward evil. What is crucial for our considerations is the fact that it is the historical side of religion, embodied in the life of the visible church, which plays the key role in Book III in the gradual victory of the good principle.

This does not appear to be a casual, arbitrary, or accidental result, but the effect of a carefully considered scheme. Closer analysis will suggest the specific role the visible church plays in Kant's view.

The introduction of Book III of Religion is important for the way it unequivocally establishes a much-neglected aspect of Kant's ethical and religious thought. Specifically, Kant clearly promotes here a theory of the social context of the establishment of the good in human life. Kant perceives a paradoxical relation between social conditions and the enhancement of the morally desirable: on the one hand, life in community has a corruptive influence on the individual, insofar as life with others engenders "envy, the lust for power, greed, and the malignant inclinations bound up with these" (p. 85); but on the other hand, life in community is the only means whereby the good can be effected, since the individual in isolation is an ethically meaningless entity.

> [The] sovereignty of the good principle is attainable, so far as men can work toward it, only through the establishment and spread of a society in accordance with, and for the sake of, the laws of virtue, a society whose task and duty it is rationally to impress those laws in all their scope upon the entire human race. For only thus can we hope for a victory of the good over the evil principle (p. 86).

An odd doctrine of the morally beneficial effects of social conflict had previously (1784) been promoted by Kant in his "Idea for a Universal History from a Cosmopolitan Point of View."[94] What is significant is the way Kant, at key points, would take into consideration the phenomenal context of ethical problems, a procedure notably absent from his formal establishment of moral principles in works such as the Foundations and the second Critique.[95]

Kant's sensitivity toward the social context of the attainment of ethical ends is the basis of his systematic concern for the institutional church. Kant's desired end--what he calls a "union of men under merely moral laws" (p. 86)--is a kind of ethical state or commonwealth, distinguished from a political state by

121

virtue of its unification "under non-coercive laws, i.e., laws of virtue alone" (p. 87). The principle of heteronomy appropriate to a civil state is, by Kantian standards, wholly inappropriate for an ethical commonwealth. To a great extent, the bulk of Book III of Religion is Kant's account of how his ideal ethical commonwealth is achieved by means of-- and only by means of--the historical church. Kant has to turn to the church, because only there, he feels, can his coveted notion of ethical autonomy be protected. Like the theory of schematism, then, Kant's theory of the church is symptomatic of his philosophical strategy of bridging the gap between rationality and the worldly, sensuous conditions of human life.

Kant's concept of an ethical commonwealth is closely tied to his theory of the highest good, which will be examined in greater detail in the final chapter. What is of interest now is the way the historical side of religion plays a positive role in Kant's scheme. At its introduction, the concept of an ethical commonwealth is essentially a regulative idea for Kant--it is an ideal which is held up to influence and shape the strivings of actual human communities. It is both significant and characteristic that Kant introduces the topic of the visible church just at that point when he wishes to translate an ideal and regulative principle into earthly, phenomenal terms (pp. 90ff.). This is because the historical side of religion functions here as the means of the worldly implementation of what otherwise would remain philosophically ideal. And, as suggested earlier, it is not wholly arbitrary of Kant to utilize the church, rather than some other institution, in this way. For, given his theory of what genuinely obeying the moral law implies (i.e., viewing moral duties as divine commands), the concept of an authentic ethical commonwealth can be meaningful only when understood in reference to God.

> [If] the commonwealth is to be ethical, the people, as a people, cannot itself be regarded as the law-giver. For in such a commonwealth all the laws are expressly designed to promote the morality of actions (which is something inner, and hence cannot be subject to public human laws)...Hence only he can be thought of as highest lawgiver of an ethical commonwealth with respect to whom all true duties, hence also

the ethical, must be represented
as at the same time his commands;
he must therefore be 'one who knows
the heart...' But this is the concept of God as moral ruler of the
world. Hence an ethical commonwealth
can be thought of only as a people
under divine commands, i.e., as a
people of God, and indeed under laws
of virtue (pp. 90-1).

Thus, because of certain implications built into
Kant's ethical theory, the idea of an ethical commonwealth, once proposed, leads automatically to religious
concerns. The final link with the visible church is
established by Kant's claim that his "idea of a People
of God can be realized (through human organization)
only in the form of a church" (p. 91). The argument
for this claim stems from the doctrine of radical evil.
That is, the founding of a people of God is such a
morally prodigious task that its "consummation can be
looked for not from men but only from God Himself"
(p. 92). This line of reasoning, of course, runs
headlong into conflict with the Kantian claim that human salvation lies in human will and not in the passive
acceptance of divine grace, but the tension between
grace and free will is nowhere satisfactorily resolved
by Kant.[96] At this point in Kant's thinking, at any
rate, human frailty and wickedness prevail, thereby
necessitating his postulating the need of a church for
the attainment of a people of God. Whether Kant could
have reached this conclusion prior to his articulation
of a doctrine of radical evil is doubtful.

Kant summarizes his results at the start of Book IV.

We have...seen that such [an ethical]
commonwealth, being a KINGDOM OF GOD,
can be undertaken by men only through
religion, and, finally, in order that
this religion be public (and this is
requisite to a commonwealth), that it
must be represented in the visible form
of a church; hence the establishment of
a church devolves upon men as a task
which is committed to them and can be
required of them (p. 139).

Certain specific details of Kant's doctrine of the
church are not important for our purposes, partly be-

cause he uses the doctrine as an opportunity to import some rather artificial epistemological considerations as a means of making his doctrine appear systematic. For example, the four "tokens" of the true church just happen to correspond directly to the four logical categories found in the first Critique (p. 93). The one important distinction Kant does draw is between the invisible church—a "mere idea of the union of all the righteous under direct and moral divine world-government, [which serves] as the archetype of what is to be established by men"—and the visible church, which is the "actual union of men into a whole which harmonizes with that ideal" (p. 92). Although the invisible church is a "mere idea," it is regulative for Kant, in the sense that it is the rational and moral archetype against which all empirical religious communities are measured. The idea of the invisible church, in other words, is objectively "real" in the same sense that the Son of God as a "disposition well-pleasing to God" is real—they both reside a priori in practical reason. Thus, the dominant rationalistic strand in Kant's ethical thinking continues as the benchmark by which the life of the church is to be judged.

The visible and phenomenal church, on the other hand, is a concession to the worldly conditions of human life. No visible church can itself be normative, just as belief in a particular historical revelation can never be rightfully compelled. Rather, any historical church is commendable and worthy of one's devotion to the extent that it approximates the ideal archetype of the invisible church. Accordingly, "the true (visible) church is that which exhibits the (moral) kingdom of God on earth so far as it can be brought to pass by men" (p. 92). The entire process of balancing the notions of an invisible and visible church is symptomatic of Kant's efforts, in religious matters, to maintain a rational standard of reference while acceding to the demands imposed by human sensibility.

The whole doctrine of the visible church becomes especially significant when we view it as a perhaps necessary way-station on the road toward pure moral faith. This, indeed, seems to be the ultimate purpose of Kant's consideration of historical religion and is the specific point of potential contact between Kant and a thinker like Lessing. In effect, the empirical, historical aspects of religion apparently

cannot be reduced away at any given point, leaving a
pure moral core; only if man were not subject to conditions of finitude and the corruption of his will
could this be possible. Rather, precisely because
man is limited in certain crucial ways, the historical dimensions of religion assume a significant systematic role in Religion. The human race, Kant seems
to be suggesting, must experience the historical aspects of religion before it can genuinely appreciate
the moral aspects. At the same time, however, the
role played by the historical side of religion is
obviously only instrumental for Kant, since man implicitly "knows" all he needs to know about morality
from the outset. Kant, then, looks forward to a time
when historical concerns can be left behind. All historical, ecclesiastical religion

> must contain within itself, along
> with the statutory articles with
> which it cannot as yet wholly dis-
> pense, still another principle, of
> setting up the religion of good life-
> conduct as the real end, in order,
> at some future time, to be able
> entirely to dispense with the stat-
> utory articles (p. 163).

In other words, Kant hopes for an ultimately full
coincidence of the empirical representation with the
rational, moral idea being represented. Should this
full coincidence ever occur, the jettisoning of the
empirical, historical aid would become possible.
Since, presumably, humanity would remain sensuous
even at this ideal rational stage, it is not clear
how Kant imagines that we would be able to express
our religious concerns, if not symbolically. Even
so, Kant is making it unmistakably clear that the
crucial role of the historical aspect lies in its
heuristic function, a function which is part of a
larger teleological scheme.

> [In] the end religion will gradually
> be freed from all empirical determin-
> ing grounds and from all statutes which
> rest on history and which through the
> agency of ecclesiastical faith pro-
> visionally unite men for the require-
> ments of the good; and thus at last
> the pure religion of reason will rule
> over all...(p. 112).

Thus, the era of an undefiled pure moral faith is, for Kant, somewhere in the future. However clearly he claims that an historical faith is ultimately dispensable, he equally clearly claims that the time for dispensing with it has not yet come. The interpreter of Kant, then, is left wondering whether the question of the necessity of an historical faith is answered along with the question of the sufficiency of such a faith. Traditional views of Kant have assumed that a negative answer to the latter involves a negative answer to the former as well; a pure religion of reason is alone sufficient, which leads to the conclusion that an historical faith must be unnecessary. But Kant himself appears to be endorsing the necessity, while at the same time claiming the ultimate insufficiency, of an historical faith. As I have shown, this potential necessity is based upon the need to adapt rational religious ideas to the conditioned nature of the life of a finite humanity. The process of mediation occurring here is reflected in the mediating powers of the schematizing process. Without acceding to the claims of those espousing the adequacy of revealed religion, Kant yields to the human need to have tangible, representative, symbolic aids which bring supersensuous religious concerns into touch with our sensuous human situation.

By focusing on a doctrine of the visible church, then, Kant brings into view a clearer picture of the problem at stake, if not its solution. The church, like historical religion itself, is purely instrumental in forwarding rational religious ends; its role is not sufficient, but it is not clear whether it is necessary. It seems to be necessary for pedagogical purposes, but the necessity of any historical aspect whatsoever would appear to violate the rational and universal norms of practical reason. My own view is that this is a conflict not satisfactorily resolved by Kant. That is, history in its pedagogical aspect is intrinsically in tension with a Kantian religion of reason, but cannot be dismissed by Kant since that would violate his principle of human limitations. The resulting impasse is just that--an impasse. Despland, on the other hand, locates this tension and then uses it to justify certain conclusions which I find unwarranted. A modern example of the same issue might usefully preface the clarification of my disagreement with Despland.

The distinction between a "soteriological" and a

"pedagogical" necessity is implicitly still operative in contemporary Protestant theology, as the difference between Rudolf Bultmann and certain left-wing Bultmannians like Schubert Ogden and Herbert Braun suggests.[97] For Bultmann, the move from "inauthentic" to "authentic" (i.e., Christian) existence is made possible only through a once-for-all act of God hidden in the so-called "cross-resurrection event." Thinkers like Ogden, on the other hand, claim that Christian existence is forever an "original" possibility for man which is simply given with the human situation and is not reliant on a putatively divine "act." From Ogden's point of view, Jesus' function is not soteriological but simply illustrative and formative, in that he illuminates an extant existential possibility and marks the historical beginning of the Christian church. Thus, whereas Bultmann's stress is on the grace of God as redeemer (i.e., in his "act" in Jesus Christ), Ogden's stress is on the grace of God as creator.[98] In my view, Despland is placing Kant on Bultmann's side of this line, whereas Kant's rightful place is clearly on Ogden's side.

Despland relies heavily on the assumption that Religion is a new and vigorous inquiry resulting from Kant's growing awareness of problems posed to his religious thought by human historicity.[99] He pinpoints the conflict between historicity and the standpoint of Kant's pre-Religion critical writings, and then, with a view to the new contributions of Religion itself, he offers two strong and interesting claims. First, he claims that, because of the doctrine of radical evil, Kant's Jesus serves a genuinely soteriological function and is not merely the personification of a rational archetype. Despland's view is worth quoting at length.

> [Kant] discerned at the time of the Gospels not just the acquisition of new moral ideas but also the beginning of an actual moral liberation from enslavement to the evil principle...[The] significance of [Jesus'] life is not only what he taught but also that he broke the power of the evil principle over mankind...Kant here was very cautious, because he was very afraid of naive designations of Jesus as loving Saviour into whose arms we should flee, but the presenta-

127

> tion of Jesus as mere teacher
> does not account for the full rev-
> erence he had for him...Kant did
> not want any mercenary devotion
> to a Saviour, but he did find
> Jesus to be a liberating figure
> who exercises saving power over
> his disciples, and gives fresh
> power to their freedom in the rela-
> tive sense in its struggle against
> the evil principle.[100]

Despland's documentation for this sort of claim is
disappointing. The third of the sentences I have
quoted, for example, is followed by the following
footnote.

> Book Two [of Religion] focuses on
> the life of Jesus. The presentation
> of Jesus as a teacher of pure religion
> appears in Book Four...in the context
> of a discussion of the problem of
> reason and revelation, a standard
> discussion of deism.[101]

It is unclear how this simply descriptive footnote
serves as a warrant for the important claim being made.

Furthermore, in making this claim about Kant's
Jesus, Despland has lost sight of the overall intention lying behind Religion. To be sure, Christianity
is the dominant example of an historical faith utilized
by Kant, but this is hardly because Kant is pursuing
an apologetic on behalf of that religion. On the contrary, Religion is not in any way a Christian apologetic (except insofar as Christianity conforms to moral
religion), but a strictly philosophical inquiry into
the moral aspects of historical faith. Kant, as I
emphasized in Chapter II, is operating strictly as
philosopher; consequently, Jesus (whom Kant does not
even refer to by name) is but an example of a founder
of an historical faith. As my analysis of Kant's theory of scriptural interpretation demonstrated, Kant's
inquiry into the Christian faith could be echoed by a
parallel inquiry into any other historical faith.
Kant's aim in Religion, in other words, is not to
legitimate or commend Christianity, but to "start
from some revelation or other," examine this revelation "in the light of moral concepts," and then determine whether this procedure leads back to the rational

religion produced by Kant's own philosophy (p. 11).
Kant's project, in other words, has methodological
and epistemological roots. Despland, on the other
hand, courts the danger of imputing to Kant certain
soteriological and ontological interests which simply
are not clearly evident in Religion. This tendency
of Despland's doubtless derives from the slight attention he devotes to the epistemological underpinnings
of Kant's concern for historical religion. It is, in
my view, crucial to view the constructive aspect of
Kant's theory of an historical faith from the standpoint of the principle of human limitations rather
than from the standpoint of an assumed Kantian Christian apologetic. Apparently because Despland thinks
that the only alternative to his interpretation is to
categorize Kant as a full-fledged deist, he ends up
pushing Kant too hard in a direction not altogether
amenable to Kantian norms.[102]

The second locus of Despland's attribution to Kant
of the necessity of an historical faith appears in
connection with the problem of revelation. Despland
claims that there are two competing theories of revelation in Religion. On the one hand, he isolates the
view of revelation which I outlined in the previous
chapter. On this view, the idea of a revelation can
serve as a valuable communicative process, insofar as
a supposed revelation can tangibly represent supersensuous moral ideas. History, in other words, merely
illustrates what rational beings already know in principle.[103] This is the sort of theory of revelation
with which the Platonist would be comfortable.

But Despland goes on to claim that there is another,
more significant, view of revelation lurking in the
pages of Religion.

> In Religion there are repeated at-
> tacks on the disjunction of reason
> and history, and reason appears not
> as an a-historical sum of eternal
> principles but as historically con-
> ditioned, dependent on the community
> of thought and action...Reason is
> never finished and complete; it
> grows in its capacity to deal ra-
> tionally with more and more aspects
> of the world, and it grows under a
> divine education which orients it
> to its own true goal. In this case,

history does not merely illustrate
what reason knows, but educates
reason...[Kant's] handling of revelation leads to a historicization
of reason, and a view of divine education of the human race.[104]

Certainly such a view helps to account for the teleological strand in Kant's doctrine of the church. Yet
one gets the impression here that Kant is being mys-
teriously transformed into a combination of Lessing
and Hegel.[105] Despite the possible distortions, however, Despland is clearly putting his finger on a
crucial issue, namely, the problem of the relationship between history (understood in terms of temporality) and reason (understood--in its practical
sense--as belonging to the a-temporal noumenal realm).
On the one hand, Kant is claiming the moral and religious significance of the temporal sequence embodied
by the life of the historical church. But on the
other hand, the very condition of the possibility of
the moral and religious life (i.e., the noumenal
realm) is intrinsically a-temporal. It is simply not
clear how Kant assumes that our moral and religious
life can be affected by time, even though it is clear
in _Religion_ that this assumption is being made.

We have arrived, then, at a point of unresolved
tension in Kant's religious thought. Unfortunately,
Despland assumes all too easily that Kant's apparent
sensitivity toward the historical dimensions of man's
religious life results in a potential resolution of
the conceptual conflict involved. Thus, he attributes
to Kant a doctrine of the "historicization of reason"
which, in my view, assumes a Kantian synthesis of opposing strands of thought which Kant never actually
effected. The elements for such a solution may well
have been there; but to attribute to Kant the solution
itself is to view him with too much of the subsequent
history of German philosophy in mind.

In contrast to Despland, then, I consider the tension between reason and history to be largely unresolved in _Religion_, and this is why it is impossible
to give a definitive answer to the question regarding
the pedagogical necessity of an historical faith. It
is crucial to emphasize the source of this tension:
Kant's theory of an historical faith, particularly
as it is expressed in his view of the church, suggests
a vision of moral and religious "progress" occurring

130

historically; but by Kant's own standards (as laid down in the Critiques and the Foundations), our moral and religious life is intelligible only in terms of a timeless noumenal realm.106 To admit a phenomenal point of contact with our moral life is to threaten the very notion of human freedom, given the deterministic workings of the phenomenal sphere. Interestingly enough, then, by raising the question of the pedagogical necessity of an historical faith, we have arrived at the highly complex problem of the relation between nature and freedom in Kant's philosophy. By asking a seemingly simple question, we are left with some exceedingly difficult ones. What could possibly serve as the link between moral progress and the phenomenal, historical transition from an historical to a moral faith? How can history possibly impinge upon morality and religion if--being noumenal--morality and religion are genuinely "timeless"?

It is worth noting that the problem posed here by Kant's notion of an historical faith is simply the social and cultural expression of a problem which, on the personal and individual level, is posed by his view of religious conversion.107 From a Kantian standpoint, what can it possibly mean to speak (as Kant himself does) of a personal "change of heart" which is "a departure from evil and an entrance into goodness" (p. 68). Even in the Critique of Practical Reason, Kant speaks of the possibility of a "finite rational being...making continuous progress" toward a state of true virtue.108 In Religion, the reference is even more explicit.

> Since [moral discipline] leads only
> to a progress, endlessly continuing,
> from bad to better, it follows that
> the conversion of the disposition of
> a bad man into that of a good one is
> to be found in the change of the high-
> est inward ground of the adoption of
> all his maxims, conformable to the
> moral law, so far as this new ground
> (the new heart) is now itself un-
> changeable (p. 46, my emphasis).

As in the case of his view of the visible church, Kant is obviously talking about a moral revolution which requires a temporal span for its accomplishment. And, again as in the case of his view of the church, Kant nowhere specifies how this claim is to be reconciled

131

with the doctrine of the noumenal quality of the moral
life.[109] What we seem to be discovering, both on the
individualistic-personal level and on the socio-histor-
ical level, is that Kant's Religion is not altogether
consistent with certain basic teachings of the critical
philosophy. Kant is forced, by virtue of his principle
of human limitations, to incorporate the historical aspects of religion into his religious philosophy. At
the level of history as a representative and symbolic
mediator, this poses no problem. But at the level of
the question of pedagogical necessity, there is a
serious conflict: to speak of man's religious development in terms of an historical progression is, from
the standpoint of Kant's writings prior to Religion,
to make a kind of category mistake. For to make good
on the notion of an historical religious development
is to risk claiming that freedom can somehow "appear,"
a highly un-Kantian claim, to say the least.[110]

    I conclude, then, that Kant opens up problems in
Religion which he is not quite equipped to resolve.[111]
We can be clear about the fact that, by Kantian standards, an historical faith lacks sufficiency; it is
less clear what we are to say about its necessity.
One gets the feeling that, were he asked, Kant would
firmly deny that an historical faith is pedagogically
necessary in any strict sense. But one also senses
that the Kantian principle of human limitations--repre-
sented in this context by the doctrines of radical evil
and of human sensibility--prohibits Kant from consistently disclaiming the pedagogical necessity of an historical faith. It could be that Kant's commitment to
rationality cannot ultimately be reconciled with his
numerous limiting concepts.

    Despite the apparent impasse, there are a number
of ways left open for discussing the relationship between history and religion, nature and freedom, in
Kant's philosophy. The key here is perhaps Kant's
philosophy of history and its relation to the progressive element apparent in his religious thought.
Such an issue, of course, revolves not only around
Kant's understanding of human freedom and its relation to the phenomenal world, but around the teleological element apparent in almost all of Kant's thinking. Insofar as these highly complex issues fuse into
a neat pattern, they eventually relate to Kant's concept of the highest good, since this concept unites
the teleological and the moral interests at work in
Kant's thought. These issues will conclude this study.

132

CHAPTER IV

RELIGION, HISTORY, AND THE HIGHEST GOOD

The various conceptual threads I have been exploring so far suggest that the historical dimensions of a rational faith are important to Kant for at least three reasons. First, history assumes the role of a valuable mediator, insofar as it is only within the phenomenal realm that a sensuous humanity can grasp supersensuous moral ideas. This is the specifically heuristic function performed by an historical faith, a function which stems directly from Kant's principle of human limitations.

Second, the historical realm is important to Kant for the way it establishes the social context of man's religious life. The individualistic ethical doctrines of Kant's Foundations of the Metaphysics of Morals and Critique of Practical Reason constitute only one aspect of Kant's overall view; Religion within the Limits of Reason Alone clearly establishes an additional aspect which is essentially social and historical in its thrust. And the social context of religion is important, not simply because it is only in his communal aspect that man genuinely assumes the role of an ethical being, but because the possibility of moral "progress" can, in Kant's view, be understood only in the context of an ethical commonwealth or community. And this, as I have suggested, leads to Kant's deep concern for the life of the visible, historical church.

Finally, Kant's notion of an ethical community or visible church has a teleological component which requires a temporal span for its fulfillment. Thus, history is important to Kant for the way it provides the medium within which man might realize his destiny as a free and rational being. The basis of the social context of religion is also the basis of the worldly realization of man's moral potential.

133

It is this third feature of the historical dimensions of a rational faith which is the subject of this final chapter. As I have suggested, the apparent reliance of moral progress upon a temporal span seems to conflict with the noumenal basis of Kant's theory of morality and religion. But Kant's commitment to the link between religion and history seems unmistakable: on the personal and individualistic level, the link is implied by Kant's notion of religious conversion; and on the social and cultural level, the link is implied by Kant's hope that the ethical community, embodied in the visible church, will gradually approximate the moral idea of the kingdom of God.

> When...(in conformity with the unavoidable limitation of human reason) an historical faith attaches itself to pure religion, as its vehicle, but with the consciousness that it is only a vehicle, and when this faith, having become ecclesiastical, embraces the principle of a continual approach to pure religious faith, in order finally to be able to dispense with the historical vehicle, a church thus characterized can at any time be called the true church...[1]

It is difficult to know what Kant means here, if not a theory of historical progress.

As I indicated in the previous chapter, there is a point at which the tension between temporality and religion in Kant's thought becomes an impasse. He anticipated certain aspects of the historicistic thinking of the nineteenth century, but his transcendental theory of reason and his phenomenal-noumenal dichotomy both worked against a fully successful integration of history into the critical philosophy. Indeed, to locate this tension in Kant's philosophy is to help explain why the course of nineteenth and twentieth century German thought is dominated by attempts to come to grips with the problem of history. We only need to draw a line through the major thinkers of the period--Hegel, Marx, Nietzsche, Dilthey, Troeltsch, Heidegger, and Gadamer--to get a sense of the problem which Kant left his successors.

At the same time, however, there are indications in Kant's philosophy of potential solutions to the problems at stake. Thus, in what follows, I intend to weave together a variety of themes in order to offer the best possible case for a Kantian synthesis of the religion and history problem. The fact that no potential synthesis is completely satisfactory should come as no surprise, given the fact that the deeper-lying issue here is the problem of the relation between freedom and nature in Kant's philosophy. The ultimate issue at stake in this final chapter, then, is the question of a potential "splice" between the world of Newtonian determinism--the world of "is"--and the world of free and rational action--the world of "ought."

The best way to begin this task is, in my view, to isolate the teleological element in Kant's thinking, determine its epistemological status, and to relate the teleological issue to Kant's hopes for man's moral and religious development. There is, as I have indicated, a strong teleological element running through the argument of Kant's Religion, especially in Book III. But whereas teleology remains at a merely implicit level in that book, it becomes considerably more explicit in Kant's writings on the philosophy of history. We might rightfully expect a family resemblance to exist between these different teleological components, at least to the point where an investigation of the one should shed light on the other. For example, Kant's inquiry into history begins with an examination of the notion of purposiveness in the natural world. Our job will be to determine how such a concern for the purposiveness of a purely phenomenal environment can be made epistemologically respectable by Kantian standards, and then to see if this type of purposiveness links up in intelligible ways with Kant's religious thought. Particularly since we want to bring together the phenomenal world (nature and history) with the noumenal realm (morality and religion), teleology would seem to be an important clue, since, for Kant, it plays a dominant role in both spheres.

Once we have come to an understanding of the force of Kant's view of teleology, it will be possible to see how, from the point of view of "purposiveness," the moral realm conceivably impinges upon the natural world in significant ways. Our best guide here will be the recent explorations of Yirmiahu Yovel into Kant's concept of the highest good.[2] Yovel argues that Kant scholarship has been dominated by "a one-sided picture of Kant's practical philosophy which becomes restricted to the realm of personal, internal morality."[3] Yovel's proposed corrective is to consider the communal and historical connotations of Kant's theory of the highest good and to show that the individualistic and eudaemonistic aspects of the doctrine evident in the second Critique do not constitute the heart of the theory.

> The combination of virtue and happiness serves only as the starting-point for the discussion, constituting the personal level of the concept... [The] Highest Good is also understood as the synthesis of the moral Idea with empirical reality...In this context, God must be conceived as the power which guarantees historical progress in the full sense, namely, the ability of human praxis to embody its intentions in the given world and to re-shape it as a 'good world.' It can be shown that [this] is the most comprehensive meaning of the Highest Good and includes all the others.[4]

Yovel's discussion, quite obviously, will be helpful for the way it unifies the inquiry into teleology with our concern for the relation between history and religion.

The Teleological Principle in Kant's Philosophy of History

Kant's philosophy of history, to put it somewhat mildly, has not traditionally been one of the most popular areas of serious inquiry within modern Kant studies. To begin with, there is a deep-seated suspicion within contemporary philosophical circles of all so-called "speculative" philosophies of history. Kant's work on history is, after all, not an investigation of the nature of historical knowledge, but a bold inquiry into the possibility of historical progress and development. Furthermore, there is the lingering sense that Kant's brief and informal essays dealing with history are the casual and unsystematic products of his leisure hours. Recently, however,

efforts have been made, not only to take Kant's philosophy of history seriously, but to demonstrate its
intimate connection with the critical philosophy as a
whole.[5] Hopefully, the preceding sections of this inquiry have indicated--at least provisionally--why Kant's
reflections on history are significant, particularly
within the context of his religious thought. If the
problem of temporality is in fact implicated in Kant's
religious philosophy, then his views on history would
seem to have an important systematic connection to
his understanding of our religious life.[6]

Not the least of the reasons for taking Kant's philosophy of history seriously is the way such a project
helps to counter the stereotype of the Enlightenment
as a radically a-historical period. Wilhelm Dilthey
inaugurated a revisionist view of the Enlightenment
by specifying the advances in modern historical consciousness which the eighteenth century contributed.[7]
Furthermore, it has recently been suggested that the
relative neglect of Kant's views on history, as well
as the popular view of the Enlightenment as an essentially a-historical age, are both due to certain pe-
culiarities of nineteenth century German philosophy.
On the one hand, anything the eighteenth century might
have said about history seemed superseded by emerging
Hegelian thought patterns; and on the other hand, most
neo-Kantians--those most likely to give a sympathetic
hearing to Kant's views on history--focused narrowly
on scientific and epistemological issues to the exclu-
sion of any real concern for Kant's theory of history.[8]
Only the so-called Baden or Heidelberg school of neo-
Kantians, besides Dilthey, attempted to make sense of
history from the standpoint of critical philosophy.
But the Heidelberg thinkers (Rickert and Windelband)
ultimately found themselves entangled in a variety of
value-laden and questionable metaphysical commitments,
whereas Dilthey left only the enigmatic and sometimes
confused fragments of his promised "critique of historical reason."[9]

Thus, a serious interest in Kant's philosophy of
history for its own sake has been apparent only recently. And, as I have already suggested, this area
of Kant's thought is important for our understanding
of his religious philosophy because of the way it illuminates Kant's view of the teleological principle
and the relation between teleology and the phenomenal
world. This is clearly not the place to attempt a
comprehensive examination of every feature of Kant's

philosophy of history. Accordingly, in what follows I shall simply attempt to isolate and evaluate the teleological principle in Kant's thinking on history, with a particular regard for the epistemological status of this principle. In this way, it will be possible to clarify the meaning of the progressive element which seems to be implicated in Kant's theory of historical religion.

It is important to note that Kant's various essays on history appeared after the publication of the first edition of the Critique of Pure Reason. Thus, these essays are all informed by the fully-matured critical viewpoint. During the six-year period between the publication dates of the two editions of the first Critique (1781-1787), Kant published four important works on history. In 1784, his well-known essay, "What Is Enlightenment?,"[10] appeared. This work, of course, reflects Kant's awareness of the cultural importance of the historical era in which he was living. In the same year, Kant's "Idea for a Universal History from a Cosmopolitan Point of View"[11] appeared, and this work perhaps constitutes Kant's most sustained and systematic inquiry into the nature of history and the dynamics of historical progress.

In 1785, Kant wrote three separate reviews of the various parts of Herder's Ideas for a Philosophy of the History of Mankind.[12] These reviews are interesting and helpful for the way they suggest the sorts of speculations about history which Kant is against. In particular, the reviews of Herder suggest the important contrast between Kant's approach to history and the idiom and outlook of romanticism. For example, Kant anticipates the style of a later philosophical school when he wonders aloud

> whether the poetic spirit that en-
> livens [Herder's] expression does
> not sometimes also intrude into
> [his] philosophy; whether synonyms
> are not valued as definitions here
> and there and allegories as truths;
> whether instead of neighborly ex-
> cursions out of the area of the
> philosophic into the sphere of
> poetic language the limits and do-
> mains of both are not completely
> disarranged...13

Whatever philosophy of history is for Kant, it obviously must be governed by the same strict standards as all other forms of philosophical discourse.

Finally, in 1786, Kant wrote his "Conjectural Beginning of Human History."[14] I briefly examined parts of this essay in Chapter III in order to isolate Kant's utilization of the Genesis narrative. This essay occupies an important place in Kant's speculations on history, because it is devoted to the highly complex issue of the emergence in the phenomenal realm of human freedom.

Thus, a series of important essays on history appeared just at that time when Kant was revising the first Critique, composing the second Critique, and publishing the Foundations of the Metaphysics of Morals. Given these various and extremely difficult tasks, it seems unlikely that Kant would have devoted so much time to the problem of history were he not genuinely interested in the issue.

Following a seven-year gap, a new set of essays on history appeared. Again, this would seem to be evidence that history, particularly in the sense of the progress and destiny of the human race, was a continual preoccupation of Kant's. Thus, in 1793 (the year of the publication of Religion), Kant published his essay, "On the Old Saw: That May Be Right in Theory but it Won't Work in Practice."[15] This neglected work contains a lengthy analysis of the relation between morality and political institutions and places a discussion of international law in the context of the concept of "providence." The following year, Kant published "The End of All Things" (though new parts were added to this essay as late as 1798).[16] This work is essentially a philosophical eschatology and carries a strong endorsement of the Christian world view. The year 1795 saw the publication of "Perpetual Peace," one of Kant's key political works, which is also an important statement on the course and purpose of history.[17] Finally, in 1798, Der Streit der Fakultäten appeared, the second part of which is an essay entitled, "An Old Question Raised Again: Is the Human Race Constantly Progressing?"[18] Unless Kant was deeply preoccupied with the issue of historical progress, it would be odd to find him taking up this issue at the advanced age of seventy-four. As Kant himself said in that same year (1798), the state of his health "is that of an old man," who, though free from any serious illness, is

> nevertheless an invalid, a man
> above all who is superannuated for
> the performance of any official or
> public service, who nevertheless
> feels a little bit of strength
> still within him to complete the
> work at hand.[19]

An important part of the "work at hand," apparently, was the philosophy of history.

Thus, what is surprising is not that there should be growing interest in Kant's thoughts on history. What is surprising is that these thoughts have not been integrated into the main tradition of Kant studies all along. For our immediate and limited purposes, it is perhaps best to focus on Kant's clearest and most succinct discussion of the teleological component in the philosophy of history, namely, that which appears in his "Idea for a Universal History." This essay is extremely easy to misunderstand, because it seems to offer an unequivocal account of what the future will necessarily be like. But this, it goes without saying, would be a highly un-Kantian project, insofar as Kant's epistemology hardly allows for such prognostication. Thus, although this essay does contain a theory of progress, and though it does appear to predict future states of affairs, it is not quite right to criticize Kant on the basis that he not only tells us _that_ history has a plot, but even presumes to tell us _what_ that plot is.[20] Such a criticism fails to take seriously the technical connotation of the term "Idea" in the essay's title. But before examining this aspect in detail, it is perhaps best to have before us a summary of the contents of this essay.

The basic purpose of Kant's "Idea for a Universal History" reflects the aim of all his speculations on history. That is, his aim is to give an account of the course and destiny of the life of rational beings who can genuinely "know" only about the world of appearances. There is consequently a tension within the essay between the freedom of rational beings and the deterministic workings of a Newtonian universe. Indeed, Kant's writings on history are perhaps the main locus of his efforts to reconcile the worlds of is and ought. His writings on history, in other words,

140

are a prime example of Kant's attempt to reconcile
his commitment to rationality with his principle of
human limitations.

Not surprisingly, then, the thrust of Kant's "Idea"
is to inquire into the purposiveness of nature in order
to see if this sheds any light on human destiny. This
notion by itself suggests Kant's desire to explore the
potential connection between freedom and nature. Accordingly, Kant proposes as the purpose of his essay
what he calls a "justification of Nature."[21] The need
for such a justification is obvious once we understand
the conflict between the deterministic world of Newtonian physics (supported by the first Critique) and
the moral realm based upon the presupposition of freedom (explored by Kant's ethical and religious writings).
Kant's writings on history seem to imply that to remain
content with Newton's universe as a sheer brute fact
would be to abandon the moral concerns which shape the
practical side of the critical philosophy. But this
very implication betrays a Kantian sensitivity toward
a potential link between the phenomenal and noumenal
realms. The very fact that Kant feels obliged to demonstrate that the natural world is something more than
simply a mechanistic showcase, devoid of purpose or
value beyond its own efficiency, suggests that the
phenomenal realm must, after all, be capable of reflecting the concerns of free and rational beings.
If this is not the case, then the natural world simply
remains unintelligible to our innate moral sensibili-
ties.

Kant's strategy is to overcome this potential moral unintelligibility by applying the teleological idea
to the natural world, a procedure that would later be
formalized in the second part of the Critique of Judgment.[22] This strategy typifies Kant's readiness to
employ teleological themes throughout his philosophy
and clearly characterizes him as a true representative
of the eighteenth century Enlightenment. More importantly, it suggests that Kant turns to teleology when
he wants to bridge the gap between the worlds of nature
and freedom. As Fackenheim has put it, the third
Critique "seeks to join together what the first two
Critiques have put asunder."[23] In the "Idea for a
Universal History," the teleological assumption which
gets Kant's project going is quite simple: "Nature
does nothing in vain."[24] Given this initial premise,
Kant's essay can be read as the search for a hidden
"plan of Nature." "Is it reasonable," he asks, "to

141

assume a purposiveness in all the parts of Nature
and to deny it to the whole?"[25] From this teleological viewpoint, an investigation into Nature's
"plan" should reveal the ultimate end which every
quality, capacity, and disposition in the natural
world is destined to realize. The question implicitly raised by Kant in his "Idea" will be explicitly
formulated in the Critique of Judgment: "We can ask
about an organized being the question: What is it
for?"[26]

· Accordingly, Kant can effect a philosophy of history by applying this teleological principle to reason itself. The substance of Kant's philosophy of
history is his reflection on what Nature must intend
to be the final purpose or fulfillment of this uniquely human quality. It should be recalled at this point
that, in the Foundations, Kant denied that the end or
purpose of rationality could be the production of human happiness, since reason seemed to be so poorly
suited for this task.[27] Thus, assuming that rationality is in fact the distinguishing characteristic
of man, the course of a specifically human history
must have for its end something other than the satisfaction of human happiness. More importantly, there
has to be a "history" if this end--whatever it is--is
to be realized. Just as we discovered in his view of
man's religious progress, Kant's view of the fulfillment of man's rational powers requires a temporal
span if this fulfillment is to be realized. Consequently, by raising the issue of history in terms of
the teleological idea, Kant has, in the words of R.G.
Collingwood, achieved "the remarkable feat of showing
why there should be such a thing as history."[28] His-
tory--as a phenomenal, temporal span--is necessary if
man's rationality is to be fulfilled.

What we have, then, seems to be this. Practical
reason's need to discover meaningfulness in the natural world results in an examination of Nature from
the standpoint of teleology. When applied to human
life, the teleological principle produces considerations which, taken together conceptually, suggest an
ultimate goal implicit in the historical dimension.
The moral justification of Nature thereby yields the
clue to proposing a philosophy of history. Put more
strongly, the moral justification of Nature necessi-
tates proposing a philosophy of history, since historical progress is the only means of yielding the
results required for the moral justification of Nature.

The fact that prior examination of Nature is necessary to understand history is not so surprising as it might at first seem. For, as Kant points out, the "folly," "childish vanity," "malice," and "destructiveness" of mankind suggest that there is no reason to "presuppose any individual purpose among men."[29] The only alternative is to initiate the search for "a <u>natural</u> purpose in this idiotic course of things human."[30] What is crucial to note in all this is, first, the predominantly practical thrust in Kant's procedure and, second, Kant's characteristic unwillingness even to consider the possibility that "things" may not have a purpose after all. Essentially, Kant is simply applying the "what is it for" question to Nature with an implicit view to discovering man's ultimate destiny.[31] This discovery of human destiny is the hidden agenda in the inquiry into the purposiveness of Nature.[32]

Kant develops the "Idea for a Universal History" by working through a series of nine theses. He proceeds from certain essentially a priori assumptions about the relation of man to Nature's plan to relatively concrete predictions about the ultimate course of human history. Kant articulates his teleological principle in the first thesis: "All natural capacities of a creature are destined to evolve completely to their natural end."[33] Then, in theses two through four, Kant faces the difficult problem of accounting for the "natural" appearance of a "free and rational" being; he maintains the seemingly self-contradictory proposition that Nature "wills" the full development of reason in the human race, but that this development is to be effected by man entirely on his own.[34] These theses embody the main task of the essay, which is "to establish the links and distinctions between the end pursued by Nature and the fact that men choose the ends they set before themselves."[35]

Theses five through eight go on to outline the way social antagonism, far from being something wholly destructive, will eventually produce a universal civic society.[36] This is Kant's famous doctrine of the "unsocial sociability of men"[37] and is noteworthy for two reasons. First, it betrays Kant's faith that even evil, in the form of human discord, can be turned to good account. This Enlightenment-like optimism would be tempered somewhat nine years later in <u>Religion</u> but would never disappear altogether from Kant's reflections on history and society.[38] Secondly, the fact that Kant predicts a "universal civic society" to result from this social antagonism suggests that, at the time of the writing of this essay, Kant is thinking of man's moral fulfillment primarily in terms of a political and civic, rather than religious, context. As we clearly saw in Chapter III, Kant's later position in Religion places the historical development of man's moral capacity within the context of the life of the visible church. This shift is obviously quite intentional, insofar as Kant introduces the notion of the church as an ethical commonwealth (and hence a community of autonomous beings) in direct contrast to the notion of the state as a civic body (and hence a community regulated by coercive laws).[39] This suggests that the role of historical religion becomes increasingly important for Kant and that the idea of the visible church can embrace certain moral issues--especially the demand for moral autonomy and the doctrine of radical evil--that remain intractable from a purely political or civic point of view.

The reasons for this shift can be clarified if we consider Kant's earlier speculations on the ethical community in the Foundations of the Metaphysics of Morals. In that work, Kant's "kingdom" or "realm" of ends is the logical product of his principle of autonomy.[40] The principle of autonomy, it is important to note, does not simply mean freedom from external coercion. Rather, it means the free self-legislation of maxims which can be intelligibly understood as universal laws.

> Autonomy of the will is that property
> of it by which it is a law of itself
> independently of any property of ob-
> jects of volition. Hence the principle
> of autonomy is: Never choose except
> in such a way that the maxims of the
> choice are comprehended in the same
> volition as a universal law...[The
> categorical] imperative commands neither
> more nor less than this very autonomy.[41]

Just as Kant's most basic epistemological doctrines betray his empiricistic tendencies, his most basic ethical principles betray his rationalistic tendencies.

The introduction of the principle of autonomy is perhaps the major leap which the Foundations makes over against the first Critique. Whereas in the first Critique freedom is understood primarily as spontaneity, in the Foundations it is articulated in terms of autonomy, and this move to autonomy is necessary if

144

practical reason is to be freed of all phenomenal components.[42] The important point involved in the principle of autonomy is the freedom from any <u>material</u>
cause of the determination of the will. The will still
has a determining ground; it is just that this ground
is the moral law, which only a rational being can grasp
and appreciate. Thus, to borrow a Kantian phrase,
rationality is the condition of the possibility that
there will be such a thing as autonomous beings. Man
is distinct from the rest of the natural world because
he has a self-legislating will. This is why, as
Richard Kroner has argued, the autonomous will, in its
very <u>acting</u> and not in our speculations <u>about</u> its acting, is the core of Kant's philosophy.[43]

This familiar point suggests why it is that a
political context cannot be an entirely satisfactory
basis for the creation of an ethical community. This
insight is further reinforced when we consider that
the kingdom or realm of ends in the <u>Foundations</u> is the
somewhat formalistic precursor of the ethical community
discussed in <u>Religion</u>.[44] The whole point of the realm
of ends is that its members are self-legislating: each
member legislates the laws to himself and is therefore
autonomous, yet is simultaneously subject to those
same laws and thereby treats each other member as an
end in himself.

> Thus there arises a systematic union
> of rational beings through common
> objective laws. This is a realm which
> may be called a realm of ends (certain-
> ly only an ideal), because what these
> laws have in view is just the relation
> of these beings to each other as ends
> and means.[45]

This realm of ends is analogous to the realm of nature--
the self-imposed laws of the former parallel the causal
laws of the latter.[46]

It is interesting to note that, at the time of the
writing of the <u>Foundations</u>, Kant speaks of this realm
of ends as "certainly only an ideal." It may be that
his writings on history, as well as <u>Religion</u>, constitute a gradual effort on Kant's part to consider
whether this "ideal" might not be actually realizable
in one degree or another. This issue, having to do
with the possible phenomenal status of the highest
good, will be taken up directly in the following sec-

tion of this chapter. For now, it is important simply
to note that, according to the basic principle of
autonomy laid down in the Foundations, religious institutions offered Kant certain conceptual possibilities
which political institutions did not. That Kant himself is aware of this is made clear by the comparison
of political and ethical communities at the start of
Book III of Religion. As Kant says with no equivocation,

> it would be a contradiction...for
> the political commonwealth to compel
> its citizens to enter into an ethical
> commonwealth, since the very concept
> of the latter involves freedom from
> coercion.[47]

All of this enhances the status of the historical
side of religion within Kant's view of human destiny.
At the same time, however, Kant's increasing emphasis
on the religious context of man's moral progress never
completely replaces the emphasis on social and political institutions. Five years after the publication of
Religion, in that section of Der Streit der Fakultäten
dealing specifically with historical progress, Kant
again speaks in the concrete terms of political improvement.[48] He is particularly concerned to consider
the correlation between forms of political constitu-
tions and the tendency to engage in warfare: the more
the constitution is "in harmony with the natural rights
of man," says Kant, the less likely is war.[49] Kant
is essentially optimistic about the future in this
essay, which can be read as a kind of up-dating of the
concerns raised in his "Idea for a Universal History."
At the same time Kant expresses his optimism, however,
he retains a characteristic note of caution:

> A doctor who consoled his patients
> from one day to the next with hopes
> of a speedy convalescence, pledging
> to one that his pulse beat better,
> to another an improvement in his
> stool, to a third the same regarding
> his perspiration, etc., received a
> visit from one of his friends. 'How's
> your illness, my friend,' was his
> first question. 'How should it be?
> I'm dying of improvement, pure and
> simple!'[50]

Thus, Kant retains a lively but cautious concern for the political realm even subsequent to his reflections on the "ethical community" in _Religion_. Given his celebrated low opinion of the ecclesiastical institutions of his own time, it is not surprising that Kant's positive outlook on the visible church, once introduced in _Religion_, did not blossom into an ongoing philosophical inquiry into the relation between the church and moral progress. Yet it would have to have been such sociological considerations which kept Kant from pursuing this inquiry, for his philosophy is not only open to such a project, but appears to demand it. This is the sort of point regarding Kant's religious thought that needs to be stressed, over against the sort of stereotype offered by T.M. Greene's introduction to his translation of _Religion_.

There are, then, two strands composing Kant's reflection on the problem of moral progress. One strand is political and dominates Kant's philosophy of history. The other is religious and is embodied by the doctrine of the church in _Religion_. The metaphor of "strands" perhaps suggests the "loose ends" with which Kant leaves us, for he never really unites the political and religious elements in a single synthetic vision. Despland has suggested that the two tendencies at work in Kant's thought simply reflect a distinction between progress in its "ethico-juridical" sense and in its "ethico-religious" sense: the former conceptualizes progress which is social and political; the latter conceptualizes progress which is personal and individualistic.[51] But such an interpretation ignores the fact that there is a crucial social dimension to the so-called "ethico-religious" side of Kant's thinking. This is the whole point of the doctrine of the church and, indeed, is the whole point of the difference between _Religion_ and the _Critique of Practical Reason_. Thus, Kant is not working out two features of a single strategy. Rather, he has produced potentially incompatible strategies to serve a larger philosophical aim.

None of this should obscure the fact that Kant's "Idea for a Universal History," the most clearly teleological of his writings on history, essentially deals with a political context. In this essay the full realization of human potentialities is attainable "only in society, and more specifically in the society with the greatest freedom."[52] This terminology does not in itself exclude religious considerations, but the thrust

of the entire essay is obviously political rather than
religious. Yet the phrase, "with the greatest freedom," suggests the direction Kant's thinking would
have to take if his viewpoint were to yield a genuinely _ethical_ community, by Kantian standards. In any
event, Kant views the "right result" for history--as
determined by the demands of practical reason--to be
intimately related to the nature of political consti-
tutions and the relations among states. Moral freedom
and political freedom condition one another. Consequently, "Nature has as her ultimate purpose" a "universal cosmopolitan condition" which alone can be most
conducive to the full realization of man's rational
nature.[53] Kant even suggests that we can perceive in
the preceding course of history a movement toward this
goal. Although these indications are slight, Kant
maintains that "from the little that has been observed,
we can confidently infer the reality of such a revolution."[54]

The specific contours of Kant's vision of history,
then, are conditioned by what he deems to be the necessary requirements for the realization of man's rational
potentialities. It is not as though there is a predetermined end or goal of history which man must somehow fit into. Rather, the goal of history is simply
the kind of social arrangement which will be most conducive to the growth of freedom and rationality. The
end of history is not so much "inevitable" as it is a
kind of "humanizing process," and this fact betrays
the anthropological anchor of Kant's philosophical
reflections. Furthermore, the stake involved in this
humanizing process is the rational capacity itself and
not individual persons. Of course, as Kant tells us,
it seems "strange that the earlier generations appear
to carry through their toilsome labor only for the
sake of the later."

> However puzzling this may be, it is
> necessary if one assumes that a
> species of animals should have reason,
> and, as a class of rational beings
> each of whom dies while the species
> is immortal, should develop their ca-
> pacities to perfection.[55]

Kant's eighth thesis in his "Idea" succinctly summarizes his main point:

> The history of mankind can be seen,

in the large, as the realization
of Nature's secret plan to bring
forth a perfectly constituted state
as the only condition in which the
capacities of mankind can be fully
developed, and also bring forth
that external relation among states
which is perfectly adequate to this
end.[56]

Far more than in Religion, Kant is establishing his
credentials here as a genuinely "enlightened" thinker.
Human aspirations and potentialities ultimately find
fulfillment, not an abyss. Still, the strength of
this claim as a prediction seems to be qualified
somewhat in the discussion of his ninth thesis. The
ninth thesis itself makes the following point.

A philosophical attempt to work out
a universal history according to a
natural plan directed to achieving
the civic union of the human race
must be regarded as possible and,
indeed, as contributing to this
end of Nature.[57]

But in the subsequent discussion, Kant admits that
his "Idea of a world history...is to some extent based
upon an a priori principle," and he claims that he has
no desire "to displace the work of practicing empirical historians."[58] It would, he notes in an apparent
softening of his position, be "strange" and "apparently
silly" to write a history in accordance with "an Idea
of how the course of the world must be if it is to
lead to certain rational ends."[59] But Kant immediately goes on to endorse such a history.

Nevertheless, if one may assume that
Nature, even in the play of human
freedom, works not without plan or
purpose, this Idea could still be of
use. Even if we are too blind to
see the secret mechanism of its
workings, this Idea may still serve
as a guiding thread for presenting
as a system, at least in broad out-
lines, what would otherwise be a
planless conglomeration of human
actions.[60]

149

Kant is here reaffirming all the major points he
has already made. The assumption that Nature "does
nothing in vain" simply has to stand--we may "assume"
it, because the alternative, from the standpoint of
practical reason, is unthinkable. Given this assumption, we are justified in employing the idea of a
plan of Nature as a "guiding thread" for our study
of history.

By suggesting the utility of this idea as a
"guiding thread," Kant clarifies the sense in which
he intends this "idea" to be understood. The idea
of a plan of Nature--indeed, the "Idea" mentioned
in the title of his essay--is to be understood as
a heuristic device (a "guiding thread"), of the sort
discussed in detail in the Appendix to the Transcendental Dialectic in the Critique of Pure Reason (i.e.,
Idee).[61] That is, Kant is speaking here of an "idea
of pure reason," something which has no cognitive
function but merely a regulative role. Such an idea
does not increase our knowledge; rather, it is to be
a guide to our research, helping us to discover what
we might otherwise miss. Within the context of the
ninth thesis, the specific idea Kant is endorsing as
a useful "guiding thread" is this: the "Idea of how
the course of the world must be if it is to lead to
certain rational ends."[62] The operative phrase here
is "must be"--practical reason places demands on the
way the world "has" to be if it is not sheer brute
fact. The idea employed here heuristically is for
the purpose of explaining how things "must be" if
they are to make sense to our innate moral sensibil-
ities.

It is important to emphasize the regulative function that the teleological principle plays in Kant's
thinking. Indeed, teleology is always understood by
Kant in a purely regulative, as opposed to constitutive, manner.[63] This means that whenever Kant speaks
of the "purpose" or "end" of something, he is not
making a knowledge claim but is proposing an angle of
vision for reflecting intelligently and creatively on
a particular issue. Within the critical philosophy,
the function of any idea of pure reason is to give
"stimulus" and "guidance" to the operation of the
understanding with the aim of providing theoretical
reason with the maximum amount of unity and totality
in its outlook on the world. Whereas sensibility and
understanding have a genuinely cognitive role to play,
it is the "business of reason [simply] to render the

150

unity of all possible acts of the understanding systematic."[65] Thus, an _idea_ of reason is "of service to the understanding as a canon for its extended and consistent employment."[66] An idea of reason, in other words, operates upon the empirical world. In an odd sort of way, ideas are once removed from genuine cognition (by Kantian standards), because no schema of sensibility corresponds to the ideas of reason.[67] Kant's theory of reason, and the associated theory of the ideas of reason, is his means of indulging man's "natural and unavoidable" propensity for thinking metaphysically,[68] but without violating critical standards. From Kant's perspective, the crucial point is that if there exists this natural propensity to think metaphysically (i.e., to think beyond the limits imposed on knowledge by the Aesthetic and the Analytic), then this propensity must serve some useful and necessary purpose. The theory of reason and the ideas it produces is Kant's way of indicating what this useful purpose might be. And the teleological principle embodied in his philosophy of history is a prime instance of one of these ideas of pure reason.

Consequently, clarifying the sense in which Kant utilizes the term "idea" illuminates the meaning of the "idea of a plan of Nature." And, once we have illuminated this, we have a better sense of the epistemological status of Kant's reflections on the future. This applies as much to his doctrine of the visible church and its future as to his philosophy of history. There is no object given in sense experience corresponding to an idea of reason (otherwise the "idea" would be an "empirical concept");[69] and no specific idea is necessary as a condition of the possibility of experience (otherwise, that "idea" would be a "category"). The ideas are "transcendent and overstep the limits of all experience."[70] Their utility lies only in their regulative employment, which directs the understanding towards a certain goal.[71] From Kant's viewpoint, the mistake of traditional metaphysics has been to treat this "goal" as an object of knowledge. To think in these terms, Kant stresses, is to fall into the constitutive employment of a purely regulative device;[72] it is to take a good _logical_ principle and turn it into a bad _metaphysical_ principle.[73] Thus, the ideas of pure reason, being heuristic rather than cognitive devices, should simply be thought of as "pointing the way" for our reflections on nature, history, and religion by means of providing us with ideals of unity and synthesis. An idea is like an "imaginary

point on which actual lines of investigation converge
but which they never reach."[74] The purpose of the
ideas is not to posit real objects, but to "secure
coherence in every possible way" for the understanding
by giving unity and system, under a single principle,
to the "numerous and diverse rules of the understanding."[75]

The regulative-constitutive distinction is not an
arcane theoretical doctrine which Kant invokes in the
first Critique and then leaves behind. To the contrary, it functions in important ways throughout his
thought, and, it is perhaps fair to say, its main purpose is ultimately to serve Kant's practical, not
theoretical, philosophy. Thus, for example, the distinction is mentioned numerous times in Religion (usually in notes) as a means of emphasizing the epistemological safeguards built into Kant's religious thought.

> In general, if we limited our judg-
> ment to regulative principles, which
> content themselves with their own
> possible application to the moral
> life, instead of aiming at constitu-
> tive principles of knowledge of
> supersensible objects, insight into
> which, after all, is forever impos-
> sible to us, human wisdom would be
> better off in a great many ways...[76]

And the regulative-constitutive distinction plays the
same role in Kant's writings on history as in his
religious philosophy. It is intended to offer a way
of reflecting on certain demands of reason without
overstepping our cognitive limitations.

Given this critical standpoint, there should be no
question concerning the force of Kant's reflections on
the future of man's civic and religious life. These
reflections are not so much predictions as they are
"rational hopes." These hopes are generated by the
demands of practical reason (and are thereby rational)
and are articulated through the strategy of the ideas
of pure reason (and are thereby epistemologically
respectable). The demands of practical reason are
paramount: they keep Kant's view of the future from
being the random product of a guessing game precisely
because they demarcate the way things "must be" for
man's moral life to fall into any intelligible relation
to the phenomenal world. What is actually "given" as

152

a priori for Kant is not the future course of human history, but the innate moral sense which Kant everywhere presupposes. Kant is not so much telling us what the plot of history "is" as he is demonstrating what it "must be" if the moral life is to have any purchase on empirical states of affairs. His hopes for the future are simply ways of thinking out the consequences of this "must be." Consequently, Kant is not really deriving what "is" from what "ought to be" but is reflecting on what is <u>necessarily entailed</u> by his ethical theory. After all, it is not so much a matter of "ought to be" anyway, but rather a matter of "must be," as Kant himself makes clear in the discussion of his ninth thesis.

It is clear, then, that the teleological principle, operating as a regulative idea, functions in the manner of a presupposition for Kant. J.D. McFarland has helpfully illuminated the structure of this presuppositional status.[77] Kant's approach, suggests McFarland, is not necessarily based on the assumption that a certain presupposition (e.g., the purposiveness of Nature) is true. Rather, it might simply be based upon the assumption of the <u>non-rejection</u> of that presupposition, which is quite a different thing. It is not a matter of assuming P to be the case before reflecting on A; it is a matter of refusing to deny P prior to reflecting on A, because to do so would make reflection on A futile and senseless.

> For example, if it were a presupposition of making an automobile trip of 100 miles that the motor would hold up for that distance, it would be futile and senseless to undertake the trip believing the statement, 'The motor will hold up for 100 miles,' to be false. But this is <u>not</u> to say that before making the trip we must know, or even believe, the statement to be true. We can undertake such a trip without making any assumptions about the trustworthiness of the motor.[78]

McFarland's inquiry has to do with the purposiveness of Nature which must not be rejected if systematic scientific inquiry is to be possible. But his interpretation would seem to hold for the purposiveness relevant to Kant's view of history as well, since in

both cases the notion of purposiveness is operating
as a regulative idea. And, if this is genuinely the
way Kant means for us to take his doctrine, then the
epistemological status of his view of the future seems
compatible with the standards of the first Critique.
Kant is simply proposing what practical reason would
require to be the case if we refuse to deny the idea
of purposiveness in Nature. He is not adopting the
concept of purposiveness as a fact. Rather, he is
proposing it as an idea of reason, with the assumption
that this idea helps to systematize and explain what
might otherwise remain unintelligible. To deny the
notion of purposiveness at the outset would bring an
abrupt end to our attempts to reflect on history.

All of these considerations suggest that the real
threat to Kant's view of history is not that his predictions will be proven to be wrong or illegitimate.
Rather, the real threat is that the world may turn
out to be irrational or--what amounts to the same
thing--that his ethical presuppositions might be shown
to be ill-founded (something which Hegel tried to
demonstrate). Putting the point in this way suggests
an illuminating analogy: Kant's future civic and cosmopolitan realm, as well as his envisioned ethical
community (realized through the life of the visible
church), are to our morally-based sense of "must be"
what God, freedom, and immortality are to the full
exercise of practical reason in the second Critique.
In other words, there exists a family resemblance
(epistemologically considered) between Kant's hopes
for the future and his postulates of practical reason.
In each case, rationalistic ethical presuppositions
are determining the boundaries of Kant's speculative
freedom of movement. Kant's hopes for the future, as
well as his postulates, are necessitated by these
limited boundaries.

The relevance of this to the progressive strand
evident in Kant's Religion is assured if we assume
that Kant did not significantly alter his understanding
of teleology between 1784 and 1793. Interceding between these two dates, of course, is the Critique of
Judgment. For our purposes, the significance of this
work is that it reflects Kant's growing preoccupation
with the teleological theme, it emphasizes the epistemological respectability and even necessity of teleological principles, and it denotes a shift in Kant's
emphasis from a purely physical and natural teleology
to what he calls a moral teleology.[79] This last

characteristic firmly establishes the link between
religion and the teleological principle in Kant's
philosophy.[80] The theory of the church in Religion is
simply the refinement of this link, considered from
the point of view of man's worldly and sensuous life.
Kant's understanding of the church, in other words,
is an example of his reflection on the relation between teleology and religion from the standpoint of
the principle of human limitations.

Thus, if the themes of purpose, goal, and end
operate in Religion in the same way as in Kant's "Idea
for a Universal History," then our examination of the
latter offers important clues for understanding the
progressive element in Kant's theory of historical
religion. The one significant alteration, as I have
already suggested, is Kant's transition from the civic
to the (institutionally) religious as the locus of
his reflection on the future. Indeed, it is not too
much to suggest that the theory of the church effectively displaces Kant's philosophy of history. This
helps to account for Weyand's suggestion that, for
Kant, secular world history becomes identified with a
rationally constituted Heilsgeschichte: the telos of
profane history is reconciled with the providence of
God.[81] Though this might be putting the case a bit
strongly, it underlines the seemingly inescapable fact
that the historical mode of man's religious life played
an increasingly important role in Kant's thinking.

In any event, Kant is clearly drawing on the notion
of purposiveness in order to give unity to a body of
explorations and to offer a vision of moral progress.
This fact remains the same whether the locus of speculation is the civic or religious realm. The object of
hope itself--which, in the case of Religion, is the
ethical community or commonwealth--is at the same time
an ideal for human aspiration, insofar as it encourages
the sort of moral attitudes which would hasten the day
of its actual realization. Furthermore, this whole
scheme is fashioned by Kant in an epistemologically
respectable way, assuming we take seriously his understanding of the teleological principle as an idea of
pure reason. The result is a theory of moral progress
worked out in terms of what James Collins has called
the "religious history of humanity."

> As distinct from various church
> histories, the religious history
> of humanity is the story of the

developing teleological relations
between the visible church and the
invisible church or family of God.
Thus the perspective of transition
taken by the philosophy of religion
has a historical connotation, insofar as it studies the movement from
ecclesial to religious history. This
perspective constitutes the passage
from Hume's natural history of religion to Kant's moral history of
religion.[82]

It ceases to seem like hyperbole, then, to speak
of teleology as the "mainspring of Kant's thought all
along," and to suggest that "it is only in the consideration of man's ultimate end that Kant feels it
necessary openly to declare his position."[83] Kant's
increasing emphasis on the teleological idea reflects
the fact that this principle serves as the natural
solution to various problems growing out of the critical philosophy. For example, as Kant's "Idea for a
Universal History" clearly shows, teleology extricates
Kant from certain dilemmas posed by Newton's mechanistic world view, a world view which--taken at face
value--is morally unintelligible. And, it goes without saying, it is a short step from the "hidden plan
of Nature" in Kant's "Idea" to a full-fledged Kantian
theodicy;[84] the discovery of natural purposiveness
introduces a means of talking about divine providence.
Thus, teleology not only solves certain theoretical
problems for Kant, it is a natural transition point
between theoretical and practical concerns within
Kant's philosophy as a whole.

To pursue this line of thought, then, helps to
account for certain themes drawn from Kant's theory
of historical religion, particularly his view of the
church. Furthermore, all of this reinforces an important claim made in the previous chapter: Kant's
understanding of the moral and religious destiny of
man requires a temporal sequence for its fulfillment.
Kant's increasing concern for teleology reflects a
highly effective strategy of employing an idea of
reason as a purely regulative device in order to cope
with certain demands of practical reason. The author
of the critical philosophy, in other words, was creating a means of extricating himself from certain serious
dilemmas into which that very same philosophy had put
him. But none of this serves to explain exactly how

156

it is that a temporal, historical sequence can be influenced by the noumenal realm of religion and morality. The teleological idea explains why the temporal span is needed by Kant, it suggests the epistemological status of the objects of rational hope, and it reinforces the suspicion that Kant is trying to bring the worlds of "is" and "ought" together. But it does not explain how the worlds of "is" and "ought," nature and freedom, history and religion, are to find common ground within the contours of the critical philosophy; nor does it explain how rational yet sensuous beings could ever know that such a synthesis was occurring. Put otherwise, many of the same problems which the theory of the church in Religion poses for us are posed by Kant's speculations in his "Idea for a Universal History." The latter may shed light on the teleological theme implicit in the former; but it does not resolve the question of the interaction of morality and the phenomenal realm. For that problem, it is necessary to turn to the relation between history and the highest good in Kant's philosophy.

The Phenomenal Dimensions of the Highest Good

The preceding investigation of the teleological element in Kant's thought has suggested that Kant is ultimately seeking some kind of rapprochement between the natural world and man's moral and religious life. The need for this rapprochement arises out of Kant's inquiry into the "purposiveness" of Nature, since such an inquiry yields a vision of the fulfillment of human potentialities within the context of man's social and historical existence. As I mentioned in the previous section, the fact that Kant feels compelled to raise the question of the purposiveness of Nature at all suggests a desire on his part to demonstrate the way the natural or phenomenal realm might exhibit moral ends. And, as I have been claiming all along, Kant's theory of historical religion increasingly becomes the instrument by which he effects this demonstration. Just as the symbols of an historical faith mediate supersensuous moral ideas to a sensuous humanity, so also does the career of historical religion itself serve as the mediation point between man's phenomenal, worldly existence and his existence as a free and rational being.

The problem with this Kantian vision is the appar-

157

ent absence in the critical philosophy of a conceptual
means suited to bridging the gap between man's phenomenal and noumenal aspects. The theme of teleology, at
first glance, appears to offer a possible solution,
but closer examination of the teleological principle
suggests that, far from solving the problem at stake,
it actually sharpens and magnifies it. If, as I have
suggested, the teleological component in Kant's view
of the life of the visible church is in fact a regulative idea--in the way teleology is a regulative idea
in Kant's "Idea for a Universal History"--then teleology does not bridge the gap between nature and freedom
but simply clarifies the demand that the gap be bridged.
The whole point of an idea of reason as regulative is
to give us a way of looking at an issue rather than a
means of solving a problem. Furthermore, the teleological theme running through all of Kant's thinking reinforces the notion that his theory of man's moral and
religious fulfillment is indeed reliant on a temporal
span. His whole approach to history, as the earlier
quotation from Collingwood indicated, has the remarkable quality of demonstrating why such a thing as
"history" is necessary at all. But this is precisely
the problem: in what way can the required temporal span
be linked to man's moral and religious aspect, which is
noumenal and therefore timeless? Even assuming that
the temporal span is genuinely necessary, how does it
gain any purchase on our existence as moral beings?
And if there were such a thing as a phenomenal-noumenal
connection, how could we--as phenomenal beings--know
it? The answers to questions like these, it would
seem, should help determine the ultimate importance in
Kant's philosophy of his theory of historical religion.

Yirmiahu Yovel, of Hebrew University, has spent
much of the past decade clarifying these problems and
proposing what he takes to be Kant's solution.[85] In
his view, the key is to understand Kant's theory of
the highest good as the regulative idea of history.
Yovel takes this insight to be the clue to the true
relationship between Kant's phenomenal and noumenal
realms. His interpretation of Kant relies on a distinction between different forms of Kant's theory of the
highest good: it can be personal, individualistic, and
otherworldly (up through the second Critique); or it can
be communal, historical, and this-worldly (the third
Critique and Religion).[86] For Yovel, Kant's notion of
the kingdom of God on earth, articulated in Religion in
his theory of the church, is the ultimate expression of
the highest good and unmistakably suggests that Kant

158

aimed for a worldly realization of this concept.

> In [Kant's] later writings, the HG
> [i.e., highest good] becomes the
> 'final end of creation' itself, i.e.,
> the consummate state of this world.
> Its realization is conceived as 'the
> kingdom of God on Earth,' and des-
> pite its infinite remoteness, it
> involves a concrete synthesis, to be
> realized in time, between the moral
> will and empirical reality. The HG
> and the given world no longer signify
> two different worlds, but two states,
> present and utopian, of the self-same
> world. In other words, the HG becomes
> a historical ideal.[87]

Yovel's proposed solution amounts to a depiction
of the worldly or phenomenal dimensions of a Kantian
doctrine which, as it is commonly known, has only an
otherworldly and transcendent meaning. That is, the
most direct and specific Kantian approach to the notion
of the highest good is the discussion of it in the
second Critique.[88] In the context of the Dialectic of
that work, the highest good--signifying the unity of
virtue and happiness in equal proportion--clearly assumes the status of a necessary premise which Kant
needs to include if his arguments for the immortality
of the soul and the existence of God (both, to be sure,
established as postulates and not by way of proofs) are
to succeed. In other words, the status of the highest
good in its most familiar setting is highly abstract,
unmistakably transcendent, and crucial as a link in a
piece of reasoning and not as a description of any empirical state of affairs. Its relation to its worldly
referents (i.e., the virtue and happiness of sensuous
beings) is ideal rather than real. In contrast, by
proposing that there is a version of the highest good
doctrine which intends that the "natural orders of the
world exhibit a moral pattern or meet...a moral demand,"[89] Yovel is clearly asking us to shift our sights
to emphases other than those found in the Critique of
Practical Reason. And there are hints of such a shift
in the second Critique itself, as when Kant speaks of
"the exact harmony of the realm of nature with the
realm of morals as the condition of the possibility of
the highest good."[90]

There are two preliminary issues to be sorted out

159

at this point. It is one thing to propose that Kant's
theory of the highest good comes in different versions;
it is quite another thing to propose that one of these
versions amounts to the phenomenal exhibition or manifestation of moral ends. It is as though something
like the theory of schematism has been transposed to
the level of the highest good, providing for the sensible rendering of what is intrinsically supersensuous.
Such a procedure would, it seems clear, solve or at
least modify the problem posed by the interaction of
moral ends with an historical or temporal span. But
how such a process is to work, and whether this is what
Kant really means by the highest good, appear to be
serious difficulties.

Yet regarding Yovel's initial premise--the claim
that Kant's theory of the highest good assumes different versions--there is a reasonable amount of agreement. John Silber, for instance, has convincingly
probed the ambiguity inherent in Kant's doctrine. This
ambiguity is largely a product of the fact that the
second Critique, in which the most familiar treatment
of the highest good doctrine appears, hardly constitutes the complete word on Kant's ethical theory.

> The second Critique does not occupy
> the position of unique importance
> for the understanding of Kant's ethics
> that the first Critique has for the
> understanding of Kant's metaphysics.
> The best possible commentary on the
> Critique of Practical Reason...could
> not possibly provide a definitive
> account of Kant's ethics either in
> whole or in part.[91]

The thrust of the present inquiry suggests that one
could justifiably add that the second Critique does
not tell the full story regarding Kant's religious
views either. In any case, Silber's perspective is a
corrective to the perennial problem of taking one of
Kant's writings in isolation from the rest and con-
structing an exhaustive interpretation on the basis of
that work alone. But at the same time that this problem is being solved, new ones are created, given the
potential discrepancies involved in a variety of separate discussions of the same issue. The threat of
such discrepancies is increased by the frequent obscurity of Kant's writing style. Indeed, this "discrepancy" problem is guaranteed, given the fact that

160

the one concept that receives its
greatest elaboration in the second
Critique--the concept of the good,
including the highest good--is [also]
considered at great length in the
Metaphysics of Morals, in the Religion, in the Anthropology, and in
several essays.[92]

Consequently, regardless of the validity of his
eventual claims, Yovel's starting point seems to be
valid.

[The] Kantian concept of the Highest
Good is ambiguous; its meaning varies
not only from one work to the next,
but occasionally even in the same
chapter. In fact, there is no single
text in which Kant discusses it ex-
haustively, and all his treatments
of the notion must be taken as frag-
mentary and as calling for reciprocal
supplementation and illumination.[93]

The key to Yovel's interpretation is his suggestion
that, in order to understand the way Kant's theory of
the highest good ultimately brings history and morality
together, it is important to discriminate between two
stages in Kant's practical philosophy. There is, he
suggests, both a "formal" and a "material" aspect to
Kant's ethical and religious thought.[94] The formal
stage is embodied in the Foundations of the Metaphysics of Morals and in the Analytic of the Critique of
Practical Reason: it is concerned with examining the
structure of the good will and with establishing an
absolutely categorical imperative. This area of Kant's
practical philosophy, of course, is the most familiar
and has traditionally attracted the most attention
among students of Kant.

But there is, says Yovel, a second or material
stage in Kant's practical philosophy. This stage
serves the purpose of fulfilling the need, of which
Kant speaks in Religion, "to conceive of some sort of
final end for all our actions and abstentions, taken
as a whole."[95] This material stage, instead of determining the absolute principle of the moral will, goes
on to define the total object of such a will.

Its axis is the formulation of a new

> imperative with a definite content
> ('act to promote the Highest Good
> in the World')--to Kant a more com-
> plete and comprehensive imperative
> than the basic categorical one.
> The latter instructs how one should
> act, while the former perpetuates
> the 'how,' and also ascertains what
> should, in the final analysis, be
> [realized].[96]

In other words, this "material" stage of Kant's moral
thought is concerned with the worldly realization and
totalization of the acts of a morally good will, rather
than with the mere establishment of the definition of
a moral will. The theory of the categorical impera-
tive--established, it should be recalled, in a foundations of the metaphysics of morals--is logically prior
to the worldly, material stage. But the material
stage is the necessary fulfillment of the demands of
the imperative, given Kant's notion of the double "need
of pure reason":[97] there is the logical need, requiring
that the sphere of human action be unified and totalized, in accordance with the theory of reason laid out
in the Dialectic of the first Critique; and there is
the psychological or subjective need, requiring that
men justifiably possess the confidence that their acts
relate purposefully to certain ultimate ends.[98]

This logical and psychological need of reason is
the ultimate expression of Kant's rationalistic demand
(and confidence) that life is ultimately meaningful.
There is no Angst on Kant's part when the issue of the
need of reason arises, for the alternative--the possibility that the universe is absurdly out of whack--is
outside of the peripheries of Kant's philosophical
vision. In his interpretation of the highest good
doctrine, Yovel relies heavily on the Kantian notion
that reason has certain needs that require satisfaction. Specifically, the material side of the practical
philosophy is, from Yovel's perspective, what satisfies
certain needs arising out of the formal side.[99]

Yovel suggests that the second or material stage
of Kant's practical philosophy is hinted at in the
Dialectic of the second Critique and articulated explicitly in the last part of the Critique of Judgment
and in Religion.[100] "The complete practical system of
Kant thus tries to determine not only the absolute form
of moral action but also its supreme content..."[101]

Somewhat like Despland, Yovel bases his approach to Kant on the assumption that Kant is continually opening up new problems, reformulating old doctrines, and generally trying to bring the competing strands in his thought together into some kind of unity. The main locus for these various efforts, thinks Yovel, is Kant's speculation on the relation between history and the highest good, since--particularly considering the various needs of reason--this topic offers the most promising possibility that the moral and natural orders might be reconciled.

On the basis of his formal-material distinction, Yovel claims that Kant's notion of the highest good assumes a variety of meanings.[102] The familiar form of the highest good, understood as the proper proportioning of virtue and happiness, remains at the formal level only. Just as the material stage of the practical philosophy logically succeeds and includes the formal stage, so does the material form of the highest good succeed and embrace the formal form. This material form of the highest good, claims Yovel, is the concept of the highest good as the regulative idea of history, since only an historical span provides for the ultimate realization and totalization of moral action.[103] By the "regulative idea of history," Yovel essentially means the representation of an ideally ethical world which, through both divine guarantee and man's concerted moral endeavor, is realizable in fact as well as in principle. It is regulative in the sense that it is the "end" or "goal" which a rational humanity is meant to seek, if moral endeavor is to be totalized, fulfilled, and therefore be ultimately meaningful. Only through this totalization process will the "need of reason"--both logical and psychological-- be met.

An example of Yovel's notion of the material form of Kant's theory of the highest good appears in the preface to the first edition of Religion. Kant's discussion there of certain "ends" to which moral conduct leads seems at first glance to inject an uncharacteristic note of heteronomy into his moral theory.[104] But, in fact, Kant is not specifying certain ends which "precede the determining of the will" but is considering the "representation" of a rational end which is the sum of "inevitable consequences of maxims adopted as conformable to that end."[105] Put otherwise, Kant is suggesting a picture of what the world would ultimately look like were men to behave in a genuinely

163

moral fashion. Again, this "picture" is not intended by Kant to serve as the basis of moral decisions; rather, it is necessarily entailed by rationally thinking through the consequences of human action in the world. To stop short of reflecting on this potential end is to cut off the exercise of reason prior to its complete satisfaction. Thus, Kant is not jeopardizing the autonomous aspect of his moral theory but is indulging a "need" of reason at the practical level.

It is this sort of procedure, thinks Yovel, which leads Kant to reflect on the worldly consequences and manifestations of moral action. As Kant puts it, an end does not determine morality but it does arise out of morality.

> [For] how the question, What is to
> result from this right conduct of
> ours? is to be answered, and towards
> what, as an end--even granted it may
> not be wholly subject to our con-
> trol--we might direct our actions
> and abstentions so as at least to be
> in harmony with that end: these can-
> not possibly be matters of indiffer-
> ence to reason.106

The "end" which Kant speaks of here is what he calls the highest good. It is the combination of

> the formal condition of all such ends
> as we ought to have (duty)...with
> whatever is conditioned, and in har-
> mony with duty, in all the ends which
> we do have (happiness proportioned to
> obedience to duty).107

As in the Critique of Practical Reason, Kant stipulates that such an idea requires the postulation of a "higher, moral, most-holy, and omnipotent Being which alone can unite the two elements of the highest good."108

> Yet (viewed practically) this idea
> is not an empty one, for it does meet
> our natural need to conceive of some
> sort of final end for all our actions
> and abstentions, taken as a whole, an
> end which can be justified by reason
> and the absence of which would be a
> hindrance to moral decision.109

Kant is obviously walking a tightrope here. The notion of an end of human praxis, embodied in a theory of the highest good, must never be the basis of morality, since that would undermine the mandates of the categorical imperative. But that very same end fulfills a need of human reason, and this fulfillment is necessary if men are to act in the expectation that their actions will make a lasting difference in the world. Whether this hope--however carefully defined by Kant--taints his moral theory with a heteronomous element is a sensitive problem, one which (in one form or another) affects all of his speculations on the highest good. At the same time Kant is reaching for a synthesis of nature and freedom, he is perhaps over-reaching the limits of the critical philosophy.

For our purposes, the importance of all this is the way Kant's reflections on the highest good in Religion suggest a strategy for bringing human history and human freedom together in some kind of unity. This vision of unity would solve the problem posed by the interaction of time and religion in Kant's theory of an historical faith. Yovel's contention is that it is this sort of unifying strategy which constitutes the fullest sense of Kant's theory of the highest good. And Kant himself offers substantial backing for such a claim.

> [It] cannot be a matter of unconcern to morality as to whether or not it forms for itself the concept of a final end of all things (harmony with which, while not multiplying men's duties, yet provides them with a special point of focus for the unification of all ends); for only thereby can objective, practical reality be given to the union of the purposiveness arising from freedom with the purposiveness of nature, a union with which we cannot possibly dispense.[110]

A more explicit Kantian demand for some kind of "splice" between nature and morality would be difficult to find.

Quite obviously, Yovel is relying heavily on Kant's concept of the "need of reason" in his proposed interpretation. It is this "need" which underlies the potential Kantian synthesis of morality and empirical reality. In particular, the psychological aspect of

165

the need is crucial, since it results in the claim
that human action can affect and re-shape the phenomenal world. If man has no confidence that his actions
will produce a fruitful effect, then his sense of
moral duty will be undermined.[111] But if he believes
that there is something inherent in the structure of
reality itself which guarantees a correspondence between moral endeavor and empirical reality, then his
sense of duty will be enlivened, not by a hope for
personal reward, but by a hope for the rational fulfillment of the empirical order. As Yovel puts it,
Kant maintains that man

> is by nature incapable of intending
> to do what one may call Sisyphan
> deeds, but demands that his actions
> integrate in a productive and mean-
> ingful continuity--or totalization--
> within the concrete world. His
> action must, therefore, be accom-
> panied first by a representation of
> a final or total end, and secondly
> by the assurance that it can be
> realized.[112]

The ground of this assurance, of course, is God.[113]
Just as God, in the second Critique, arises as the
guarantor of the correspondence of virtue and happiness, so he also arises as the guarantor of the possibility that the duality of nature and freedom, history
and morality, can be bridged by man. There is in God
a fundamental unity of opposites underlying the dual-
ities--cognitive, moral, and religious--characteristic
of Kant's description of the human situation.[114] The
fact that this primordial unity exists is crucial,
since it establishes the sheer ontological possibility
that moral action can significantly affect the phenomenal realm. The establishment of this possibility is
what Yovel takes to be the key metaphysical role played
by God in Kant's philosophy. But although God is the
source of this possibility, man must be the agent of
its realization.

> What God guarantees is not the real-
> ization of the Highest Good but only
> its ontological possibility, and this
> guarantee, moreover, is furnished not
> by special action on God's part but
> by his very existence. Since there
> is a God, namely, since there is one

166

> 'supersensible substratum' of the
> whole of creation, the synthesis
> of the Highest Good is possible.
> But the realization of this possi-
> bility, its translation from po-
> tentiality into actuality, is the
> duty of Man and not the action of
> God. At most, God helps us to
> help ourselves.[115]

God, then, guarantees the sheer possibility that
the need of reason can be fulfilled. Yet what is
worrisome in this whole procedure is the psychological
aspect of this need of reason. It is one thing to
postulate a third term because of the _logical_ relationship between two other terms; it is quite another
thing to postulate a third term because of a _psycho-
logical need_ generated by two other terms. As an
earlier critic of Kant pointed out, "the existence of
a need does not imply the existence of the object which
satisfies it."[116] Yovel claims that the existence of
God is inferred by Kant on the basis of a logical
rather than psychological need of reason.[117] But it
would seem that this inference is preceded by the dual
demand that (1) virtue and happiness be justly propor-
tioned and (2) the empirical order give some evidence
of moral action. And these steps, it seems hard to
deny, are manifestly _psychological_ in their power to
convince. In fact, as Yovel himself is quick to point
out, "the Kantian doctrine of the deity is subservient to a strictly _human_ interest."

> The ultimate object of the system
> is not God but the _Highest Good_,
> grasped as the ideal of historical
> realization, while 'the existence
> of God' is only an auxiliary thesis
> that derives its meaning and its
> justification from the double role
> that it plays, both as enabling the
> maintenance of the doctrine of the
> Highest Good and as encouraging
> those who act upon it. To put it
> more figuratively, God has been ex-
> plicitly transformed into the assis-
> tant of Man.[118]

To emphasize in this way the human element is, it would
seem, to threaten Kant's whole procedure by underscor-
ing the psychological element.

Thus, it is time to raise some questions about Kant's actual ability to unify history and morality, nature and freedom. Yovel's interpretation does not so much succeed in outlining a Kantian solution to the problem at stake as it helps to emphasize the enormity of the difficulty. It is important to re-state the specific problem at this point, a problem which is generated by two opposing Kantian principles:

> 1) man's moral and religious life is lived at the level of the noumenal realm, which is timeless;

> 2) yet moral and religious "progress" is a real possibility, particularly in the context of the visible church as an ethical community; such progress is gradualistic and therefore reliant on a temporal span (i.e., history).

The first principle is built into the whole fabric of the critical philosophy; it is the guarantee that religion and morality will not be threatened by the demands of Newtonian science. And the second principle comes unmistakably into focus whenever Kant abandons the formal and individualistic emphases of works like the Foundations and the second Critique and treats the social and communal aspects of man's life, as in Religion and the writings on history. Thus, each principle has its place--it is just that they appear to be in conflict with one another.

Now Yovel, as I have indicated, suggests that the theory of the highest good, understood in its "material" aspect, is the key to the Kantian solution to this impasse. This is because this theory provides for:

> 1) the primoridal possibility (in God) that nature and freedom can be unified;

> 2) the exhibition of moral endeavor in the phenomenal realm as the fulfillment of a particular "need" of reason; and

> 3) the representation of this final "end" of moral action as the regulative idea

168

> of history (in the sense that it
> is the rational "goal" to which
> rational beings aspire, though
> without allowing it to become the
> ground of moral volition).

This scheme of moral teleology, claims Yovel, constitutes the universalized sense of the highest good.[119]
This not only means that it includes the results of
universal (rather than individual) moral endeavor; it
also means that it includes the natural or phenomenal
realm in Kant's ultimate speculations on the end result
of moral action. For Yovel, this incorporation of the
natural realm in final speculations regarding man's
moral capacities simply reflects reason's characteristic drive for totality in the course of its reflections. As a result, the highest good should not be
understood as a separate and transcendent world, but
as "the consummate state of this world," embodying the
"kingdom of God on earth," which, to repeat the key
quotation,

> despite its infinite remoteness,
> [involves] a concrete synthesis, to
> be realized in time, between the
> moral will and empirical reality.[120]

And this concrete and historical synthesis of the moral
will and empirical reality is provided for by Kant's
theory of the church, in tandem with genuinely enlightened social and political institutions.[121]

Yovel's interpretation of Kant is not only ambitious but extremely tempting, since it points to the
resolution of some of the key problems uncovered in
the present inquiry. Above all, of course, Yovel's
approach suggests a Kantian method of overcoming the
apparent gap between religion and temporality. If,
indeed, the theory of the highest good is ultimately
constituted by a regulative idea of history, then it
would seem that the temporal span permeating Religion
coalesces intelligibly with the noumenal basis of religion and morality. Unfortunately, however, there
appears to be a variety of weak links in Yovel's interpretation, exhaustive as it is. It is worth specifying
what these weaknesses are, since the problems involved
lie at the heart of what I have been referring to as
the ultimate "impasse" in Kant's thinking on the religion and history issue.

In the first section of this chapter, I emphasized that Kant maintains a consistent distinction between the regulative and the constitutive uses of an idea of reason--in this case, the teleological idea involving the "end" or "plan" of nature. To employ a regulative idea in a constitutive fashion is to turn a good logical principle into a bad metaphysical principle. Now this basic epistemological ground rule seems in no way changed when we shift from Kant's view of nature and history to his view of the highest good. Yovel speaks of a representation of the "end" of concerted moral action as the universalized form of the highest good as though the compelling force of such a representation suffices to insure its ultimate reality. Yet such a claim is inconsistent with Yovel's own characterization of this representation as the "regulative idea of history."[122] For the whole point of a <u>regulative</u> idea--to put it crudely--is that we never <u>get</u> there. A certain representation of the end of moral action, which involves the empirical expression of moral endeavor, is actually analogous to the regulative influence which the concept of infinity exerts on certain mathematical inquiries: not only do we never <u>get</u> there, we possess no criteria for recognizing the goal even were we to reach it. The influence exerted by the concept of the highest good, like that exerted by the concept of infinity, helps to situate a type of inquiry and to fashion a particular perspective. It does not hold out the promise of actually reaching a specifically defined goal.

A good way of posing the issue is to ask what else must be the case if Kant's material version of the highest good yields a successful synthesis of morality and nature. The synthesis itself would be reliant on the completion of a moral teleology. Yet if we can draw such an inference from a teleological principle, then what is to keep us (or Kant) from embracing the teleological proof for the existence of God? In fairness to Yovel, it must be pointed out that he concludes one of his articles with a discussion of this issue, and he recognizes the discrepancy in Kant's uses of teleology.[123] But he does not seem to realize that, by pointing out this discrepancy, he is undercutting his own argument concerning the Kantian synthesis of morality and nature in the theory of the highest good. In the first <u>Critique</u>, of course, Kant has criticized the teleological argument as an illegitimate passage from a "natural necessity" of reason (the idea of design and purpose) to an existential claim.[124] Yet--

170

again as Yovel points out--if Kant refutes the validity of this procedure, how could he possibly endorse the passage from man's psychological need to believe in the worldly fulfillment of moral behavior to a claim about a world in which morality and the empirical order are actually united? Amazingly enough, Yovel, after locating this difficulty, goes on to claim that Kant's view amounts to

> the assertion that the given world is the Highest Good in potentia, and that human praxis can make it so actually. This is a teleological principle which enriches the concept of freedom. For it affirms that in the world itself...there is 'something' which makes it susceptible of moral transformation in response to the free and intentional action of man, and that we are therefore able to act fruitfully upon it.[125]

In the end, then, Yovel seems overwhelmed by the "primacy of the practical," even at the cost of violating a key theoretical mandate which he himself has recognized. The specific violation involves the exploitation of a regulative idea concerning the end of moral endeavor for the purpose of positing an historical goal which will be actually realized. Unless the goal is realized, Yovel's claims about the Kantian synthesis of morality and the empirical order will be falsified; but if the goal is in fact realized, then the purely regulative status of the teleological idea has been corrupted. Yovel is willing to pay the price of the theoretical violation in order to guarantee the practical mandate. It may well be that he is simply following Kant himself--especially the Kant of Religion--in this endeavor.

My first criticism, then, is that, in order to effect his interpretation of Kant and posit a Kantian synthesis of morality and nature, Yovel undermines the regulative status of Kant's ideas of pure reason. This criticism is not as damning as it might be, because it is perhaps Kant's problem more than it is that of a highly sympathetic interpreter of Kant. But my second criticism goes to the heart of a telling gap in Yovel's analysis. Even if the notion of an historical version of the highest good could be defended, what could possibly serve as the conceptual mechanism by which--to

borrow Yovel's formulation--"a new 'nature' which embodies a moral and human meaning" is being created?[126]
One can understand the moral demand or requirement
that man "should make the world good";[127] but it is
impossible to conceive of how man could ever determine
if he is being successful, given the gap between the
phenomenal and noumenal spheres. Something analogous
to the transcendental schema is obviously needed here.
What this "something" is, Yovel never tells us.

The problem facing Yovel at this highly conceptual
level is exemplified by the extravagance of one of his
more interesting claims. Kant's theory of the highest
good, he has told us, has, in its universalized and
material sense, a far wider meaning than it has in the
individualistic and formal sense endorsed in the second
Critique.

> The Highest Good remains a 'synthesis'
> of moral and empirical elements, but
> not of virtue and happiness alone, but
> of 'freedom' and 'nature' at large;
> and to realize it now means to imprint
> the demands of the moral idea upon the
> whole range (the 'totality') of our
> empirical environment, transforming
> the patterns of our psychological dis-
> positions, our social and political
> institutions, as well as the surround-
> ing physical and ecological systems--
> in so far as they relate to the sphere
> of human needs and moral interests.[128]

The thrust of my present criticism has to do with the
mechanisms by which this "imprinting" process can
either occur or be known, by Kantian standards. God
may provide the sheer possibility for such a process,
but the actual "imprinting" is, presumably, man's job
alone. And even assuming that man could get this job
done, there would remain the epistemological problem
of how he could possibly know that this "imprinting"
process was occurring.

From my vantage point, then, to speak of a Kantian
strategy for "transforming" empirical patterns--be
they psychological, socio-political, or ecological--is
to pose the problem, not to solve it. Yovel speaks
somewhat vaguely of human "culture" as the arena in
which this imprinting or synthesizing process will
occur, but this seems only to be a new way of stating

172

the same problem.[129] Thus, even if we can speak of an
immanent, historical goal--which preserves the ultimate unity of morality and nature at the cost of
threatening the regulative status of moral teleology--
it is still unclear how this goal can be reconciled
with the stereoscopic perspective imposed by Kant's
phenomenal-noumenal dichotomy. It is one thing to
propose what Kant's vision is; it is quite another
thing to explain how this vision could possibly be actualized.

A way to clarify this criticism is to indicate the
difficulties involved in the relationship between the
moral law and the highest good. How does the highest
good, as a moral ideal, stand in relation to the categorical imperative, which must be the sole determining
ground of moral volition? For Yovel, the highest good,
standing as the synthesis of morality and nature, is
important partly for the way it shapes and influences
the behavior of rational beings. We are obligated to
transform this world so that it will more closely approximate the world embodied by a universalized version of the highest good. Such, after all, is the
impact of the highest good as the "regulative idea of
history."

Now even supposing that there is a version of the
highest good doctrine matching this description, the
obligation to promote the highest good leads to serious
problems. In the first place, it is not altogether
clear whether Kant is actually (and consistently)
claiming that rational beings are obligated to promote
the highest good. For example, he says "the command
to further the highest good is objectively grounded"
in practical reason,[130] speaking of this command in
the sense of an imperative. Yet, as Beck has pointed
out, none of the formulations of the categorical imperative has the highest good as its content.[131] Furthermore, Kant--immediately following his statement
concerning "the command to further the highest good"--
appears to change his emphasis. The "voluntary deci-
sion" of our judgment to assume the existence of the
highest good

> and to make it the foundation of
> further employment of reason, con-
> ducing to the moral (commanded)
> purpose and agreeing moreover with
> the theoretical need of reason...
> is itself not commanded. It rather

173

springs from the moral disposition itself.[132]

This passage is symptomatic of a number of confusions in Kant's approach to the problem of the relation
between the moral law and the highest good. John
Silber has attempted to lend some clarity to the issue
by distinguishing between a duty to <u>attain</u> the highest
good and a duty simply to <u>promote</u> it.[133] Silber speaks
of the former as the "transcendent" version of the
highest good; it cannot possibly be a moral duty, since
finite beings are incapable of effecting it. The
latter, says Silber, is the "immanent" version of the
highest good; it <u>is</u> a moral duty and consistent with
the limits of our powers.[134] In other words, we are
obligated to <u>promote</u>, but not to attain, the highest
good in the world. The <u>attainment</u> of the highest good
remains a regulative idea, and not a true moral obligation.

Silber's strategy offers a nice distinction which,
on the face of it, seems to clarify the ambiguity in
Kant's own comments on the issue. But a recent critic
of Silber has noted serious difficulties attending the
notion of a duty to "promote" the highest good, and
these same difficulties affect Yovel's interpretation
as well. Jeffrie Murphy has suggested that an obligation to promote the highest good would severely undermine the autonomous basis of Kant's ethics.[135] Yovel
himself steers away from this danger by emphasizing
Kant's claim that it is not the private interest, but
the universal human interest (and therefore my moral
duty), to promote the highest good.[136] Yet the danger
of heteronomy persists, infecting any deviation from
the categorical imperative as the sole norm of the determination of the will. By siding with Kant at the
point of one of Kant's weakest conceptual claims,
Yovel is perpetuating a long-standing problem, rather
than correcting it.

More important, suggests Murphy, are the epistemological problems accompanying any obligation to promote the highest good. Any such obligation would
presumably involve the requirement that we attempt to
proportion happiness to virtue. But how are we to do
this, if moral action occurs only noumenally?[137] Kant
himself, as the commentators never tire of reminding
us, emphasizes that "ought implies can." Thus, if we
cannot possibly specify true virtue or moral endeavor,
we must not be obligated to proportion it to happiness.

174

> We cannot legitimately infer from
> phenomenal actions to noumenal dis-
> position...At best we can judge the
> legality of actions and apportion
> happiness according to that...Though
> it is legitimate to require us to
> act without sufficient knowledge, it
> would be strange indeed to ask that
> we act without necessary knowledge.[138]

To ask us to "promote" the highest good, then, would
be to ask us to violate one of the foundational premises of the critical philosophy.

My final criticism of Yovel's approach involves
the formal-material distinction he invokes in order
to generate a variety of ways of defining Kant's
theory of the highest good. The whole thrust of
Yovel's interpretation is centered on the implicit
notion that there is something essentially unfinished
or incomplete regarding the formal side of Kant's
ethics. Thus, this formal side requires a corresponding material side if practical reason's various needs
are to be fulfilled. The formal side is the "how" of
moral endeavor: it concerns the good will, the structure of such a will, and the categorical imperative
establishing the absolute duty of such a will.[139] The
material side, on the other hand, is the "what" of
moral endeavor: it defines the total object of the
moral will and thereby "fulfills the need 'to conceive
of some sort of final end for all our actions and abstentions, taken as a whole.'"[140] Yovel's entire
interpretation relies, not only on the formal-material
distinction, but on the further claim that the material side completes and includes the formal side
(though, to be sure, the formal side is <u>logically</u>
prior to the material).

> The formal (categorical) imperative
> is already included in the material
> imperative as an absolute condition,
> the latter being its necessary com-
> plement. Lacking the second stage
> the moral system would remain pure,
> absolute and incomplete.[141]

A kind of rehabilitation of Kant is occurring here,
such that Kant's putative excessive formalism in ethical matters will be balanced by an emphasis on the
worldly effects of the moral will. The depiction of

175

these worldly effects follows directly from Yovel's notion of the highest good as the regulative idea of history.

Thus, the operative distinction here is between the formal condition of a good will (i.e., the categorical imperative) and the material object of that same will (i.e., Yovel's universalized version of the highest good). Just as the categorical imperative has an obviously moral dimension (indeed, it _defines_ the moral dimension), so also does the universalized version of the highest good have a moral dimension, since it specifies the ultimate object of the moral will. The problem with this is Yovel's imputation of a genuinely _moral_ quality to the material side of Kant's practical philosophy.[142] It is true, by Kantian standards, that every act of will must _have_ an object. But such an object--or material content--is present only in a _non-moral_ capacity, since only the formal aspect, embodied in the categorical imperative, defines morality.[143] In Kant's words, every volition

> must have an object and therefore
> a material; but the material cannot
> be supposed, for this reason, to be
> the determining ground and condition
> of the maxim...The mere form of a
> law, which limits its material, must
> be a condition for introducing this
> material but not for presupposing it
> as a condition of the will.[144]

The material component is something which can only be _described_ and never _prescribed_. It is true, as Yovel argues, that a vision of the totalization of the objects of the will fulfills a metaphysical need of reason.[145] But it is wrong to impute to this vision or representation a moral worth, since the formal moral law has nothing to do with this or any other end but only with what is stipulated by the categorical imperative.

This problem elevates us to the most abstract levels of Kant's moral theory--we are quickly approaching what Beck has appropriately called that "repellently technical level" which is "of interest only to Kantian adepts."[146] But the clear adjudication of this issue is essential for a fair evaluation of Yovel's thesis. The solution to the problem is basically a matter of correctly sorting and categorizing a variety of Kantian claims. The key distinction is this: it is one thing to claim that the highest good (in whatever form) is the object of the moral will; it is quite another thing to propose that we _ought_ to make the highest good the object of our will. The _former_ is merely a description of a state of affairs arrived at through reason's need to totalize and unify the objects of its speculation. The _latter_ is a genuine moral imperative which, Yovel claims, fulfills and completes the merely formal demand pronounced by the categorical imperative. But Yovel has taken a strictly _logical_ issue, based upon a feature of Kant's theory of _reason_ (i.e., its drive for totality) and freighted it with a moral implication. And then, recognizing that the product of this strategy totalizes and unifies our perspective on moral issues in a way not provided for by the categorical imperative alone, he jumps to the conclusion that the resulting material and universal form of the highest good somehow completes Kant's ethical and religious system. Thus, Yovel has recognized a demand of pure reason and forced it to serve a moral aim. In a peculiar way, this is analogous to his exploitation of a regulative idea for constitutive purposes.

What is ultimately problematic in Yovel's interpretation, then, is the relationship between moral volition and the highest good. He is anxious to achieve a synthesis of moral acts, and this leads him to utilize Kant's theory of the highest good in ways which are not clearly accounted for by the critical philosophy. In fairness to Yovel, it must be repeated that Kant is indeed guilty of certain ambiguities concerning the meaning of the highest good, ambiguities which, as I have indicated, revolve around the problem of our duty to "promote" the highest good. But one thing Kant is reasonably clear about is the relation between the categorical imperative and the highest good--or, borrowing Yovel's formulation, between the "formal" and the "material" aspects of his ethical theory.

> The moral law [i.e., the categorical
> imperative] is the sole determining
> ground of the pure will. Since it
> is merely formal, requiring only that
> the form of the maxim be universally
> legislative, as a determining ground
> it abstracts from all material and
> thus from every object of volition.

> Consequently, though the highest
> good may be the entire object of
> a pure practical reason, i.e., of
> a pure will, it is still not to be
> taken as the determining ground of
> the pure will; the moral law alone
> must be seen as the ground for mak-
> ing the highest good and its reali-
> zation or promotion the object of
> the pure will.[147]

By giving the categorical imperative the dominant role
which Kant clearly means it to have, we can best understand the highest good as the descriptive product of
reason's drive for totality. When Kant says, the
"achievement of the highest good in the world is the
necessary object of a will determinable by the moral
law," he means it "happens to be" this necessary object, not that it "ought to be."[148] In other words,
the idea of the highest good "arises out of morality
and is not its basis; it is an end the adoption of
which as one's own presupposes basic ethical principles."[149]

Now it may seem that Yovel could be justly criticized only on the grounds that he makes the highest
good the "determining ground" of the moral will. He
is, however, reasonably careful about the introduction
of such a note of heteronomy into his interpretation
of Kant.

> [The] end-concept necessarily accom-
> panies the moral act, without deter-
> mining it. The latter function is
> fulfilled by the formal aspect of the
> imperative, while the representation
> of the final-end only posits my par-
> ticular act in the same context with
> my other moral actions, and with the
> moral actions of others. It is only
> an accompanying consciousness and not
> a direct motivation, removing the
> danger of heteronomy.[150]

Thus, although Yovel (along with Kant himself) courts
the dangers posed by heteronomy, I am not relying
solely or even mainly on the charge that the heteronomy
issue undercuts his interpretation. What I am claiming
is that Yovel has underestimated the systematic utility
of the formal side of Kant's practical philosophy and

has consequently assigned too great a moral function to the material side.[151] Perhaps another way of stating the same criticism is to suggest that Yovel has exaggerated the distinction between the so-called formal and material sides of Kant's ethical thought. If, in fact, there is something "incomplete" about what is laid down by the categorical imperative (i.e., the formal side), it is not a _moral_ incompletion. All that is left incomplete is the demand of reason to totalize and unify its objects--in this case, the objects of the moral will. But _this_ form of incompletion does not constitute or in any way inform moral endeavor, but is simply the by-product of reflection on the results of moral action. In other words, the incompletion which generates Yovel's claims about the highest good does not constitute a genuinely moral issue at all, but simply a need of reason. Thus, to claim that the material side of Kant's ethical thought, represented by a universalized version of the highest good, fulfills and completes the formal side is to make a kind of category mistake. The material side does not meet any _moral_ demand but simply indulges an unavoidable metaphysical interest. The fact that we are dealing with the practical rather than theoretical sphere does not alter the way the intellect operates in meeting this metaphysical interest.

Beck has put this issue in proper perspective by emphasizing that "the truth of the matter is that the concept of the highest good is not a practical concept at all, but a dialectical Ideal of reason."

> It is not important in Kant's phi-
> losophy for any practical conse-
> quences it might have...It is im-
> portant for the architectonic pur-
> pose of reason in uniting under one
> Idea the two legislations of reason,
> the theoretical and the practical
> ...Reason cannot tolerate a chaos of
> ends; it demands the a priori synthe-
> sis of them into a system.[152]

Thus, Yovel's attempt to propose a version of the highest good which completes and thereby meets a moral demand is to confuse the issue. Yovel's entire approach is based on a smearing of the line Kant draws between the theoretical and practical.

If my view is correct, then what I am proposing

179

suggests the enormity of the gap between Kant's moral concerns and his theory of the natural world. Yovel, after all, is attempting to demonstrate that through a particular version of the doctrine of the highest good, Kant is bringing the worlds of "is" and "ought" together in one systematic vision. The ultimate point of the highest good as the "regulative idea of history" is that the highest good "becomes an ideal of a coordination between the natural order and moral legislation."[153] But this entire interpretive enterprise rests on the assumption that the so-called material side of Kant's practical philosophy carries with it a genuinely moral dimension, without which the formal side remains incomplete and ultimately unintelligible. If, then, I am correct in denying that the material side carries any moral qualities, then the empirical, phenomenal order has been pushed farther away from any genuine reconciliation with moral demands. The impasse between religion and history remains.

What leads Yovel astray is his assumption that certain "needs of reason" have a practical rather than strictly theoretical import. The "need of reason" which requires that men be able to act with the expectation that their actions will have an ultimate purpose and effect is simply not the moral issue Yovel tries to make it. It may be poignant and affecting, but, by Kant's stringent standards, such psychological attributes do not accumulate in such a way as to score a moral point. Rather, what is at stake in these so-called "needs of reason" is an <u>aesthetic</u>, and not a moral, ideal.[154] Human reason has an unavoidable interest in the achievement of synthesis, unity, and proportion, but the ground rules underlying this achievement are not moral ones. Kant's theory of the highest good simply happens to be the product of reason's reflection on the ends of moral endeavor, and this is a speculative side-effect of the practical philosophy and not constitutive <u>of</u> it. The one truly moral demand laid on us is embodied solely by the categorical imperative. The highest good, in fulfilling a need of reason, functions aesthetically and not morally.

Thus, Yovel's reading of the doctrine of the highest good runs into a variety of conceptual difficulties. His problems seem to stem from two main sources: he tries to impose an unwarranted moral meaning on the various needs or interests of reason; and he fails adequately to keep in proper focus the point of Kant's

180

regulative-constitutive distinction. The combination of these two failings leads Yovel to propose that mankind both can and should reach a goal which, in actual fact, has only a regulative meaning. And the meaning of something that is regulative is that we are indulging reason's "natural" and "unavoidable" propensity to seek the unified and absolute end of its objects of speculation.[155] But no legitimate inference can be made from the end point of this reflective process to an existential claim. Kant is clearest on this point in the theoretical realm, but the ground rules remain the same when we shift to the practical realm.

Concluding Remarks

Like my earlier inquiry into Kant's view of teleology and history, Yovel's ambitious interpretation simply sharpens the demand for an ultimate synthesis of freedom and nature, without explaining how the synthesis occurs. And this, to reemphasize my earlier claim, is to put one's finger on a serious impasse in the critical philosophy. The ultimate problem here betrays a somewhat bitter irony. Kant has preserved morals and religion from the threats of Newtonian science by invoking a phenomena-noumena distinction. But this very distinction denies Kant the conceptual means of ever articulating the genuinely worldly manifestation of moral ends. Consequently, the very style and method of Kant's philosophy work against the possibility that certain dualities can ever be brought together in a higher synthesis. The present inquiry has demonstrated how this is the case with respect to the relation between history and religion. But, as I have suggested, the history and religion issue can ultimately be understood as a particular way of viewing the relation between nature and freedom within Kant's philosophy. The apparent inability of Kant ever to reconcile the latter pair means that history and religion--however much they may need each other within Kant's system--can never meet on common ground. For Kant to have posited such a common ground would have involved him in the creation of a higher metaphysical unity more characteristic of Hegel than of the author of the Critique of Pure Reason.[156]

Interestingly enough, the problem of the impasse between religion and history serves to enhance the importance of historical religion within the Kantian framework. This is because the apparent impossibility of ever attaining a true synthesis of morality and the empirical order requires the maintenance of the historical aspect of religion as a mediator between supersensuous moral ideas and a sensuous humanity. Thus, although in the previous chapter I was unable to determine Kant's answer to the question of the pedagogical necessity of historical religion, my own inquiry suggests that this necessity is very real.

. This conclusion is suggested by the trajectory of the entire inquiry. Chapter II located and explored the important mediating role played by historical religion, given Kant's sensitivity toward human limitations. History does not impinge upon the ultimate truth and source of authentic Kantian religion, but it has an enormous impact on the communication of that religion. This is why the same religion, to recall Kant's own suggestion, can be both "objectively natural" and "subjectively revealed."[157]

Then, Chapter III explored the intimate conceptual relations existing between the historical and moral elements in a given faith. This inquiry reinforced Kant's own emphasis on the rationalistic basis of religion, and the issue of schematism exemplified the cognitive stringency characteristic of Kant's religious thought. At the same time, however, the role of history as an ongoing, temporal process, and not simply as the sphere of religious concretion and symbolization, was isolated through a consideration of Kant's view of the church. This suggested a more important role for history, insofar as the temporal span itself appeared to be bound up with Kant's religious aims. Yet the teleological aspect of this Kantian vision, as well as Kant's comments on the ultimate dispensability of the historical "vehicle," posed the problem of an historical faith in a new and troublesome way. Was historical religion to be understood as a necessary "stage" in man's moral and religious progress? And if so, how were we to conceive of the relationship between moral and religious ends and the historical process, given the noumenal character of the former and the phenomenal character of the latter?

This fourth and final chapter has suggested that there is no means, within the ground rules of the critical philosophy, of synthesizing religion and his-

182

tory, freedom and nature, in a way that makes history ultimately dispensable. History as a medium--whether it be the medium for the symbolic representation of moral ideas or the medium for the moral progress of humanity--can never be jettisoned without invoking the kind of metaphysical synthesis with which Kant could not possibly be comfortable. The one consistent Kantian caveat is that the historical aspect must always be in the service of moral mandates, and not the other way around. As long as this principle is observed and safeguarded, history can never be a threat but only an aid to the authentic religious life. And the so-called "end" of moral and religious endeavor--whether we call it the kingdom of ends, the ethical commonwealth, or the kingdom of God on earth--will, as the teleologically-conceived "highest good," serve as the regulative representation of the goal which man, as rational, can conceptualize, but which man, as finite, will never reach. Kant's ideal ethical kingdom may be approximated, but it cannot possibly be actualized. As a result, history remains the ongoing medium of man's religious endeavors, and the ideal relation between rationality and the empirical order remains one of balance rather than of complete synthesis.

NOTES

Wherever possible, references to works by Kant are to the standard English translations.

Introduction

1. Kant was actually quoting Lord Shaftesbury when he said this. Cf. Kant, The Metaphysical Elements of Justice, tr. J. Ladd (New York: Bobbs-Merrill, Library of Liberal Arts, 1965), p. 8.

2. J. Collins, Interpreting Modern Philosophy (Princeton: Princeton University Press, 1972), Ch. V.

3. Cf. J.E. Smith, Reason and God (New Haven: Yale University Press, 1961), pp. 3-20; J.H. Gill, The Possibility of Religious Knowledge (Grand Rapids: Eerdmans, 1971).

4. T.M. Greene, "The Historical Context and Religious Significance of Kant's Religion," Introduction, Religion within the Limits of Reason Alone, tr. Greene and H. Hudson (New York: Harper Torchbook, 1960), pp. lxxvi-lxxvii. Hereafter referred to as Religion. The heart of Greene's interpretation--that Kant executes a reduction of religion to morality and that his views reflect a rationalistic world view--is echoed in numerous surveys of modern religious thought, as well as in another standard English-language account of Kant's religious philosophy, C.C.J. Webb's Kant's Philosophy of Religion (Oxford: Oxford University Press, 1926). The situation within European scholarship is somewhat different, owing to the tendency on the Continent to utilize "Kant interpretation" as the starting point for an original constructive position. Cf. the overview of approaches to Kant's religious thought in M. Despland, Kant on History and Religion (Montreal: McGill-Queens, 1973), pp. 1-14, 299-302, as well as the overview of recent research interests in Kant studies generally in M.J. Scott-Taggart, "Recent Work on the Philosophy of Kant," in L.W. Beck (ed.), Kant Studies Today (La Salle: Open Court, 1969), pp. 1-71. A recent work of French scholarship offering a useful and balanced view of

185

Kant's religious thought is J.L. Bruch, La Philosophie Religieuse de Kant (Paris: Aubier, 1968).

5. The work of Despland, op. cit., is the most ambitious attempt to build a bridge between Kant's views on history and religion. Cf. also J. Collins, The Emergence of Philosophy of Religion (New Haven: Yale University Press, 1967), Chs. 3-5, esp. pp. 197-204; G.A. Kelly, Idealism, Politics, and History: Sources of Hegelian Thought (Cambridge: Cambridge University Press, 1969);C.A. Raschke, Moral Action, God, and History in the Thought of Immanuel Kant (Missoula, Montana: American Academy of Religion, Scholars Press); H. Saner, Kant's Political Thought, tr. E.B. Ashton (Chicago: University of Chicago Press, 1973); K. Weyand, Kants Geschichtsphilosophie: Ihre Entwicklung und ihr Verhältnis zur Aufklärung (Köln: Kölnuniversitäts-Verlag, 1964), pp. 183-85;Y. Yovel, "The Highest Good and History in Kant's Thought," Archiv für Geschichte der Philosophie 54, Heft 3 (1972), pp. 238-83. Despite its title, William Galston's Kant and the Problem of History (Chicago: University of Chicago Press, 1975) is a disappointing work which commits the unforgivable sin of making Kant more, rather than less, confusing.

6. I particularly have in mind Allen Wood's excellent, if sometimes turgid, book, Kant's Moral Religion (Ithaca: Cornell University Press, 1970).

7. Despland, op. cit.

8. In what follows, I will only be offering a very general explication and justification of this principle. A more detailed and more closely documented justification will appear in Chapter I. My principle of human limitations can perhaps be taken as a greatly broadened version of the "principle of significance" which P.F. Strawson attributes to Kant. Cf. Strawson, The Bounds of Sense (London: Metheun, 1966), pp. 16-18.

9. Cf. J. Collins, The Emergence of Philosophy of Religion (New Haven: Yale University Press, 1967), p. 410.

10. Such a claim, of course, brings to mind Heidegger's controversial interpretation of Kant. More will be said on this issue in the second section of the Introduction.

11. Cf. the Critique of Pure Reason, tr. N. Kemp Smith (New York: St. Martin's Press, 1965), B 307-309, pp. 268-71. Hereafter referred to as Pure. The human-divine contrast involved in the distinction between a sensible and an intellectual intuition has recently been explored in an unpublished Yale University doctoral

dissertation by J. Hicks, "Divine and Human Subjectivity in Kant," (1969).

12. Foundations of the Metaphysics of Morals, tr. L.W. Beck (New York: Bobbs-Merrill, Library of Liberal Arts, 1959), pp. 22-3.

13. Goethe's reaction to Kant's doctrine is typical: he claimed that Kant "'had criminally smeared his philosopher's cloak with the shameful stain of radical evil, after it had taken him a long human life to cleanse it from many a dirty prejudice, so that Christians too might yet be enticed to kiss its hem,'" quoted in K. Barth, Protestant Thought from Rousseau to Ritschl, tr. B. Cozens (New York: Simon and Schuster, 1969), p. 178.

14. Religion, pp. 23ff.

15. Cf. Kant's Critique of Practical Reason, tr. L.W. Beck (New York: Bobbs-Merrill, Library of Liberal Arts, 1956), pp. 84-5; Beck, A Commentary on Kant's Critique of Practical Reason (Chicago: University of Chicago Press, 1961), p. 50n. According to Hicks, op. cit., the contrast case in the third Critique is the so-called "archetypal intellect," which stands over against man's discursive intellect. E.g., Critique of Judgment, tr. J.H. Bernard (New York: Hafner, 1972), pp. 256-7.

16. Religion, p. 122.

17. Kant's most important essays on history have been collected by Beck in Kant on History (New York: Bobbs-Merrill, Library of Liberal Arts, 1963). For a chronology of the key historical writings, cf. Despland, op. cit., p. 300, n. 13. Most important secondary works are Despland's Kant on History and Religion, op. cit., and Weyand's Kants Geschichtsphilosophie..., op. cit. Cf. also Beck's Editor's Introduction to Kant on History, op. cit., pp. vii-xxviii; E. Fackenheim, "Kant's Concept of History," Kant-Studien XLVII (1957), pp. 381-98; and B.T. Wilkens, "Teleology in Kant's Philosophy of History," History and Theory V (1966), pp. 172-85.

18. An argument establishing this view of Kant's summum bonum has been illuminatingly conceived in a lengthy and laborious essay by Y. Yovel, "The Highest Good and History in Kant's Thought," op. cit., esp. pp. 273-83. Cf. also Yovel's essay, "The God of Kant," Scripta Hierosolymitana XX (Jerusalem: Magnes Press, 1968), pp. 88-123.

19. Religion, p. 92.

20. Yovel, "The Highest Good and History in Kant's

187

Thought," op. cit., p. 239.

21. Heidegger's highly controversial interpretation of Kant is presented in Kant and the Problem of Metaphysics, tr. J.S. Churchill (Bloomington, Indiana: Indiana University Press, 1962), with additional remarks in What Is a Thing?, tr. W.B. Barton, Jr. and V. Deutsch (Chicago: University of Chicago Press, 1967), Part B. Heidegger has been taken to task for his supposed distortions of Kant by E. Cassirer, "Kant and the Problem of Metaphysics: Remarks on Heidegger's Interpretation of Kant," now in M.S. Gram (ed.), Kant: Disputed Questions (Chicago: Quadrangle Books, 1967), pp. 131-57. Cassirer suggests that Heidegger is perhaps overreacting to the neo-Kantian emphasis on the problem of knowledge: "What Heidegger regards as the dominant idea of his interpretation of Kant is doubtless the effort to overcome that neo-Kantianism that sought to found the entire Kantian system in his critique of knowledge and finally to let it disappear into mere epistemology. Heidegger opposes this with the thesis of the primarily metaphysical character of Kant's problem. For him, Kant's doctrine is not a theory of experience but is primarily and originally ontology... [But] Heidegger's fundamental ontology...must put all Kant's concepts from the very beginning--however much Heidegger attempted to do justice to their purely logical sense--into a changed atmosphere and thus, as it were, cover them up...Goethe once said to Schopenhauer that, when he read a page of Kant, he felt as if he were entering a bright room. From the very outset Heidegger's philosophy obeys, as it were, a different principle of style," pp. 149-50, 155. Discussions of the Heideggerian approach to Kant can be found in J. Collins, Interpreting Modern Philosophy, op. cit., pp. 297-314; and N. Rotenstreich, Experience and its Systematization 2nd ed. (The Hague: Martinus Nijhoff, 1972), pp. 190-202. Cf. also the remarks of Allen Wood, op. cit., pp. 3-4. Useful, and generally sympathetic, expositions of Heidegger's view of Kant are contained in two articles by C. Sherover, "Heidegger's Ontology and the Copernican Revolution," The Monist 51 (1967), pp. 559-73; and "Kant's Transcendental Object and Heidegger's Nichts," Journal of the History of Philosophy VII (1969), pp. 413-22. Finally, cf. C.O. Schrag, "Heidegger and Cassirer on Kant," Kant-Studien 58 (1967), pp. 87-100.

22. Cf. Cassirer, op. cit., pp. 151ff.

23. Kant and the Problem of Metaphysics, op. cit.,

pp. 28-30; Schrag, op.cit., p. 93.

24 The phrase is borrowed from Rotenstreich's characterization of Heidegger's approach to Kant, op. cit., p. 196.

25. It is interesting to note that, prior to the publication of the first Critique, Kant had planned to publish a work entitled, "The Limits of Sense and Reason." Cf. Philosophical Correspondence, A. Zweig (ed.) (Chicago: University of Chicago Press, 1967), p. 71.

26. An exception is the provocative if difficult work of Wilfred Sellars, Science and Metaphysics (London: Rutledge and Kegan Paul, 1968).

27. Rotenstreich, op. cit., p. 193.

28. Ibid., p. 161.

29. As James Collins has recently pointed out, Husserl, Heidegger, and Jaspers were all life-long "existential grapplers" with Kant. Cf. Interpreting Modern Philosophy, op. cit., pp. 283ff.

30. Strawson, op. cit., p. 11.

31. J. Bennett, Kant's Analytic (Cambridge: Cambridge University Press, 1966), p. viii.

32. J.N. Findlay, "Kant and Anglo-Saxon Criticism," in L.W. Beck (ed.), Proceedings of the Third International Kant Congress (Dordrecht: D. Reidel, 1972), p. 128.

33. Allen Wood rightly perceives the potential distortions involved in such an approach to Kant. Cf. Wood, op. cit., pp. 1-9.

34. Strawson, op. cit., p. 44.

35. Pure, A 805=B 833, p. 635.

36. Collingwood, An Autobiography (Oxford: Oxford University Press, 1970), p. 41. One might also consider O.K. Bouwsma's three methods of "frisking" a philosophical theory: "You may try to misunderstand it which in philosophy requires almost no effort at all...You may...try to refute the theory in question. In this case you settle upon some clear and plausible import of the theory, and then you discover some contradiction. The contradiction must be hidden, subtle, and for the best results should pop out like a jack-in-the-box... You may try to understand the theory in question. This is, of course, a very dangerous expedient. It is clear that having understood the theory you may be taken in by it, and so suffer the corruption which you certainly intended at the outset to avoid." Philosophical Essays (Lincoln: University of Nebraska Press, 1969), p. 75.

37. G. Buchdal, Metaphysics and the Philosophy of Science (Cambridge, Mass.: M.I.T. Press, 1970), p. 470.

189

38. R. Kroner, Kant's Weltanschauung, tr. J.E. Smith (Chicago: University of Chicago Press, 1956).

39. Ibid., pp. 84-5. Kroner was one of the later members of the Heidelberg school of neo-Kantians. In contrast to the Marburg neo-Kantians (one of whom was E. Cassirer), the Heidelberg school emphasized the axiological, rather than the scientific-epistemological, side of Kant's thinking. The difference in emphasis is clearly reflected in the divergent scholarly careers of Kroner and Cassirer.

40. Critique of Practical Reason, op. cit., p. 10.

41. Smith in Kroner, op. cit., p. v.

42. Smith, Reason and God, op. cit., p. ix.

43. On the problem of Kant and the "system," cf. the Appendix of Rotenstreich, op. cit., pp. 160ff.

44. Despland, op. cit., p. 1. In fairness to Despland, it should be pointed out that he characterizes this comment as the "maximal form" of his interpretive contention. "The minimal form is that the interpretation of [Kant's] philosophy of religion through his philosophy of history should be placed alongside the interpretation through the results of his ethics." I am in full agreement with the "minimal form" of Despland's contention. In Chapter III, I shall criticize certain specific points of Despland's interpretation.

45. Wood, op. cit., p. 2.

46. Philosophical Correspondence, op. cit., p. 205.

Chapter I

1. A. Wood, Kant's Moral Religion (Ithaca: Cornell University Press, 1970), pp. 32-3.

2. Critique of Pure Reason, tr. Kemp Smith (New York: St. Martin's Press, 1965), B XXX, p. 29. Hereafter referred to as Pure.

3. W.H. Walsh, "Kant's Moral Theology," Proceedings of the British Academy XLIX (1963), p. 286.

4. P.F. Strawson, The Bounds of Sense (London: Methuen, 1966), p. 44.

5. Quoted in L.W. Beck, A Commentary on Kant's Critique of Practical Reason (Chicago: University of Chicago Press, 1960), p. 4.

6. H. Fain, Between Philosophy and History (Princeton: Princeton University Press, 1970), p. 11. Fain actually makes this comment with regard to Hegel, but it seems to apply equally--if not better--to Kant.

7. Kant, <u>Prolegomena to Any Future Metaphysics</u>, tr. Carus, ed. Beck (New York: Bobbs-Merrill, Library of Liberal Arts, 1950), p. 9.

8. Ibid., pp. 3-4.

9. P. Tillich, <u>Systematic Theology</u>, Vol. II (Chicago: University of Chicago Press, 1957), p. 27.

10. <u>Pure</u>, A 856=B 884, p. 669.

11. <u>Ibid</u>., B XVIff., pp. 22ff.

12. Ibid., B XIV-XV, pp. 20-1.

13. Ibid., B XVI, p. 22.

14. Ibid., A 11-12=B 25, p. 59.

15. D. Pears, <u>Wittgenstein</u> (New York: Viking Press, 1970), p. 18. Pears' book on Wittgenstein, in the "Modern Masters" series, contains an extremely lucid and jargon-free discussion of critical philosophy, pp. 17-35. Most helpfully, Pears draws illuminating connections between the classic instance of critical philosophy, found in Kant, and the "critical" nature of modern linguistic philosophy, found especially in Wittgenstein. In both cases, Pears emphasizes the metaphysical issues at stake. On the methodological relation between Kant and Wittgenstein, cf. also J. Hartnack, "Kant and Wittgenstein," <u>Kant-Studien</u> 60 (1969), pp. 131-4; R. Rorty, "Strawson's Objectivity Argument," <u>Review of Metaphysics</u> 24 (December, 1970), pp. 236-44; W.H. Walsh, "Philosophy and Psychology in Kant's <u>Critique</u>," <u>Kant-Studien</u> 57 (1966), pp. 189-98.

16. <u>Pure</u>, B XXV, p. 32.

17. Paton, <u>The Categorical Imperative</u> (Philadelphia: University of Pennsylvania Press, 1971), p. 19.

18. Cf. Kant's "History of Pure Reason," <u>Pure</u>, A 852-56=B 880-84, pp. 666-9.

19. <u>Pure</u>, B 1, p. 41.

20. J. Smith, "Hegel's Critique of Kant," <u>Review of Metaphysics</u> 26 (March, 1973), p. 447.

21. E.g., cf. <u>Pure</u>, A 50-57=B 74-82, pp. 92-7; also, cf. N. Rotenstreich, <u>Experience and Its Systematization</u> 2nd edition (The Hague: Martinus Nijhoff, 1972), Ch. I.

22. <u>Pure</u>, A XIII, p. 10, my emphasis.

23. <u>Ibid</u>., A 19=B 33, p. 65.

24. Cf. the exploration of the so-called "myth of the given" in Wilfred Sellars' essay, "Empiricism and the Philosophy of Mind," in <u>Science, Perception and Reality</u> (London: Routledge and Kegan Paul, 1963), pp. 127-96. Though critical of the notion of "foundational" knowledge, Sellars provides a detailed account of what kind of epistemological commitment is involved in a theory like Kant's theory of sensibility.

25. <u>Pure</u>, A 24=B 38-39, p. 68; A 29-32=B 46-48, pp. 74-5.

26. Cf. ibid., B XVII-XVIII, pp. 22-3.

27. Ibid., A 19=B 33, p. 65.

28. This is the specific point of my agreement with Heidegger's approach to Kant and is basically limited to Heidegger's treatment of Kant's doctrine of sensibility. It seems possible to maintain this limited, qualified agreement without running the risk of "ontologizing" the sense of Kant's "transcendental," as Heidegger is prone to do. Cf. C. Sherover, "Heidegger's Ontology and the Copernican Revolution," <u>The Monist</u> 51 (1967), pp. 559-73, esp. pp. 563-5.

29. For a good discussion of Kant's evolving view of the idea of an intellectual intuition, and an account of the reasons which led him to drop the idea, cf. the unpublished Princeton University dissertation (1972) by E.A. Langerak, "Orienting Oneself Rationally: Kant's Constructive Philosophy of Religion," pp. 19ff.

30. <u>Pure</u>, B 72, p. 90.

31. <u>Ibid.</u>, B 307, p. 268.

32. Ibid., A 286=B 342, p. 292.

33. Again, Heidegger's interpretation of this point seems defensible, op. cit., pp. 28-30.

34. Walsh, "Philosophy and Psychology in Kant's <u>Critique</u>," op. cit., p. 191.

35. Ibid., p. 186.

36. This metaphilosophical problem may in fact affect all philosophical methods. Cf. R. Rorty, "The Limits of Reductionism," in I.C. Lieb (ed.), <u>Experience, Existence, and the Good: Essays in Honor of Paul Weiss</u> (Carbondale, Illinois: Southern Illinois University Press, 1961), pp. 100-16.

37. Cf. R. Solomon, <u>From Rationalism to Existentialism</u> (New York: Harper and Row, 1972), pp. 13-15; T.D. Weldon, <u>Kant's Critique of Pure Reason</u> 2nd edition (Oxford: Oxford University Press, 1958), pp. 73, 75-6.

38. <u>Pure</u>, A 70-83=B 95-109, pp. 106-15.

39. <u>Ibid.</u>, A 66=B 91, p. 104.

40. Cf. Strawson, op. cit., p. 31. As Strawson characteristically puts it, it "requires only moderate acquaintance with formal logic to be both critical of the list of forms which is to be the basis of Kant's derivation in the Metaphysical Deduction and sceptical of the whole conception of the deduction itself."

41. <u>Pure</u>, cf. esp. A 66-83=B 91-109, pp. 104-15.

42. <u>Ibid.</u>, A 192-99=B 238-44, pp. 221-5; A 200-202= B 246-47, pp. 226-7.

43. Ibid., A 536=B 564, p. 466.
44. Ibid., A 540=B 568, p. 469.
45. Ibid., A 546=B 574, p. 472.
46. Cf. Beck, A Commentary on Kant's Critique of Practical Reason, op. cit., p. 27.
47. Pure, B XXVI-XXVII, p. 27.
48. Ibid.
49. Cf. Kant's note, ibid., B XXVII, p. 27.
50. Ibid.
51. Ibid., A 255=B 311, p. 272.
52. Ibid., B 307, p. 268.
53. Schrader, "The Thing in Itself in Kantian Philosophy," in R.P. Wolff (ed.), Kant: A Collection of Critical Essays (Garden City, N.Y.: Doubleday, 1967), pp. 174-5.
54. Ibid., p. 176.
55. This claim is, in fact, the point of Schrader's article. Schrader thinks that Kant's "dogmatic" lapses can be separated out from the rest, leaving a genuinely critical teaching intact. Cf. ibid., pp. 173-4.
56. Pure, A 255=B 311, p. 272.
57. J. Bennett, Kant's Analytic (Cambridge: Cambridge University Press, 1966), p. 56.
58. Pure, B 72, p. 90.
59. This discussion leaves unanswered the question of whether Kant's ethical and religious writings are based upon a positive sense of the noumenal. This at least appears to be the case, e.g., in Section 3 of the Foundations of the Metaphysics of Morals, tr. Beck (New York: Bobbs-Merrill, Library of Liberal Arts, 1959), where Kant argues for the reality of freedom on the basis of man's residence in an "intelligible" as well as phenomenal world, esp. pp. 70, 72, 76. Hereafter referred to as Foundations.
60. Cf. Pure, B XXVIII, p. 28.
61. Ibid., A 557=B 585, pp. 478-9.
62. Ibid., A 641=B 669, p. 531.
63. Ibid., B XXX, p. 29.
64. It is unclear whether Kant ever makes the same sort of "logical/real" distinction concerning impossibility that he makes concerning possibility. Whereas in the earlier case his aim is the demonstration of the logical possibility of a certain metaphysical reality (i.e., freedom), his aim in this second case is the demonstration of the impossibility of a certain sort of claim (i.e., the claim that freedom is logically impossible). And in this latter case, it would seem that what Kant has in mind is real impossibility. (I

am indebted to Henry Levinson, of Stanford University,
for pointing out this difficulty to me.)

65. Ibid., A 795-831=B 823-59, pp. 629-51.
66. Foundations, pp. 75-6.
67. Pure, B X, p. 18.
68. Beck, A Commentary on Kant's Critique of Practical Reason, op. cit., p. 241.
69. Foundations, p. 8.
70. The culmination of this effort is Kant's discussion of the postulates of pure practical reason, in Book II, Chapter II of the Critique of Practical Reason, op. cit., pp. 114-53.
71. Beck, A Commentary on Kant's Critique of Practical Reason, op. cit., pp. 249-50.
72. Practical, p. 6.
73. A.R.C. Duncan has pointed out the inherently paradoxical nature of ever speaking or thinking "about" practical reason, since such an activity must be theoretical rather than practical. "Practical reason is reason at work in the field of action. A discussion of practical reason is an example of speculative [i.e., theoretical] reason at work. The categorical assertion which is required in order to take us from the mere analysis of ideas to the reality to which these ideas refer cannot be a mere assertion of theoretical reason. It cannot be a declaration that something is the case, which would be the result of observation and of the intellectual conceptualization of that observation. The 'assertions' of practical reason must be made by practical reason, and practical reason is reason at work in the field of action." Duncan, Practical Reason and Morality (Edinburgh: Thomas Nelson, 1957), pp. 134-5.
74. E.g., cf. Foundations, pp. 9ff.
75. Ibid., pp. 8-9, my emphasis.
76. Ibid., p. 9.
77. E.g., cf. Beck, A Commentary on Kant's Critique of Practical Reason, op. cit., pp. 165, 235.
78. Beck, Early German Philosophy: Kant and His Predecessors (Cambridge, Mass.: Harvard University Press, 1969), p. 489.
79. E. Cassirer, Rousseau, Kant, and Goethe (Princeton: Princeton University Press, 1970), pp. 1-2.
80. Duncan, op. cit., p. 139.
81. Practical, p. 166.
82. Walsh, op. cit., p. 269.
83. Practical, pp. 126-38.
84. Ibid., pp. 139-44.
85. The phrase is Malcolm Diamond's. Cf. his Con-

temporary Philosophy and Religious Thought (New York: McGraw Hill, 1974), pp. 133-4.

86. Practical, p. 127.

87. Malcolm Diamond has consistently emphasized this point to me in private conversations.

88. J. Collins, The Emergence of Philosophy of Religion (New Haven: Yale University Press, 1967), pp. 121, 139.

89. Practical, p. 152.

90. Religion within the Limits of Reason Alone, tr. T.M. Greene and H. Hudson (New York: Harper Torchbook, 1960), pp. 3ff. Hereafter referred to as Religion.

91. Ibid., p. 167.

92. Walsh, op. cit., p. 282.

93. Ibid., p. 284.

94. Pure, A 829=B 857, p. 650.

95. M. Despland, Kant on History and Religion (Montreal: McGill-Queen's University Press, 1973), p. 116.

96. Religion, p. 142, my emphasis.

97. Collins, op. cit., and Despland, op. cit., have both emphasized the Kantian distinction between personal religion and formal institutional religion. Cf. Collins, pp. 97-9; Despland, pp. 107-20.

98. Pears, op. cit., p. 18.

99. Religion, p. 100.

Chapter II

1. The English edition is translated and edited by T.M. Greene and H.H. Hudson (New York: Harper Torchbook, 1960). Hereafter referred to as Religion, with pagination cited in parentheses in my text. Other sources with regard to Kant's view of an historical religion are Der Streit der Fakultäten (Hamburg: Felix Meiner, 1959), and Vorlesungen über philosophische Religionslehre in the Akademie edition of Kant's Werke Vol. 28 (Berlin: de Gruyter, 1972).

2. M. Despland, Kant on History and Religion (Montreal: McGill-Queen's University Press, 1973), pp. 159-60.

3. J. Baillie, The Idea of Revelation in Recent Thought (New York: Harper and Row, 1956), p. 10.

4. This interpretation of Kant's Religion as essentially a polemical treatment of the historical dimensions of faith is typified by Greene's introduction to the English translation; by C.C.J. Webb's Kant's Phi-

losophy of Religion (Oxford: Oxford University Press, 1926); and by a recent unpublished Yale University doctoral dissertation (1971) by G. Green, "Positive Religion in the Early Philosophy of the German Idealists."

5. A. Philonenko, L'Oeuvre de Kant II (Paris: Vrin, 1972), p. 223.

6. Cf. Y. Yovel, "Bible Interpretation as Philosophical Praxis: A Study of Spinoza and Kant," Journal of the History of Philosophy XI (April, 1973), pp. 194-5.

7. Kant to Friedrich Wilhelm II, after October 12, 1794, in Philosophical Correspondence, ed. A. Zweig (Chicago: University of Chicago Press, 1967), pp. 219-20. Hereafter referred to as Correspondence.

8. This view is expressed most forcefully by Ernst Troeltsch in his long essay, "Das Historische in Kants Religionsphilosophie," Kant-Studien Vol. 9 (1904), pp. 21-154.

9. E.g., in his letter to C.F. Stäudlin of May 4, 1793, Correspondence, p. 205.

10. Cf. J.L. Bruch, La Philosophie Religieuse de Kant (Paris: Aubier, 1968), p. 17; Despland, op. cit., p. 105.

11. Despland, op. cit., pp. 105-7.

12. Correspondence, p. 54.

13. J. Collins, The Emergence of Philosophy of Religion (New Haven: Yale University Press, 1967), p. 156.

14. Correspondence, p. 205.

15. M.L. Diamond, Contemporary Philosophy and Religious Thought (New York: McGraw Hill, 1974): revelation "involves a momentous self-disclosure of what could not be learned in any other way," p. 10, my emphasis.

16. H.W. Frei, The Eclipse of Biblical Narrative (New Haven: Yale University Press, 1974), pp. 52ff.

17. E. Cassirer, The Philosophy of the Enlightenment (Princeton: Princeton University Press, 1951), p. 167; G.R. Cragg, Reason and Authority in the Eighteenth Century (Cambridge: Cambridge University Press, 1964), pp. 78ff., 97; Cragg, Freedom and Authority: A Study of English Thought in the Early Seventeenth Century (Philadelphia: Westminster Press, 1975), Ch. IX.

18. Cassirer, op. cit., p. 159.

19. Ibid.

20. Collins, op. cit., pp. 155-6.

21. Bruch, op. cit., p. 13.

22. Though Kant maintains that the reader need not be familiar with the rest of his system in order to understand Religion (p. 12).

23. These same themes--plus an explicit reference to
Christianity--are echoed in Kant's letter to C.F.
Stäudlin of May 4, 1793: "In this book [i.e., Religion]
I have proceeded conscientiously and with genuine respect for the Christian religion but also with a befit-
ting candor, concealing nothing but rather presenting
openly the way in which I believe that a possible union
of Christianity with the purest practical reason is
possible," Correspondence, p. 205.
   24. Collins, op. cit., pp. 92ff.
   25. Ibid., pp. 94-5.
   26. Ibid., pp. 164-5.
   27. Strictly speaking, there is no such thing as an
historical "religion" for Kant, but only an historical
"faith." But, keeping in mind the sense of Kant's "one
true religion"--which I shall examine momentarily--the
terms historical faith and historical religion will be
used interchangeably, insofar as they both connote an
historical, rather than purely rational, point of religious reference.
   28. Cf. e.g., the Critique of Pure Reason, tr. N.
Kemp Smith (New York: St. Martin's Press, 1965),
A 836-37=B 864-65, pp. 655-7.
   29. Cf. Kierkegaard, Concluding Unscientific Postscript, tr. D. Swenson (Princeton: Princeton University
Press, 1941), pp. 42-3.
   30. Vorlesungen, op. cit., p. 1117; cf. also A. Wood,
Kant's Moral Religion (Ithaca: Cornell University Press,
1969), p. 205.
   31. Vorlesungen, op. cit., p. 1117.
   32. Cf. Collins, op. cit., Ch. 4.
   33. Cf. Bruch, op. cit., pp. 174ff.
   34. It is this issue which is the central concern of
Despland's recent work on Kant's religious thought.
Despland argues that Kant intends the latter of these
two possibilities. His interpretation, and the problems surrounding it, will be taken up in the next chapter. A major point of difference between Despland's
approach and my own is Despland's almost total lack of
attention devoted to the epistemological roots of Kant's
theory of historical religion.

CHAPTER III

   1. Religion within the Limits of Reason Alone, tr.
T.M. Greene and H.H. Hudson (New York: Harper Torchbook,

1960), p. 100. Hereafter cited as Religion, and all references to this work will appear within parentheses in my text.

2. H.W. Frei, The Eclipse of Biblical Narrative (New Haven: Yale University Press, 1974), p. 263. Frei helpfully places Kant in the context of modern hermeneutical theory, an original angle of vision which has generally been ignored by students of Kant.

3. One can easily imagine what Kant's reaction to the following century's "quest of the historical Jesus" would have been.

4. Y. Yovel, "Bible Interpretation as Philosophical Praxis: A Study of Spinoza and Kant," Journal of the History of Philosophy XI (April, 1973), p. 191.

5. Ibid., p. 193.

6. Frei, op. cit., p. 262.

7. Cf. J. Collins, The Emergence of Philosophy of Religion (New Haven: Yale University Press, 1967), pp. 121-4; M. Despland, Kant on History and Religion (Montreal: McGill-Queen's University Press, 1973), pp. 148-53.

8. Cf. Frei, op. cit., pp. 262ff., 340, n.21.

9. Despland, op. cit., p. 200.

10. This essay has been translated by Despland and included as an appendix to his recent book. Cf. ibid., pp. 283-97, esp. pp. 291-3.

11. Ibid., p. 292.

12. Ibid., pp. 292-3.

13. Ibid., p. 293.

14. Ibid.

15. For more on Kant's view of Job, cf. Collins, op. cit., pp. 207ff.

16. This essay is in the collection of Kant's essays entitled On History, L.W. Beck (ed.) (New York: Bobbs-Merrill Library of Liberal Arts, 1963), pp. 53-68.

17. On this problem, cf. E. Fackenheim, "Kant's Concept of History," Kant-Studien, Band 48 (1956-57), pp. 386ff.

18. "Conjectural Beginning of Human History," in On History, op. cit., p. 54.

19. Ibid.

20. Miracles are "events in the world the operating laws of whose causes are, and must remain, absolutely unknown to us," (p. 81).

21. Despland's alternative view of Kant's Jesus will be examined in the third section of this chapter.

22. Der Streit der Fakultäten (Hamburg: Felix Meiner, 1959).

23. Protestant Thought from Rousseau to Ritschl, tr. B. Cozens (New York: Simon and Schuster, 1969), p. 162.

24. E.g., Streit, op. cit., pp. 33-44.

25. Barth, op. cit., pp. 194-5.

26. Collins, op. cit., p. 166.

27. Frei, op. cit., p. 263.

28. Kant, Prolegomena to Any Future Metaphysics, ed. L.W. Beck (New York: Bobbs-Merrill, 1950), p. 63.

29. W.H. Walsh, "Schematism," in R.P. Wolff (ed.), Kant: A Collection of Critical Essays (Garden City, N.Y.: Doubleday Anchor Books, 1967), p. 71.

30. Critique of Pure Reason, tr. Kemp Smith (New York: St. Martin's Press, 1965), A 137-47=B 176-87, pp. 180-7. Hereafter referred to as Pure.

31. This correction in the manner of referring to the sort of judgment Kant is justifying in the Critique has been proposed recently by R.P. Wolff in his editor's introduction to Kant's Foundations of the Metaphysics of Morals (New York: Bobbs-Merrill, 1969), p. ix (note): Kant "never actually speaks of 'synthetic a priori judgments.' He speaks only of 'synthetic judgments a priori,' and this is merely an elliptical way of saying 'synthetic judgments known a priori.'"

32. For a recent criticism of the traditional understanding of Kant's concepts as "rules," cf. R. Rorty, "Strawson's Objectivity Argument," Review of Metaphysics XXIV (1970), p. 237n.

33. This notion of an "intelligible conception of experience" is what P.F. Strawson takes to be the central problem of the Critique. Cf. Strawson, The Bounds of Sense (London: Metheun, 1966), p. 44.

34. Cf. esp. Pure, B 137-39, pp. 156-7.

35. Ibid., B 137-38, p. 156.

36. Ibid., B 157, p. 168.

37. Strawson, op. cit., p. 24.

38. For an interesting critical discussion of Kant's strategy at this point, cf. J. Bennett, Kant's Analytic (Cambridge: Cambridge University Press, 1966), pp. 130-4.

39. Walsh, op. cit., p. 79.

40. Pure, A 138=B 177, p. 180.

41. Ibid., A 138=B 177, p. 181.

42. Walsh, op. cit., p. 75; S. Körner, Kant (Baltimore: Penguin Books, 1955), p. 71.

43. Pure, A 146=B 185, p. 186.

44. Ibid., A 140=B 180, p. 182; cf. Bennett, op. cit., p. 141.

45. On this issue, cf. the unpublished Princeton

University (1972) dissertation by Edward Langerak,
"Orienting Oneself Rationally: Kant's Constructive
Philosophy of Religion," pp. 23ff.

46. Pure, A 140=B 179, p. 182.
47. Walsh, op. cit., p. 82.
48. Bennett, op. cit., p. 141.
49. Körner, op. cit., p. 72.
50. Pure, A 139=B 178, p. 181; A 145=B 184, p. 185.
51. For criticisms, cf. Walsh, op. cit., pp. 86-7;
N. Kemp Smith, A Commentary to Kant's Critique of Pure
Reason 2nd edition (New York: Humanities Press, 1962),
p. 341.
52. Pure, A 141-42=B 181, p. 183.
53. Bennett, op. cit., p. 142.
54. Walsh, op. cit., p. 76.
55. Bennett, op. cit., p. 148.
56. Pure, A 137-38=B 176-77, p. 180, my emphasis.
57. Ibid., A 141=B 180, pp. 182-3; for discussions
of this discrepancy, cf. Bennett, op. cit., pp. 148ff.;
Walsh, op. cit., pp. 75-6.
58. Kemp Smith, op. cit., pp. 334ff.
59. Ibid., pp. 334-5.
60. Ibid., p. 335.
61. Ibid., pp. 339-40.
62. Ibid., p. 335.
63. Ibid.
64. Ibid., p. 336.
65. G.J. Warnock, "Concepts and Schematism," Analysis
IX (1949), pp. 77-82.
66. Ibid., p. 80.
67. Ibid., p. 82; Bennett offers a similar criticism,
op. cit., pp. 143-8.
68. M.S. Gram, Kant, Ontology, and the A Priori
(Evanston: Northwestern University Press, 1968), pp.
91-106; Walsh makes a distinction similar to that existing between Gram's (1) and (2) by speaking of the "stat-
ic" and the "dynamic" forms of Kant's theory, op. cit.,
p. 77.
69. Collins, op. cit., p. 411.
70. N. Rotenstreich, Experience and its Systematization 2nd edition (The Hague: Martinus Nijhoff, 1972),
p. 34.
71. Kant, Critique of Practical Reason, tr. L.W.
Beck (New York: Bobbs-Merrill, 1956), p. 71.
72. Ibid.
73. Rotenstreich, op. cit., p. 35.
74. H.J. Paton, The Categorical Imperative (Philadelphia: University of Pennsylvania Press, 1971), pp.

158-9.

75. L.W. Beck, A Commentary on Kant's Critique of Practical Reason (Chicago: University of Chicago Press, 1960), p. 156.

76. Walsh, op. cit., p. 83.

77. Strictly speaking, the theory of schematism in the first Critique has as its analogue in the second Critique Kant's theory of "types." This term refers to the "types" of the moral law which mediate between nature (what is) and morality (what ought to be), and thus--like the schema itself--serve as a mediating "third thing." Cf. Kant, Critique of Practical Reason, op. cit., pp. 72ff.; Beck, op. cit., pp. 154ff.

78. Kant, Critique of Judgment, tr. J.H. Bernard (New York: Hafner, 1972), p. 197, my emphasis.

79. Ibid., p. 198.

80. Walsh, op. cit., pp. 84-5.

81. Collins, op. cit., p. 411.

82. Kant, Critique of Judgment, op. cit., p. 198.

83. Collins, op. cit., pp. 164, 412.

84. On this terminology, see ibid., pp. 161ff.; Despland, op. cit., pp. 119, 127.

85. Collins, op. cit., p. 163.

86. T.M. Greene, "Editor's Introduction," Religion, pp. li, lxxv.

87. It is with regard to this sort of soteriological necessity that Kant proposes his antinomy in Book III of Religion (pp. 107ff.). The real theme of this antinomy is not historical faith as a "vehicle"; rather, it is the problem of divine grace and atonement, an issue Kant obviously has to confront, given his aversion to all forms of moral and religious heteronomy. Although I am not concerned in this inquiry with Kant's view of grace, it is important to emphasize the difficulties this doctrine poses for him once he embraces simultaneously the doctrines of moral autonomy and radical evil. For more on this issue, cf. G. Green, "Positive Religion in the Early Philosophy of the German Idealists," unpublished Yale University Ph.D. dissertation (1971), esp. p. 110.

88. J. Bohatec, Die Religionsphilosophie Kants in der 'Religion innerhalb der Grenzen der blossen Vernunft' (Hildesheim: Georg Olms, 1966), p. 636; cited by Despland, op. cit., p. 221. Friedrich Paulsen has suggested that whenever Kant "expresses himself directly in his own personal thinking, as in lectures and lecture-notes, we find everywhere the pure Platonist." Cf. Paulsen, Immanuel Kant: His Life and Doctrine (New

York: Frederick Ungar, 1963), p. xiii.

89. Beck, A Commentary on Kant's Critique of Practical Reason, op. cit., p. 233.

90. For a helpful clarification of the way Kant's discussion of radical evil in Religion marks a significant advance in his thinking (by way of justifying the very possibility of evil--a possibility which seemed logically impossible on the basis of Kant's earlier writings), cf. E. Frackenheim, "Kant and Radical Evil," University of Toronto Quarterly 23 (1953-54), pp. 339-52.

91. Kant, Foundations of the Metaphysics of Morals, tr. L.W. Beck (New York: Bobbs-Merrill, Library of Liberal Arts, 1959), pp. 51ff.

92. J. L. Bruch, La Philosophie Religieuse de Kant (Paris: Aubier, 1968), p. 166.

93. Ibid., p. 157.

94. This essay is contained in the collection of Kant's essays entitled On History, op. cit., pp. 11-26.

95. At points like this--i.e., concerning the theme of man-in-community--it is worth recalling the profound influence which Rousseau had on Kant. Cf. Bruch, op. cit., p. 161n.; E.P. Van de Pitte, Kant as Philosophical Anthropologist (The Hague: Martinus Nijhoff, 1971), pp. 49-69.

96. E.g., cf. the tortured discussion of this in Religion, pp. 107ff.

97. Cf. Bultmann, "The Historicity of Man and Faith" in Existence and Faith, ed. S. Ogden (Cleveland: World Publishing Co., 1960), pp. 92-110, esp. pp. 107-10; Ogden, Christ without Myth (New York: Harper and Row, 1961), esp. pp. 146-64.

98. T.C. Oden, "The Alleged Structural Inconsistency in Bultmann," Journal of Religion 44 (July, 1964), p. 198.

99. Despland, op. cit., pp. 159-60.

100. Ibid., pp. 222, 198-9, my emphasis.

101. Ibid., p. 330, n.91.

102. Ibid., pp. 198-202.

103. Ibid., p. 222.

104. Ibid., pp. 223, 232.

105. A revealing passage from an earlier chapter of Despland's book is the following: "I believe...that following the examples of post-Kantians such as Dilthey and Troeltsch, as Raymond Aron did, for instance, a full contemporary philosophy of history can be developed on an ultimately Kantian basis." Ibid., p. 83. The fact that certain details of Despland's work may prove unsatisfactory should not obscure the fact that the work

as a whole is clearly the most comprehensive and historically informed work on Kant's religious thought in
English.

106. Kant's own awareness of this issue is evident in
his claim that we can have a history of ecclesiastical
faith but not a universal history of religion, "for,
since [religion] is based upon pure moral faith, it has
no public status," (p. 115).

107. Cf. esp. pp. 40-9, 60-72. For a clear statement
of the two "trajectories"--personal and social--in
Kant's philosophy of religion, cf. Bruch, op. cit.,
p. 219.

108. Critique of Practical Reason, op. cit., p. 33.

109. J.L. Bruch suggests that, in his view of conversion, Kant intentionally draws upon the Pauline motif
of a "new birth" in order to minimize the problem posed
by temporality. Cf. Bruch, op. cit., p. 80.

110. On the problem of having freedom "appear," cf.
Fackenheim, "Kant's Concept of History," op. cit.,
pp. 389ff.; Collins, op. cit., pp. 198ff.

111. The same conclusion is reached by G. Green with
regard to the element of grace implicit in the Kantian
concept of "positive" religion. Cf. Green, op. cit.,
p. 110.

Chapter IV

1. Kant, Religion within the Limits of Reason
Alone, tr. T.M. Greene and H. Hudson (New York: Harper
Torchbook, 1960), p. 106. Hereafter referred to as
Religion.

2. Yovel, "The God of Kant," Scripta Hierosoly-
mitana XX (Jerusalem: Magnes Press, 1968), pp. 88-123;
"The Highest Good and History in Kant's Thought,"
Archiv für Geschichte der Philosophie 54, Heft 3 (1972),
pp. 238-83. Hereafter referred to as "The Highest
Good..."

3. Yovel, "The Highest Good...," p. 239.

4. Yovel, "The God of Kant," op. cit., p. 89.

5. E.g., cf. L.W. Beck, "Editor's Introduction,"
Kant on History (New York: Bobbs-Merrill, Library of
Liberal Arts, 1963), pp. vii-xxviii; J.L. Bruch, La
Philosophie Religieuse de Kant (Paris: Aubier, 1968),
Ch. VIII; M. Despland, Kant on History and Religion
(Montreal: McGill-Queen's University Press, 1973);
E. Fackenheim, "Kant's Concept of History," Kant-Studien

XLVII (1957), pp. 381-98; K. Weyand, Kants Geschichts-philosophie: Ihre Entwicklung und ihr Verhältnis zur Aufklärung (Köln: Kölnuniversitäts-Verlag, 1964); B.T. Wilkens, "Teleology in Kant's Philosophy of History," History and Theory V (1966), pp. 172-85.

6. Kant's basic writings on history have been collected in Beck (ed.), Kant on History, op. cit.

7. Cf. Weyand, op. cit., pp. 19-20.

8. Ibid., pp. 29-31.

9. Cf. L.W. Beck, "Neo-Kantianism," Encyclopedia of Philosophy Vol. V, ed. P. Edwards (New York: Macmillan, 1967), pp. 468-73; E. Cassirer, The Problem of Knowledge, tr. W.W. Woglom and C.W. Hendel (New Haven: Yale University Press, 1950), Part III; H.S. Hughes, Consciousness and Society (New York: Vintage Books, 1958), Ch. 6; R.A. Makkreel, "Wilhelm Dilthey and the Neo-Kantians: The Distinction of the Geisteswissenschaften and the Kulturwissenschaften," Journal of the History of Philosophy VII (1969), pp. 423-40.

10. In Kant on History, op. cit., pp. 3-10.

11. Ibid., pp. 11-26. Hereafter referred to as "Idea."

12. Ibid., pp. 27-52.

13. Ibid., p. 45.

14. Ibid., pp. 53-68.

15. Tr. E.B. Ashton (Philadelphia: University of Pennsylvania Press, 1974).

16. In Kant on History, op. cit., pp. 69-84.

17. Ibid., pp. 85-136.

18. A translation of this section of Streit is in ibid., pp. 137-54.

19. Philosophical Correspondence, op. cit., p. 252.

20. W.H. Walsh, Philosophy of History (New York: Harper Torchbook, 1967), p. 128.

21. "Idea," p. 25.

22. Critique of Judgment, tr. J.H. Bernard (New York: Hafner, 1972), esp. Sections 83-4, pp. 279-86.

23. Fackenheim, op. cit., p. 389.

24. "Idea," p. 13.

25. Ibid., p. 20. For a discussion of the way in which Kant's notion of a "hidden plan of Nature" anticipates certain developments in Hegel and Marx, cf. L. Goldmann, Immanuel Kant (London: NLB, 1971), pp. 218ff.

26. Critique of Judgment, op. cit., p. 275.

27. Kant, Foundations of the Metaphysics of Morals, tr. L.W. Beck (New York: Bobbs-Merrill, Library of Liberal Arts, 1959), pp. 11ff. Hereafter referred to

as Foundations.

28. R.G. Collingwood, The Idea of History, ed. T.M. Knox (New York: Oxford University Press, 1957), p. 98.

29. "Idea," p. 12.

30. Ibid., my emphasis.

31. Wilkens, op. cit., pp. 182-3.

32. Cf. Fackenheim, op. cit., on the problem of the relation between the natural and moral realms, esp. pp. 384ff.

33. "Idea," p. 12.

34. Thesis Two: "In man (as the only rational creature on earth) those natural capacities which are directed to the use of his reason are to be fully developed in the race, not in the individual," ibid., p. 13.

Thesis Three: "Nature has willed that man should, by himself, produce everything that goes beyond the mechanical ordering of his animal existence, and that he should partake of no other happiness or perfection than that which he himself, independently of instinct, has created by his own reason," ibid.

Thesis Four: "The means employed by Nature to bring about the development of all the capacities of men is their antagonism in society, so far as this is, in the end, the cause of a lawful order among men," ibid., p. 15.

35. Despland, op. cit., p. 22.

36. Thesis Five: "The greatest problem for the human race, to the solution of which Nature drives man, is the achievement of a universal civic society which administers law among men," "Idea," p. 16.

Thesis Six: "This problem is the most difficult and the last to be solved by mankind," ibid., p. 17.

Thesis Seven: "The problem of establishing a perfect civic constitution is dependent upon the problem of a lawful external relation among states and cannot be solved without a solution of the latter problem," ibid., p. 18.

37. Ibid., p. 15.

38. As I pointed out in the last section of the previous chapter, the doctrine of "unsocial sociability" is explicitly operative in Kant's account--in Religion--of the visible church.

39. Religion, pp. 87ff.

40. Foundations, pp. 50-2.

41. Ibid., p. 59.

42. Cf. L.W. Beck, A Commentary on Kant's Critique of Practical Reason (Chicago: University of Chicago

Press, 1961), pp. 14, 177, 181. Hereafter referred to as Beck, Commentary. This distinction between two types of freedom is what underlies John Silber's discussion of Wille and Willkür in his essay, "The Ethical Significance of Kant's Religion," Religion, pp. lxxix-cxxic, esp. pp. xciv-cvi.

43. Kant's Weltanschauung, tr. J.E. Smith (Chicago: University of Chicago Press, 1956), pp. 6-11.

44. Foundations, pp. 51-9.

45. Ibid., p. 52.

46. This parallel is perhaps what Beck means by the "practical translation of a natural law," Commentary, p. 179.

47. Religion, p. 87.

48. "An Old Question Raised Again: Is the Human Race Constantly Progressing?," in Kant on History, op. cit., pp. 137-54, esp. p. 151.

49. Ibid., p. 150.

50. Ibid., p. 153.

51. Despland, op. cit., pp. 275-7.

52. "Idea," p. 16.

53. Ibid., p. 23.

54. Ibid., p. 22.

55. Ibid., p. 14.

56. Ibid., p. 21.

57. Ibid., p. 23.

58. Ibid., p. 25.

59. Ibid., p. 24.

60. Ibid.

61. Cf. Beck, "Introduction," Kant on History, op. cit., pp. xixff.; Fackenheim, op. cit., pp. 392ff.

62. "Idea," p. 24.

63. Cf. G. Schrader, "The Status of Teleological Judgment in the Critical Philosophy," Kant-Studien 45 (1953-54), pp. 204-35.

64. N. Kemp Smith, A Commentary to Kant's Critique of Pure Reason 2nd ed. (New York: Humanities Press, 1962), p. 452.

65. Critique of Pure Reason, tr. N. Kemp Smith (New York: St. Martin's Press, 1965), B 692, p. 546. Hereafter referred to as Pure. For a detailed discussion of Kant's view of reason's drive toward unity and totality, cf. N. Rotenstreich, Experience and its Systematization 2nd ed. (The Hague: Martinus Nijhoff, 1972), pp. 53-5, 60-3.

66. Pure, B 385, p. 320.

67. Ibid., B 692, p. 546.

68. Ibid., B 354-55, pp. 299-300.

69. Ibid., B 383-84, pp. 318-9.
70. Ibid., B 384, p. 319.
71. Ibid., B 672, p. 533.
72. Ibid.
73. This characterization has been suggested by Richard Rorty, of Princeton University.
74. T.D. Weldon, Kant's Critique of Pure Reason 2nd ed. (Oxford: Clarendon Press, 1958), pp. 73, 75-6.
75. Pure, B 676, pp. 535-6. For a good discussion of the way Kant can hold that the ideas of reason are (1) heuristic fictions yet (2) epistemologically useful in a genuinely positive way, cf. J.E. Dister, "Kant's Regulative Ideas and the 'Objectivity' of Reason," in L.W. Beck (ed.), Proceedings of the Third International Kant Congress (Dordrecht: D. Reidel, 1972), pp. 262-9.
76. Religion, p. 65n.
77. J.D. McFarland, Kant's Concept of Teleology (Edinburgh: Edinburgh University Press, 1970), pp. 84ff.
78. Ibid., p. 86.
79. Critique of Judgment, op. cit., Section 87, pp. 298ff.
80. It is worth recalling the respect with which Kant spoke of the teleological proof in the first Critique (just before he demolished it): "This proof always deserves to be mentioned with respect. It is the oldest, the clearest, and the most accordant with the common reason of mankind." Pure, A 623=B 651, p. 520.
81. Weyand, op. cit., p. 185.
82. J. Collins, The Emergence of Philosophy of Religion (New Haven: Yale University Press, 1967), p. 203.
83. F.P. Van de Pitte, Kant as Philosophical Anthropologist (The Hague: Martinus Nijhoff, 1971), p. 106.
84. Weyand, op. cit., pp. 183-5.
85. "The God of Kant," op. cit.; "The Highest Good...," op. cit.
86. "The Highest Good...," pp. 239-43.
87. Ibid., pp. 273-4.
88. Critique of Practical Reason, tr. L.W. Beck (New York: Bobbs-Merrill, Library of Liberal Arts, 1956), pp. 111ff. Hereafter referred to as Practical.
89. "The God of Kant," p. 89.
90. Practical, p. 151.
91. "The Importance of the Highest Good in Kant's Ethics," Ethics LXXIII (1963), p. 179.
92. Ibid., p. 180.
93. "The God of Kant," p. 88.
94. "The Highest Good...," p. 242.

95. Religion, p. 5; cited by Yovel, "The Highest Good...," p. 242.

96. "The Highest Good...," p. 243.

97. On this "need of pure reason," cf. esp. Religion, pp. 4-5. The need of reason is what implicitly grounds Kant's postulates in the second Critique. Cf. Beck, Commentary, pp. 251-5.

98. "The Highest Good...," p. 243.

99. Ibid., pp. 242-3.

100. Ibid., p. 244.

101. Ibid., pp. 244-5.

·102. Ibid., pp. 254-6.

103. Ibid., pp. 273-81.

104. Religion, pp. 4-5.

105. Ibid., p. 4.

106. Ibid.

107. Ibid.

108. Ibid., pp. 4-5.

109. Ibid., p. 5.

110. Ibid.

111. "The God of Kant," pp. 108-9.

112. Ibid., p. 108.

113. Ibid., pp. 99-105.

114. Ibid., pp. 101-2.

115. "The God of Kant," p. 103.

116. Weizenmann, quoted by Yovel in ibid., p. 111.

117. Ibid., p. 112.

118. Ibid., p. 119.

119. "The Highest Good...," p. 282.

120. Ibid., pp. 273-4.

121. Ibid., p. 269.

122. Ibid., pp. 273-81.

123. "The God of Kant," pp. 121-3.

124. Pure, A 620-30=B 648-58, pp. 518-24.

125. "The God of Kant," pp. 122-3.

126. "The Highest Good...," p. 275.

127. Ibid.

128. Ibid., p. 241.

129. Ibid., pp. 276-7.

130. Practical, pp. 150-1.

131. Beck, Commentary, p. 244.

132. Practical, p. 151.

133. "Kant's Conception of the Highest Good as Immanent and Transcendent," Philosophical Review LXVIII (1959), pp. 475-9.

134. Ibid., p. 478.

135. "The Highest Good as Content for Kant's Ethical Formalism," Kant-Studien 56 (1965), pp. 102-10. The

autonomy-heteronomy issue is most succinctly summarized by Kant in _Practical_, pp. 33-4.

136. "The Highest Good...," p. 269.
137. Murphy, op. cit., p. 107.
138. Ibid., pp. 107-8.
139. "The Highest Good...," p. 242.
140. Ibid., pp. 242-3.
141. Ibid., p. 243.
142. I am aided at this point again by J. Murphy's article on the highest good.
143. Murphy, op. cit., p. 106.
144. _Practical_, pp. 34-5; cited by Murphy, op. cit., p. 106, n.22.
145. "The Highest Good...," p. 245.
146. Beck, _Commentary_, p. 142.
147. _Practical_, p. 113.
148. Ibid., p. 126.
149. _Religion_, p. 5, my emphasis.
150. "The Highest Good...," p. 249.
151. For a defense of the material as well as the formal importance of the categorical imperative, cf. Murphy, op. cit., p. 110.
152. Beck, _Commentary_, p. 245.
153. "The Highest Good...," p. 271.
154. On this, cf. Murphy, op. cit., pp. 109-10.
155. _Pure_, A 298=B 354, p. 300.
156. Collins, op. cit., p. 410.
157. _Religion_, p. 144.

SELECTED BIBLIOGRAPHY

Works by Kant

Anthropology from a Pragmatic Point of View. Translated by M.J. Gregor. Atlantic Highlands, New Jersey: Humanities Press, 1974.

Critique of Judgment. Translated by J.H. Bernard. New York: Hafner Publishing Company, 1972.

Critique of Practical Reason. Translated by L.W. Beck. New York: The Bobbs-Merrill Company, Library of Liberal Arts, 1956.

Critique of Pure Reason. Translated by N. Kemp Smith. New York: St. Martin's Press, 1965.

Der Streit der Fakultäten. Hamburg: Felix Meiner, 1959.

The Doctrine of Virtue: Part II of the Metaphysics of Morals. Translated by M.J. Gregor. New York: Harper and Row, Harper Torchbook, 1964.

First Introduction to the Critique of Judgment. Translated by James Haden. New York: The Bobbs-Merrill Company, Library of Liberal Arts, 1965.

Foundations of the Metaphysics of Morals. Translated by L.W. Beck. New York: The Bobbs-Merrill Company, Library of Liberal Arts, 1959.

Lectures on Ethics. Translated by L. Infield. New York: Harper and Row, Harper Torchbook, 1963.

The Metaphysical Elements of Justice: Part I of the Metaphysics of Morals. Translated by J. Ladd. New York: The Bobbs-Merrill Company, Library of Liberal Arts, 1965.

Metaphysical Foundations of Natural Science. Translated by J. Ellington. New York: The Bobbs-Merrill Company, Library of Liberal Arts, 1970.

Observations on the Feeling of the Beautiful and Sublime. Translated by J.T. Goldthwait. Los Angeles: University of California Press, 1965.

211

On History. Edited by L.W. Beck. Translated by L.W.
 Beck, R.E. Anchor, and E.L. Fackenheim. New York:
 The Bobbs-Merrill Company, Library of Liberal Arts,
 1963.
On the Old Saw: That May Be Right in Theory but It
 Won't Work in Practice. Translated by E.B. Ashton.
 Philadelphia: University of Pennsylvania Press,
 1974.
Philosophical Correspondence, 1759-99. Edited and
 translated by A. Zweig. Chicago: University of
 Chicago Press, 1967.
Prolegomena to Any Future Metaphysics. Edited by L.W.
 Beck. Translated by P. Carus. New York: The
 Bobbs-Merrill Company, Library of Liberal Arts,
 1950.
Religion within the Limits of Reason Alone. Translated
 by T.M. Greene and H.H. Hudson. New York: Harper
 and Row, Harper Torchbook, 1960.
Vorlesungen über philosophische Religionslehre, Volume
 28 of Kant's Werke. Akademie Edition. Berlin:
 de Gruyter, 1972.

                    Secondary Works--Books

Allison, H.E. Lessing and the Enlightenment. Ann
 Arbor: University of Michigan Press, 1966.
Baillie, J. The Idea of Revelation in Recent Thought.
 New York: Harper and Row, 1956.
Barth, K. Protestant Thought from Rousseau to Ritschl.
 New York: Simon and Schuster, 1969.
Beck, L.W. A Commentary on Kant's Critique of Practi-
 cal Reason. Chicago: University of Chicago Press,
 1960.
_____. Early German Philosophy: Kant and His Pred-
 ecessors. Cambridge, Mass.: Harvard University
 Press, 1969.
_____, ed. Kant Studies Today. La Salle: Open
 Court Press, 1969.
_____, ed. Proceedings of the Third International
 Kant Congress. Dordrecht: D. Reidel Company, 1972.
_____. Studies in the Philosophy of Kant. New
 York: The Bobbs-Merrill Company, 1965.
Bennett, J. Kant's Analytic. Cambridge: Cambridge
 University Press, 1966.
_____. Kant's Dialectic. Cambridge: Cambridge
 University Press, 1974.

Bird, G. Kant's Theory of Knowledge. New York: The Humanities Press, 1962.

Bohatec, J. Die Religionsphilosophie Kants in der 'Religion innerhalb der Grenzen der blossen Vernunft.' Hildesheim: Georg Olms, 1966.

Bouwsma, O.K. Philosophical Essays. Lincoln: University of Nebraska Press, 1969.

Bruch, J.L. La Philosophie Religieuse de Kant. Editions Montaigne. Paris: Aubier, 1968.

Buchdal, G. Metaphysics and the Philosophy of Science: The Classical Origins. Cambridge, Mass.: MIT Press, 1969.

Cassirer, E. The Philosophy of the Enlightenment. Princeton: Princeton University Press, 1951.

_____. The Problem of Knowledge. Translated by W.W. Woglom and C.W. Hendel. New Haven: Yale University Press, 1950.

_____. Rousseau, Kant, and Goethe. Princeton: Princeton University Press, 1970.

Cassirer, H.W. A Commentary on Kant's Critique of Judgment. London: Metheun and Company, 1938.

Charlesworth, M.J. Philosophy of Religion: The Historic Approaches. London: The Macmillan Press, 1972.

Collingwood, R.G. An Autobiography. Oxford: Oxford University Press, 1970.

_____. The Idea of History. Edited by T.M. Knox. New York: Oxford University Press, Galaxy Book, 1957.

Collins, James. The Emergence of Philosophy of Religion. New Haven: Yale University Press, 1967.

_____. Interpreting Modern Philosophy. Princeton: Princeton University Press, 1972.

Copleston, F. A History of Philosophy. Volume 6, Part II. New York: Doubleday and Company, 1960.

Cragg, G.R. Freedom and Authority: A Study of English Thought in the Early Seventeenth Century. Philadelphia: Westminster Press, 1975.

_____. Reason and Authority in the Eighteenth Century. Cambridge: Cambridge University Press, 1964.

Despland, M. Kant on History and Religion. Montreal: McGill-Queen's University Press, 1973.

De Vleeschauwer, H.J. The Development of Kantian Thought. Translated by A.R.C. Duncan. London: Thomas Nelson and Sons, 1962.

Diamond, M.L. Contemporary Philosophy and Religious Thought. New York: McGraw Hill, 1974.

Duncan, A.R.C. Practical Reason and Morality. London:
Thomas Nelson and Sons, 1962.
Fain, H. Between Philosophy and History. Princeton:
Princeton University Press, 1970.
Frei, H.W. The Eclipse of Biblical Narrative. New
Haven: Yale University Press, 1974.
Galston, W. Kant and the Problem of History. Chicago:
University of Chicago Press, 1975.
Gay, P. The Enlightenment: An Interpretation. Two
Volumes. New York: Alfred A. Knopf, 1966, 1969.
Gill, J.H. The Possibility of Religious Knowledge.
· Grand Rapids: Eerdmans, 1971.
Gram, M.S., ed. Kant: Disputed Questions. Chicago:
Quadrangle Books, 1967.
_____. Kant, Ontology, and the A Priori. Evanston:
Northwestern University Press, 1968.
Hartnack, Justus. Kant's Theory of Knowledge. New
York: Harcourt, Brace and World, 1967.
Harvey, V.A. The Historian and the Believer. New York:
Macmillan, 1966.
Hazard, P. The European Mind: 1680-1715. New York:
The New American Library, Meridian Book, 1963.
Heidegger, M. Kant and the Problem of Metaphysics.
Translated by J.S. Churchill. Bloomington: Univer-
sity of Indiana Press, 1962.
_____. What Is a Thing? Translated by W.B.
Barton, Jr. and V. Deutsch. Chicago: University of
Chicago Press, 1967.
Hughes, H.S. Consciousness and Society. New York:
Vintage Books, 1958.
Jaspers, Karl. Kant. Translated by R. Mannheim. New
York: Harcourt, Brace and World, 1962.
Jones, W.T. Morality and Freedom in the Philosophy of
Immanuel Kant. Oxford: Oxford University Press,
1940.
Kelly, G.A. Idealism, Politics, and History: Sources
of Hegelian Thought. Cambridge: Cambridge Univer-
sity Press, 1969.
Kierkegaard, Soren. Concluding Unscientific Postscript.
Translated by D.F. Swenson and W. Lowrie. Prince-
ton: Princeton University Press, 1941.
_____. Philosophical Fragments. Trans-
lated by D. Swenson and H.V. Hong. Princeton:
Princeton University Press, 1962.
Körner, S. Kant. Baltimore: Penguin Books, 1955.
Kroner, R. Kant's Weltanschauung. Translated by J.E.
Smith. Chicago: University of Chicago Press, 1956.

Landgrebe, L. Major Problems in Contemporary European Philosophy. New York: Ungar, 1966.

Lessing, G. Lessing's Theological Writings. Edited and translated by H. Chadwick. Stanford: Stanford University Press, 1956.

Lieb, I.C., ed. Experience, Existence, and the Good: Essays in Honor of Paul Weiss. Carbondale: Southern Illinois University Press, 1961.

McFarland, J.D. Kant's Concept of Teleology. Edinburgh: University of Edinburgh Press, 1970.

Martin, G. Kant's Metaphysics and Theory of Science. Translated by P.G. Lucas. Manchester: Manchester University Press, 1955.

Murphy, J.G. Kant: The Philosophy of Right. New York: St. Martin's Press, 1970.

Ogden, S. Christ without Myth. New York: Harper and Row, 1961.

Paton, H.J. The Categorical Imperative. Philadelphia: University of Pennsylvania Press, 1971.

_____. Kant's Metaphysic of Experience. Two Volumes. New York: Macmillan, 1936.

Paulsen, F. Immanuel Kant: His Life and Doctrine. Translated by J.E. Creighton and A. Lefevre. New York: Ungar, 1963.

Pears, D. Wittgenstein. New York: Viking Press, 1970.

Penelhum, T., and MacIntosh, J.J., eds. The First Critique. Belmont: Wadsworth Publishing Company, 1969.

Philonenko, A. L'Oeuvre de Kant. Volume Two. Paris: Vrin, 1972.

Raschke, C.A. Moral Action, God, and History in the Thought of Immanuel Kant. Missoula, Montana: American Academy of Religion, Scholars Press, 1975.

Rotenstreich, N. Experience and Its Systematization. Second Edition. The Hague: Martinus Nijhoff, 1972.

Saner, H. Kant's Political Thought. Translated by E.B. Ashton. Chicago: University of Chicago Press, 1973.

Sellars, W. Science and Metaphysics. London: Rutledge and Kegan Paul, 1968.

_____. Science, Perception, and Reality. London: Routledge and Kegan Paul, 1963.

Sherover, C.M. Heidegger, Kant, and Time. Bloomington: Indiana University Press, 1971.

Smith, J.E. Reason and God. New Haven: Yale University Press, 1961.

215

Smith, N.K. A Commentary to Kant's 'Critique of Pure Reason.' Second Edition. New York: The Humanities Press, 1962.

Solomon, R. From Rationalism to Existentialism. New York: Harper and Row, 1972.

Strawson, P.F. The Bounds of Sense. London: Methuen and Company, 1966.

Tillich, P. Systematic Theology. Three Volumes. Chicago: University of Chicago Press, 1951-63.

Vaihinger, H. The Philosophy of 'As If:' A System of the Theoretical, Practical, and Religious Fictions of Mankind. Translated by C.K. Ogden. New York: Barnes and Noble, 1968.

Van de Pitte, F.P. Kant as Philosophical Anthropologist. The Hague: Martinus Nijhoff, 1971.

Walsh, W.H. Kant's Criticism of Metaphysics. Chicago: University of Chicago Press, 1975.

_____. Philosophy of History: An Introduction. Revised Edition. New York: Harper and Row, Harper Torchbook, 1967.

Webb, C.C.J. Kant's Philosophy of Religion. Oxford: Oxford University Press, 1926.

Welch, C. Protestant Thought in the Nineteenth Century. Volume One. New Haven: Yale University Press, 1972.

Weldon, T.D. Kant's Critique of Pure Reason. Second Edition. Oxford: Oxford University Press, 1958.

Weyand, K. Kants Geschichtsphilosophie: Ihre Entwicklung und ihr Verhältnis zur Aufklärung. Köln: Kölnuniversitäts-Verlag, 1964.

Willey, B. The Eighteenth Century Background. Boston: Beacon Press, 1961.

Wolff, R.P. The Autonomy of Reason. New York: Harper and Row, Harper Torchbook, 1973.

_____, ed. Kant: A Collection of Critical Essays. Garden City: Doubleday and Company, 1967.

_____, ed. Kant: Foundations of the Metaphysics of Morals: Texts and Critical Essays. New York: The Bobbs-Merrill Company, 1969.

_____. Kant's Theory of Mental Activity. Cambridge, Mass.: Harvard University Press, 1963.

Wood, A.W. Kant's Moral Religion. Ithaca: Cornell University Press, 1970.

216

Secondary Works--Articles

Allison, H.E. "Kant's Concept of the Transcendental Object." Kant-Studien 59 (1968), 165-86.
_____. "Transcendental Idealism and Descriptive Metaphysics." Kant-Studien 60 (1969), 216-33.

Aquila, R.E. "Categories, Schematism and Forms of Judgment." Ratio XVIII (1976), 31-49.

Chipman, L. "Kant's Categories and their Schematism." Kant-Studien 63 (1972), 36-50.

Ewing, A.C. "Kant's View of Immortality." Scottish Journal of Theology 17 (1964), 385-95.

Greene, T.M. "The Historical Context and Religious Significance of Kant's Religion." In Kant, Religion within the Limits of Reason Alone. Edited and translated by T.M. Greene and H.H. Hudson. New York: Harper and Row, Harper Torchbook, 1960, lx-lxxviii.

Fackenheim, E. "Kant and Radical Evil." University of Toronto Quarterly 23 (1953-54), 339-52.
_____. "Kant's Concept of History." Kant-Studien 48 (1956-57), 381-98.

Genova, A.C. "Kant's Three Critiques: A Suggested Analytical Framework." Kant-Studien 60 (1969), 135-46.

Kelly, G.A. "Rousseau, Kant, and History." Journal of the History of Ideas XXIX (1968), 347-64.

Makkreel, R.A. "Wilhelm Dilthey and the Neo-Kantians: The Distinction of the Geisteswissenschaften and the Kulturwissenschaften." Journal of the History of Philosophy VII (1969), 423-40.

Murphy, J. "The Highest Good as Content for Kant's Ethical Formalism." Kant-Studien 56 (1965), 102-11.

Rorty, R. "Strawson's Objectivity Argument." Review of Metaphysics XXIV (1970), 207-44.

Sherover, C.M. "Heidegger's Ontology and the Copernican Revolution." The Monist LI (1967), 559-73.
_____. "Kant's Transcendental Object and Heidegger's Nichts." Journal of the History of Philosophy VII (1969), 413-22.

Schrader, G. "Kant's Presumed Repudiation of the 'Moral Argument' in the Opus Postumum: An Examination of Adickes' Interpretation." Philosophy XXVI (1951), 228-41.
_____. "The Status of Teleological Judgment in the Critical Philosophy." Kant-Studien 45 (1953-54), 204-35.

Schrag, C.O. "Heidegger and Cassirer on Kant." Kant-Studien 58 (1967), 87-100.

Silber, J. "The Context of Kant's Ethical Thought." Two Parts. The Philosophical Quarterly 9 (1959), 193-207 and 309-18.

_____. "The Ethical Significance of Kant's Religion." In Kant, Religion within the Limits of Reason Alone. Edited and translated by T.M. Greene and H.H. Hudson. New York: Harper and Row, Harper Torchbook, 1960, lxxix-cxlii.

_____. "The Importance of the Highest Good in Kant's Ethics." Ethics LXXIII (1963), 179-97.

_____. "Kant's Conception of the Highest Good as Immanent and Transcendent." Philosophical Review LXVII (1959), 469-92.

_____. "The Metaphysical Importance of the Highest Good as the Canon of Pure Reason in Kant's Philosophy." Texas Studies in Literature and Language 1 (1959), 232-44.

Smith, J.E. "Hegel's Critique of Kant." Review of Metaphysics 26 (1973), 438-60.

Troeltsch, E. "Das Historische in Kants Religionsphilosophie." Kant-Studien 9 (1904), 21-154.

Walsh, W.H. "Kant's Moral Theology." Proceedings of the British Academy 49 (1963), 263-89.

_____. "Philosophy and Psychology in Kant's Critique." Kant-Studien 57 (1966), 186-98.

Warnock, G.J. "Concepts and Schematism." Analysis IX (1949), 77-82.

Wilkens, B.T. "Teleology in Kant's Philosophy of History." History and Theory V (1966), 172-85.

Yovel, Y. "Bible Interpretation as Philosophical Praxis: A Study of Spinoza and Kant." Journal of the History of Philosophy XI (1973), 189-212.

_____. "The God of Kant." Scripta Hierosolymitana XX (1968), 88-123.

_____. "The Highest Good and History in Kant's Thought." Archiv für Geschichte der Philosophie 54 (1972), 238-83.

Zeldin, M.B. "The Summum Bonum, the Moral Law, and the Existence of God." Kant-Studien 62 (1971), 43-54.

221